Contents

Notes on Contributors		iv
Preface		vi
Introduction		viii
1	Britain: The Mysteries of a Modus Vivendi ANTHONY SMITH	1
2	France: The Monopoly that Won't Divide ANTOINE DE TARLÉ	41
3	Italy: From Party Occupation to Party Partition FABIO LUCA CAVAZZA	76
4	Federal Republic of Germany: From Democratic Showcase to Party Domination ALFRED GROSSER	114
5	Sweden: Freedom's Boundaries ÅKE ORTMARK	142
6	Holland: The Shaky Pillars of Hilversum HERMAN WIGBOLD	191
7	Some Conclusions ANTHONY SMITH	232
	Notes and References	239
	Bibliography	249
	Index	257

. . .

. . .

Notes on Contributors

FABIO LUCA CAVAZZA is Vice-Chairman of the Board and Editor of *Il Sole 24 Ore*, the financial and economic daily paper published in Milan. He was a founder of the journal *Il Mulino* of Bologna, and of the publishing house of the same name, of which he is today a Director. Together with Stephen Graubard, Editor of *Daedalus*, he edited *Il Caso Italiano* (1974).

ALFRED GROSSER is Director of the Graduate Programme of the Institut d'Études Politiques, Paris. He was Director of International Research on Media and Politics for the International Political Science Association, chairing symposia in Bucharest and Montreal. He has written extensively on post-war Germany, and was awarded the German Peace Prize in 1975 and the Theodor Heuss Prize in 1978 for his work in 'explaining the Federal Republic of Germany to France' and for having helped to promote German democracy in Germany, by pointing out and criticising undemocratic trends.

ÅKE ORTMARK is by training an economist, who has worked on newspapers, magazines and as a commentator and producer in Swedish radio and television. He is Head of the Foreign Affairs section in the news department of Sweden's Channel One. His books include *The Power Game of Sweden* (1967), *The Unknown Holders of Power* (1969) and *The Tools of Power* (1971).

ANTHONY SMITH is a television producer who has written extensively on problems of media policy in regard to broadcasting and the press. He was for five years Research Fellow at St Antony's College, Oxford. He provided international research material for the Committee on the Future of Broadcasting, 1977 (the Annan Committee). He is the author of *The Shadow in the Cave – the Broadcaster, the Audience and the State* (1974) and *The Politics of Information* (1978).

ANTOINE DE TARLÉ is a consultant on problems of finance and management in French broadcasting. He has written for a number of journals including the *Revue Politique et Parlementaire*, *Esprit* and *Intermedia*. He is a member of the Editorial Board of the monthly *Etudes*.

HERMAN WIGBOLD has worked in Dutch journalism since 1950 as a specialist in social and international affairs. In the 1950s he wrote for the journals *International Spectator* and *Socialism and Democracy*. In 1960 he published a book calling for the expansion of the public sector. He has worked in television since 1960, for a time as a documentary-maker and then as Chief Editor of the current affairs programme of VARA Television, 'Behind the News'. He was for two years the producer of Holland's weekly satirical television programme and is currently the presenter of two regular television discussion programmes. In 1970 he became Chief Editor of the daily newspaper *Het Vrije Volk*.

Preface

This is the first in a series of research studies into problems of freedom of expression that has been commissioned by the Writers' and Scholars' Educational Trust (WSET) in London. WSET is an independent body that was established to gather information on and conduct research into all aspects of censorship and restraints on free expression and study the forces at work in this field. Most of the results of its work are published in its associated bimonthly journal, *Index on Censorship*, but the present series is designed to range more widely and deeply than is possible within the confines of a magazine. Other research studies in preparation or completed include *The Greek Press under the Dictatorship and after, 1967 – 77, The Spanish Media since the Death of Franco, Censorship in Brazil* and *The Press in Argentina 1973–8*.

The present study was commissioned from Anthony Smith in early 1977 and took just over a year to prepare. It was made possible by a generous grant from the European Cultural Foundation in Amsterdam, an international non-governmental organisation that devotes most of its income to promoting the development of European cooperation and a better understanding among European nations, and by small additional grants from Granada Television and Thames Television, to all of whom I would like to express my gratitude. Thanks are also due to the Acton Society, and especially Mrs Jackie Lebe, for secretarial and other assistance. Henry Fox translated the chapter on Germany, Geoffrey French that on Sweden and Peter Langdale the chapter on France and an earlier version of the Italian chapter. Gudi Lawaetz, Ejvor Martinus and Ludi Boeken translated early drafts in the opening stages of the work.

March 1978   MICHAEL SCAMMELL
Director, Writers' and Scholars'
Educational Trust

Introduction

The purpose of these studies is to take stock of the relationship between politics and the television medium now that the latter has reached an era of consolidation and, it might be said, maturity. For ten years now a group of new media professions active in most European societies and in North America has been exercising a new and unforeseen function within the world of political discourse. Between the world of politics and that of television lies an area of marshland obscured by fog, in which territorial rights and privileges have continually to be renegotiated and institutions rebuilt. The medium of television performs many cultural and entertainment functions in addition to its brokerage between electorate and politicians (and some would say that in these other functions it has a far greater impact) but each system of broadcasting in Europe stands upon foundations dug inside the world of politics: television drama, sport, education and entertainment cannot be secure in situations where the constitutional links between society and broadcasting are unsound.

The theories of press freedom which seemed to be firmly established within Western countries at the end of the Second World War are grossly inadequate tools for dealing with the problems of the electronic media. None of the rights seems to translate from one medium to the other. The broadcaster seems at times to be a kind of journalist, at other times a kind of public functionary. Since he is the means by which others exercise their freedom to communicate with the society, can he too have the same freedoms? Since he is dependent for his income and his legal existence upon the legislature can he ever really exercise the freedom of comment which was thought to be the mainstay of a free press? In the age of mechanical rather than electronic media, the difference between censorship and freedom was much easier to perceive. The media are not to blame for the complication: the conduct of politics has also altered.

These problems were given solutions of a kind in the 1950s and 1960s, but the institutions and assumptions which existed in those years have taken a severe buffeting in the 1970s, an era characterised by chastened ideals and depleted hopes. This project was born of the desire to see how, in practice, the relationship between these two entities has been shaping since the end of that heady period of growth in the 1960s when money and opportunity seemed to be for ever expanding. There have, of course, been many major obvious organisational changes; in France a completely new system has been constructed, in Italy the monopoly of the RAI has been overthrown, in all the other countries important national investigations have been held into the future development of the existing institutions. But it is not enough to describe structures and constitutions; what happens in practice is often very different from constitutional theory and political intention. The ways in which television presents politics and the ways in which politicians influence television have to be explained in terms of the political and journalistic culture of the societies concerned. It was decided, therefore, at an early stage of this project that the best method would be to choose a limited group of societies and a small team of people all of whom are concerned with television in one or more of the countries concerned, but each from a different professional angle. It was hoped that, by this means, the studies would contain sufficient parallel material for comparisons to be drawn but from a variety of different perspectives. The group contains a newspaper publisher, a television presenter, a newspaper editor, a civil servant, a political scientist, a television producer. Of the six, five are citizens of the countries about which they write; in the case of the chapter on Germany the writer, Professor Alfred Grosser, has acted as an influential interpreter of Germany in France (and of France in Germany).

The project was initiated by Michael Scammell, Editor of *Index on Censorship* and Director of Writers' and Scholars' Educational

Trust (WSET), and when the project had reached its middle stage a conference was held at the Aspen Institute in Berlin, where the Director, Shepherd Stone, acted as host to a conference at which the whole of the first draft was subjected to the detailed criticism of a group of German nationals drawn from the worlds of politics, broadcasting and the press. Roger Errera, Maître des Requêtes au Conseil d'État and Maître de Conférences at the Institut d'Études Politiques de Paris, and Robert McKenzie, Professor of Sociology (with Special Reference to Politics) at the London School of Economics, have acted as advisers and critics during the course of the project. The thanks of the editor and writers are thus due to a wide circle of expert and generous supporters and advisers, including Professor Jay Blumler, who provided detailed criticism of one of the chapters.

A. S.

1 Britain

The Mysteries of a Modus Vivendi

Anthony Smith

In Britain the broadcasters have come to think of the elected representatives of the people as a collective entity, 'the politicians', whose commonalty of outlook towards the business of broadcasting is assumed almost as a fact of nature. Parliament stands enviously glowering at the easy power which comes to those in command of microphones and cameras, distrustful of their casual usurpations, slightly incredulous that so much influence can come with such little responsibility. But unlike their counterparts in some other countries of Europe, the British Broadcasting Corporation and its younger rather more brazen commercial sister, the Independent Broadcasting Authority, do not live in serious fear of being dismantled and reorganised; the relationship between them and 'the politicians' is a settled question and though it is reopened and investigated from time to time, the former conduct their affairs in the knowledge that within a territory variously labelled 'impartiality', 'objectivity', 'independence', there shines an eternal summer of institutional continuity. The most recent investigation into the structures of British broadcasting, the Annan Committee,[1] concluded that the existing organisations had justified the underlying concept of the 'broadcasting authority' – that is, the placing of total editorial power in the hands of a statutory body whose members are appointed by politicians but who acquire a loyalty to the historic continuity of their respective organisations, within a sense of responsibility towards the public.[2] There is a feeling among the broadcasters that the 'enemy', if such he be, is the *collectivity* of politicians; any single party will interfere with broadcasting at its own rather than the broadcasters' peril; any broadcasting body will offend the collectivity of politicians at its rather than the politicians' peril. However, across this neat gulf there are many planks along which threats and promises travel, cautions are exchanged, business is transacted. The British system of broadcasting is not quite what it seems, though many of its most outstanding creative achievements are the direct result of its long-term security – and that has been acquired through a mysterious ability to negotiate a route way through all crises, to wield in self-defence any one of a set of swords, named Independence, Public Service, Professionalism.

At the end of the 1970s, one is aware that informal linkages, practices and processes have grown up through the era of television's most rapid growth which together amount to a kind of counter-constitution, a semi-formalised structure which lies beneath the acts and charters out of which the broadcasting institutions have been born. To take stock of where the relationship between television and politics now stands entails some examinat' n of both the outer and the inner system. Against the background of secure structures an enormous variety of conscious and unconscious 'dealing' takes place. Rows over specific programmes generate precedents of caution; contact between producers and newly acknowledged sources of expertise becomes slowly institutionalised. The powers of the broadcasting authorities become redefined and clarified through case law and through the occasional painful experience, seared into collective memories. In a *settled* system the opportunities of informal linkages are much greater. They seep through the system and make it more and more secure; they provide a wider group with access to it and therefore with a stake in it.

One reason for the desirability and effectiveness of this form of control (if that is the correct term for an essentially osmotic, incorporative process) is that so much of the public debate in British society takes place within a unified arena. The concept of censorship is of marginal value in considering the British system because it suggests too narrow and too overt a procedure. The society is geared to control through absorption rather than open conflict, or rather, by the latter leading to the former. British society continues, as it has for centuries, to depend upon a unitary public life which overlaps – though it is by no means identical – with the centres of actual power; the changing generations contribute through addition and subtraction, through alterations of emphasis and values, by accretions to institutional structures and recomposition; above all, by shifting the methods by which groups and individuals enter and leave the central arena. Each new emerging group is incorporated (or not) after a process of bargaining which may or may not begin with open encounter. That central arena consists of a network of relationships which includes in its quasi-geological strata the remnants of past economic and administrative structures, eroded social classes, faded political parties. A great barrier stands between public and non-public life; once crossed, society provides its members with access to the facilities for playing a part in the transactions of power. The arena was once identified with Parliament itself, but it is now equally dependent upon newer instruments which confer social visibility. One is reminded of Lord Chesterfield's famous advice to his son in the middle of the eighteenth century: 'You will be of the House of Commons as soon as you are of age and you must first make a figure there if you would make a figure in your country.'[3] One might today go as far as to offer the media as an alternative for the Commons. It is *social visibility* which is one important key to membership of power-holding groups in Britain, and in modern times the control of the machinery of publicity is of crucial significance to all the power processes of the society, certainly the key to fresh *admissions* to the public world. The same applies to public issues as it does men – they must first make a figure in the media if they are to make a figure in the country.

However, distinctions have to be made between those who have power within the world of broadcasting, who tend to be very nearly invisible, those who are professional broadcasters, who are public people but who are subject to the controls of the former, and those who are selected by the two previous groups as representative of the spectrum of prevailing views and issues. It is the third group who look to television increasingly as an important source of patronage and arbitrage. They 'make a figure in the country' as a result of their passage through the mesh of choices, decisions and controls of which the broadcasting system of Britain consists. Television is one of the instruments, the modern counterpart of more ancient institutions, which help to weld 'public life' into a single entity.

That is not to say that British political life is based upon or even creates a single social elite; rather, the society offers a series of concentric or overlapping groupings, within each of which a certain number belong to a world of public elites, elite through having become public and public through having been absorbed into an available elite. The more complex the relationships between the world of 'public life' and society in general the more important have the mechanics of publicity become, and the more important the professional groups who operate them. Indeed, the media which have come to dominate mass communication since the 1950s have acquired roles of historic proportions and have even provided the society with a wholly new elite sector. In a sense, broadcasting sits astride all other groupings and institutions. A little like the House of Commons of the eighteenth century it is both barometer of influence and lever of power. It is a yardstick of social visibility and at the same time the essential magnifying glass of prestige. The radio and television worlds have quickly become part of the essential paraphernalia of British political life. They are the entrepôt of influence, in which a myriad contending elements meet, to be scrutinised and to negotiate for membership of the club of public life.

Both broadcasting systems of Britain are themselves emanations of that same 'public life'. Unlike the United States where commercial broadcasting was founded on local capital with national networks building themselves out of linkages between stations, Britain has, in its commercial system, created a second public authority which operates, in the selection of its members, in much the same way as the BBC. The personalities who dominate both radio and television at its supervisory levels have all, whatever their political views, been trained in the cut and thrust of business, academia, trade unionism, public administration and sometimes politics. They are all chosen for the sake of their existing reputations in one sphere of society or another, 'roasted daily in the oven of men's tongues', as St Augustine puts it. Theirs have been careers typical of public people in the United Kingdom, monitored by publicity, encouraged for brightness of intellect, their very non-conformities gently fashioned to fit into a prescribed pattern. This is not the place to provide a detailed description of the formal workings of the two supervisory institutions,[4] but it is important to see how the constitutional life of broadcasting in Britain is conducted at its senior level at this stage in its history.

The Broadcasting Authorities

The two authorities consist of individuals appointed by the Home Secretary with very small financial recompense. In the case of the BBC there are nine Governors, three of whom are specifically designated to represent Scotland, Wales and Northern Ireland and two of whom are chosen as Chairman and Vice-Chairman. This group simply assumes all the powers provided under the Charter of the BBC to operate a wide range of broadcasting services. It is a part-time body; the BBC now has two national television services, with a variety of regional inputs and 'opt-outs', and four national radio channels, plus twenty local radio stations and a variety of regional services (especially in the three *national* regions). The Overseas Services of the BBC, responsible for several hundred hours of programmes per week in dozens of languages, are a further responsibility, as is the enormous publishing house owned by the BBC, its libraries and overseas sales sections and a variety of other activities, which have emerged from the business of broadcasting. In the case of the BBC this statutory Board of Governors acts as if it were a group of proprietors of a vast undertaking, without formal reference back to government (or any ministry) on any matter which is contained already within its terms of reference. The Home Office sits in the background checking the BBC's actions against the Charter. The BBC has a statutory obligation to set up a General Advisory Council (and in practice sets up a large number of other more specialist advisory councils) and a further statutory obligation to set up National Broadcasting Councils for Scotland and Wales, which have the 'function of controlling the policy and content of programmes' in both radio and television. Other parts of the country are accounted for by regional advisory councils with power, as their name suggests, merely to advise. The only statutory infringement of the Governors' sovereignty over the content of its broadcasting services consists first in an obligation to provide 'an impartial account day by day prepared by professional reporters of the proceedings of both

Houses of Parliament',[5] and secondly in a power retained by the Home Secretary 'from time to time by notice in writing to require the Corporation to refrain at any specified time or at all times from sending any matter or matter of any class specified in such notice'.[6] No instances exist of a minister compelling a specific broadcast to be made or prohibiting a specific broadcast, although, as we shall see, pressures have frequently been applied to this end, without this reserve power being invoked; however, instructions have been given over the years under this rubric for prohibitions on the BBC expressing editorial positions on matters of controversy. In addition, ministers and shadow ministers have direct access to the air in certain (quite frequent) circumstances for conducting both un-controversial departmental business (for example encouraging the population to post early for Christmas, or volunteer for military service) and, under various tight rules, extremely controversial political business. In the rarity with which the reserve powers are employed and in making the various appointments to the Govern-ing Body the separateness of the BBC from its governmental cradle is constantly emphasised. There have been important turning points, which will be explained, when the government has in recent times appeared to step out of frame, so to speak, to move outside the prescribed rituals, for example, in the appointment of an ex-Conservative politician to the Chairmanship of the BBC and in vehement public disapproval of certain programmes dealing with Northern Ireland: these incidents have exercised profound influence – through a kind of shock effect – over the subsequent conduct of the politics/BBC relationship.

It is axiomatic that the BBC is responsible not merely for the technical operation of channels but for every moment of pro-gramme content within them. It is a single editorial entity; its staff, numbering well over twenty thousand, and its enormous patronage, covering all the arts, sciences and forms of public discourse within society, are balanced upon the pivot of the constitutional relation-ship between Governors and Home Secretary. It may be argued that the reserve power held by government is an emergency power, a tiny fragment of supreme sovereignty; or it may be argued that the reserve power, expressed at the head of an administrative pyramid, must be magnified in its psychic conse-quences and must colour the entire activity of the Corporation.

One further link with government remains; the BBC's finances consist, almost entirely, of moneys provided for it by Parliament through the Post Office and these are raised through a licence fee on television sets, similar to that used in most other countries of Europe. The BBC is totally dependent on the government of the day for deciding when and by how much to raise the fee, which in times of economic prosperity may occur once a decade but in times of high inflation can be necessary almost annually. The BBC, therefore, has its mind permanently concentrated on impending actions by government to prevent itself simply withering away. No government is likely in practice to risk the unpopularity of allowing the programme services to collapse but no government wishes to incur the electoral opprobrium of excessive increases. A constant negotiation takes place, in which irascible ministers have been heard to utter threats and in which insistent broadcasting officials have been known to call their bluff. It is a source of tension, and one which tends to differentiate 'the politicians' into those who support increases (that is, support the BBC) and those who do not. The supplying of cash is an important element in the field of force in which broadcasting is conducted in Britain, at least in regard to the BBC.

The Independent Broadcasting Authority (IBA) is a body of similar character to the Governing Body of the BBC, but with very different functions. Its eleven members consist of private individuals, three of whom represent national regions and two of whom are Chairman and Vice-Chairman. They operate under the provisions of an Act of Parliament (1964) which empowers them to operate the transmitters of a national network of regionally based programme companies, which they enfranchise but do not possess. Like the BBC they use a set of frequencies allotted to them by the Post Office, according to prescribed techniques and standards, but the content of these wavebands (and of a score of local radio stations created under special additional legislation in 1972) is only indirectly the IBA's responsibility. In the IBA's system there now exist thirty-four separate companies each of which has been allotted its franchise after competitive hearings at which the word of the IBA is final. No challenges take place in courts of law; no word of debate between competitors is published, apart from the contents of the winning franchise.[7] Though the IBA functions as a granter of licences it also shares editorial control of content with the enfranchised companies. The 1954 Act of Parliament which created the IBA (in its previous nomenclature of ITA or Independent Television Authority) expressed the prevailing fears concerning the degree of social responsibility which could be expected from commercial companies and instructed the Authority to make certain that specific periods of time are set aside for education, religion, news, documentaries and programmes dealing with local affairs in each region. No sponsorship of programmes is allowed but the companies raise their revenue by transmitting advertisements between programmes and at certain breaks within programmes. The IBA has built up over the years an enormous body of internal statute and advice on the shaping both of advertising and of programme material, and has created in a manner similar to the BBC a network of advisory and consultative bodies dealing with a variety of specialised topics, which in all involve more than 400 members of the public. Among the more important of the internal committees with which the IBA system operates is the Programme Policy Committee presided over by the IBA's Chairman which contains the programme controllers as well as the managing directors of all the television programme companies and at which the IBA presents its own views and policies. However the bulk of the programmes which are transmitted nationally emanate from the five largest of the commercial companies; the representatives of these form the largest group within a further committee, the Network Programme Committee, which is attended by two representatives of the IBA; it is here that the programme decisions are made which result, after further consultation with all the programme controllers, in the networked material which most of the IBA's audience view. It is a federal system with an increasingly powerful statutory body at the centre – powerful but reluctant to intervene too often in daily programme matters.

The IBA is quite unlike the BBC in that it supervises without being the primary initiator of programmes. It 'controls' but does not employ the programme makers. It is legally responsible for everything transmitted but cannot possibly so much as view and hear all the thousands of hours of material which it physically transmits. Inevitably, therefore, the system has grown over the years into a seamless web of relationships and procedures, part formal, part informal. The IBA has ultimate power over the fifteen companies inside its television arm; it has all the 'clout' but selects with care the occasions when it acts. It could be swamped and destroyed if the companies were deliberately to refer to it every programme decision. It has therefore to concentrate its attention on the 'sensitive' issues, laying down rulings and setting precedents, viewing in advance of transmission programmes which might provoke public accusations that it is defaulting on its trust. In the course of the 1970s its *de facto* powers have come to resemble very closely those wielded by the senior management of the BBC, as similar problems have arisen for successive acts of adjudication.

Governing Mood and Fashion

In constitutional terms the key relationship in the whole broadcasting system is that between Chairman of the Governors of the BBC (or of the Members of the IBA) and the Director General of the respective body; the former is appointed by the Prime Minister of the day, and the latter is the senior professional appointment made by the board concerned. Any major change intended in the relationship between government and medium will be signalled in the making of that supreme appointment. A great deal of the literature of British broadcasting has been generated on the subject of this relationship, and many are the opinions about exactly how it should be conducted and developed.[8]

In the inter-war years, the Chairmanship evolved (through personalities and incidents) as the chief judge of the public interest in broadcasting; it was supposed to be a part-time task, performed by a person with knowledge of large areas of the world, a wise man able to make long-term judgements on policy. In the post-war period, the post gradually became far more executive in nature. Lord Normanbrook, chairman during the Prime Ministership of Macmillan and Home and in the early years of Wilson, once took the step of preventing a particular programme (an interview with Ian Smith of Rhodesia) before transmission; until then it had been assumed that the power of the Chairman was retrospective and long-term only. Normanbrook, who had for many years been Secretary of the Cabinet Office, a most important role in British political life, defended his constitutional right, as Chairman of the BBC; to take such decisions. A new doctrine seemed to be emerging which moved sovereign power more into the hands of the government-appointed Chairman.

Harold Wilson made one appointment as Chairman of the BBC during his term of office and one as Chairman of the IBA. In both cases he chose ex-politicians. To the BBC he gave Lord Hill, a former Conservative Cabinet Minister, and Chairman of the IBA, and to the IBA Lord Bowden, formerly Labour Chief Whip.

Hill immediately proceeded to make his BBC role far more executive in scope than it had ever been previously. His appointment was widely treated as a deliberate slight on the BBC or as an attempt to curb the excesses of its newer school of programme makers. Hill's successor was an academic, Sir Michael Swann, who, on assuming office, used a freshly minted image to describe the relationship between himself and the Director General: he was, he said, to be the 'navigator' while the Director General was the 'driver'. Certainly the expression placed the Chairman firmly in the quasi-executive position which had gradually been evolving. Swann explained the position of the Chairman in a later speech:

> Lord Hill and his Governor colleagues had no option but to strengthen their hand, and it is surely to their credit that they did so, and in the doing fended off a series of threats to the BBC's autonomy. The fact of the matter is that inadequate as the Governors may be, they are in the last resort the BBC's only guarantee of autonomy . . .[9]

Thus, a new twist to the doctrine of power was being developed, at the very top of the BBC. Its *independence* was henceforth to be guaranteed by increasing the power of a Board which is chosen by government (though seldom *in toto* by a single administration). The Governors are the cement by which the BBC is fixed to the foundations of British society; they are broadcasting's special ration of Britain's public elite who justify past actions, unruffle the infuriated, allay qualms, switch trends. The two Boards are the means by which the BBC and IBA make their deals with the other sections of the elite of public life. The Governors define the political realities of broadcasting; within the confines of the arrangements which they uphold with society in general, such crucial matters as the nature of broadcasting impartiality are worked out. Their powers of long-term policy-making are crucial powers in this respect. The Governors and board members can encourage or discourage the careers of senior people; they can in the course of time steer the medium towards certain genres of content and away from others. In their rare public pronouncements, and equally rare internal pronouncements, this is what they attempt to do. But they are aloof from the business of programme-making – so much so that senior managers of the BBC and IBA tend to influence their view of things. Some think of the Governors even as the prisoners of the officials.

The era of Hill at the BBC was the era of the greatest conflicts between senior politicians and broadcasters. The Wilson Cabinet, in office and out of it, were the source of persistent and shrill accusations against alleged unfairness in programmes. The classic row resulting from the 'Yesterday's Men' documentary about the Labour leaders one year after the departure of the Labour government in the 1970 General Election resulted in a tightening of the flow of managerial information within the BBC rather than in a growing subservience to the demands of politicians; once the allegations of bad faith on the part of the programme-makers had been cleared away by (internal) investigations, any lasting after-math of the row lay in managerial processes and in moods rather than in constitutional changes. The programme had dealt mockingly with the post-electoral affairs of the former Cabinet, and with its personalities, and the residue of the extremely vigorous and public protests of Harold Wilson and his colleagues consisted in an abiding wariness throughout the broadcasting world when it came to treating politicians in a spirit of levity. The change was inseparable from the general slow abandonment of the 1960s' mood of irreverence; it certainly contributed to such a change within broadcasting, but it produced no noticeable self-abasement towards any particular party in government or opposition. But 'Yesterday's Men' could never be made again; the atmosphere in which relations are conducted between broadcasting as a whole and politicians as a whole had changed significantly as a result of the furore and the traumas which it occasioned. Such a programme, even as an idea has acquired a dated implausible feeling. It would be impossible now to find anyone with a serious desire to make a programme of that kind. The spirit of plausibility which governs the sense of what is topical or valid at a given moment has moved on. Politicians are not for mockery. No one issued a rule about it. Many senior politicians were even rather embarrassed about the fuss which had been made. But everyone *knew* that an idea for a

'Yesterday's Men' would simply wither for its seeming irrelevance in the prior discussions between producers, heads of departments, controllers of channels. It would not be budgeted; it would not be scheduled; it would not seem an interesting idea.

The bad blood which had developed in the Wilson period between the Labour Party and the BBC simply disappeared with the change of Prime Minister. So firm is the *system* which governs the relationship that in 1977, during a Labour administration, the Governors even appointed to the Director Generalship a man widely thought to be Conservative in his views. The private political views of high officials in broadcasting are thought to be almost irrelevant to their conduct of office. Attempts by political parties to make accusations of bias against the BBC are frequent but always seem to fade away. After a recent General Election the Labour Party made a public and categoric accusation of anti-Labour bias in the coverage of the campaign and set up its own one-man enquiry; an academic was asked to report to the National Executive of the Labour Party after investigating all of the campaign coverage on television. The man duly reported that he found no bias and a slightly abashed General Secretary was obliged to make a public statement which sounded to some like an apology.

'Yesterday's Men' did help to bring about one constitutional change which was in the air at the time. The decision to transmit the programme had been taken in the last instance by a group of BBC Governors and the investigation into Wilson's allegations had also been conducted by the Governors. The demand for a complaints procedure independent of the Governors (which had been a theme of much of the discussion about broadcasting reform for many years) was intensified and the BBC proceeded to set up a new Complaints' Commission consisting of three distinguished retired lawyers who have since then undertaken the adjudication of any complaint which the BBC itself fails to satisfy. (More recently non-lawyers have been included in this panel of judges.) The IBA declined to join in the arrangement and set up its own internal complaints panel. It seems possible but not inevitable that these two procedures, set up somewhat in haste in a period of high passions, will in time be turned into a public joint body separate from the broadcasting institutions.

Behind the constitutional arrangements which create a formal separation of powers between governments and Governors/Members, there lies a penumbra of precedents, accumulating over the course of time. The degree of newspaper attention paid to a given incident in the relationship is not necessarily a guide to its impact or importance. It is often difficult to guess at the influence of a given incident on future conduct: the Governors may stand quite firm at a particular moment in support of a producer or programme and yet provide the impression internally that the conduct or policy concerned is never to be repeated. The first great 'incident' in broadcasting history was the tension between BBC and government at the time of the General Strike in 1926,[10] when the government did not quite take over the BBC as Churchill had desired, nor did the BBC act objectively or impartially between government and strikers. It helped the Government to win. Yet a precedent was established for an ambiguous independence (perhaps the most which Reith could have achieved in the circumstances) upon which a greater independence was later constructed. The precedent was manipulable in the memory of both sides, but the essential ambiguity has lingered. A similarly symbolic incident occurred in 1956 at the time of the Suez incident, when the BBC was placed under considerable pressure from the Eden government not to allow opposition to the military adventure to be expressed on the air; the BBC did allow Gaitskell, the Labour Leader, to broadcast, interpreting its duties to provide coverage of the whole Parliamentary spectrum of views, rather than to take the view that the government alone represented 'the country'. The internal mythology generated by the incident went further than the logical extension of the incident itself; the BBC's obligations were demonstrated towards Parliament, rather than towards its own autonomy. Such incidents are crucial turning points but their meaning historically is seldom clear. The Suez precedent suited both politicians and broadcasters in the conditions of the late 1950s but seemed rather lame a decade later when Ireland, the devaluation crisis, the appointment of Hill and the coverage of General Elections provided a string of further symbolic interchanges.

An 'incident' is powerful because of the sense of internal emergency which it creates, and one must include as an important category of such incidents the periodical public investigations into broadcasting. Since the 1920s there have been a total of six major, plus one or two minor, committees of enquiry set up by the government of the day to make recommendations on the future institutional and organisational arrangements for broadcasting and to enquire into the stewardship of the BBC, and latterly of the IBA system as well. The public discussion and literature thrown up by these enquiries is considerable. There is a period of a year or more during which material is gathered from the public and hearings held, then a period of press speculation as to the conclusions, followed by a lengthy public debate when the findings and recommendations are published; the government then pre-pares its own response which may take the form of a 'green' or 'white' paper, followed by a bill presented to Parliament. Each stage is attended by considerable press and public comment in which the broadcasting authorities have to reply to every criticism, lobby in their own defence publicly and behind the scenes of both Houses of Parliament, advise, warn and compromise. The whole process can take several years. The end product is a Charter renewed for a further decade, or the granting of a new channel, or a brace of new radio stations. In between these investigations there are periods when public discussion on the size of the licence fee entails a further debate about broadcasting 'standards' and 'values'. Each of these has the same effect of creating a sense of crisis within the organisations and a deep awareness that each programme broadcast will be taken by the participants in the debate as evidence for or against the stewardship of a given institution. Parliament looms over broadcasting in Britain like the Cloud of Unknowing; it is a preoccupation and a permanent source of irritation and threat. Like an ageing rich aunt suffering from a long drawn out disease and incessantly changing her will, Parliament's very presence nags at the BBC and the IBA. The most trivial discontent can set off a row. The whole history of the external relations of British broadcasting with the political establishment is an incessant pounding of complaint and rebuff, each side attempt-ing to accommodate its needs within the existing codes and precedents. Mrs Goldie's account of the evolution of political broadcasting[11] indicates very well the way in which individual politicians (Prime Ministers, in particular) shaped the evolving measures into a system, how each new election and political situation had to be interpreted afresh in terms of programme formats, styles of interviewing, formulations of debates and discus-sions; she very shrewdly makes the point that politicians 'feel diminished by the need to appear on television and resentful of the circumstances in which such appearances take place'.[12] That phase is now over. Few politicians are less than eager to use the medium, but still political communication is transmuted into anxieties in individual politicians about the handling of the medium. The politician feels that one vital element of his work is taken out of his direct control; it is he not the broadcaster who is the victim of arbitrary power. The impartiality of the broadcasters, the *sine qua non* of their continued existence, is an impartiality firmly frontiered by Parliament, which does not permit an impartiality between parliamentarism and anti-parliamentarism, nor between views held inside and outside Parliament. At the same time the incessant public enquiries and frequent occurrence of 'incidents', with the sense of internal crisis which these occasion, have encouraged both broadcasting organisations to create groups of officials especially skilled in the art of coping with pressure and fending it off, internally and externally. The professional training of a high broadcasting official consists to a great extent in the acquisition of these special political skills. It is important to emphasise that the British system has the effect of transforming the general public discussion about broadcasting into a discussion about the steward-ship of two institutions. Sometimes the actual viewed product of television is felt almost to be a waste product of the endless bargaining over institutions. Planted within British broadcasting are the seeds of an intense bureaucratism, bred of the residual impact of outside pressures. Indeed, it is surprising that the much debated growth of 'managerialism' in broadcasting, has not been greater than it has; its arrival is the most important change in the last decade.

The Power of the Parties

In its internal document 'Principles and Practice in News and Current Affairs',[13] one of the main texts of broadcasting practice, the BBC maintains that it is its express duty to uphold parliamentary life. Interpreted in the context of the Northern Ireland conflict, for instance, this means that time can be found to represent all groups which participate in elections, but not the para-military groups, whatever their standing or degree of acceptance within their respective communities. In another document,

'Principles and Practice in Documentary Programmes',[14] the BBC makes it clear that the individual employee is not empowered to make any programme the expression of his own views or position; where a producer feels he wishes to make a statement on a subject of concern in his own name, he has a clear duty to resign and see if in due course, he is invited to make a programme as a member of the public, expressing his own view. There are slight exceptions to this, where a producer is in himself of sufficient stature 'to make a personal, visual or artistic statement on some subject in which wholly black and white views do not exist'. Television production has come to involve an ever more variegated set of skills; maintaining impartiality depends upon far more than decreeing who shall or shall not 'appear'. It entails the creation of a cadre of impartial people able to administer an impartial system, at the heart of which lies the promise to the politicians as a whole that their specific needs will be catered for.

Over the years the BBC and IBA have granted important 'hostages' to parliament, in the form of systems of ministerial broadcasts and party political broadcasts. The former date back to an *aide-mémoire* of 1947, redrawn in 1969.[15] There are two categories of ministerial broadcast: in the former a minister may ask for time 'to seek the co-operation of the public in matters where there is a general consensus of opinion' and be given time within the BBC's schedule of programmes, without any equal period of time being given to a member of the opposition; the second category includes the rarer cases where a Prime Minister, or a Cabinet colleague nominated by him, wishes to 'broadcast to the nation in order to provide information or explanation of events of prime national or international importance', and here the BBC will provide the opportunity both to the minister concerned and to a leading member of the opposition, if the latter demands it. In order to accommodate the other parties in Parliament, the BBC, under the same agreement, will hold a broadcast discussion a day or so later in which senior members of government and opposition must both participate and in which other parties with a reasonable level of representation in Parliament will be invited to take part. The first two stages of the ministerial broadcast arrangement are carried by the independent channel also, but the third stage is optional. A similar procedure is adopted every year after the Chancellor of the Exchequer presents his Budget, except that the broadcast normally takes the form of an interview rather than a direct speech to camera. The system operates at the will of the politician rather than the broadcasting institutions and the deterrent to its over-frequent use lies in the rigmarole of contradiction which it automatically invokes.

Another of the current practices in political broadcasting which date back to the 1947 *aide-mémoire* are the election and party broadcasts. Section 4 states: 'A limited number of controversial party political broadcasts shall be allocated to the various parties in accordance with their polls at the last general election. The allocation shall be calculated on a yearly basis and the total number of such broadcasts shall be a matter for discussion between the parties and the BBC.' In practice a semi-formal Party Political Broadcast (PPB) Committee has come into being over the years in which the sharing out of time takes place between delegates of all the parties with representation in Parliament, of the BBC and IBA, of the party organisations, and under the chairmanship of the Lord President of the Council (a senior minister responsible for various matters including the organisation of House of Commons business). The PPB Committee tends to operate on the basis of its own precedents, government and opposition are normally given equal time, the Liberals just over half of the time given to each of the major parties. Since the arrival in parliament of the Welsh and Scottish Nationalist and Northern Irish parties in the 1970s, time is provided within their respective countries, according to their standing within those countries. Thus for example the Scottish Nationalists whose total voting strength when measured against the total for the United Kingdom is very small but which is very large when considered against the total for Scotland, are given a relatively large amount of time within Scotland alone.

The parties are permitted to use their time as they wish, and their allocation includes, of course, radio as well as television. The programmes are of varying lengths, sometimes as short as five minutes, sometimes fifteen. Although editorial control rests in practice with the parties, the BBC and the IBA are compliant publishers and are therefore bound in law for libel or other misdemeanours (for example, breaches of the laws of contempt of court or the Race Relations Act) which may occur within them. In the run-up to elections a special series of election broadcasts are transmitted within a three-week period which follow roughly the same rules as the party political broadcasts; their governance is controlled by the same semi-official PPB Committee.

The PPB Committee has thus acquired a novel role within British constitutional life. It was formed *ad hoc* and it continues to be recalled *ad hoc*. After each bout of activity it virtually ceases to exist. However, when the government decided to hold a Referendum on membership of the Common Market, the enabling legislation included a clause which instructed the broadcasting authorities to make provision for the two sides (that is, the organised campaigns for and against continued membership of the EEC, which did not correspond with party lines) to have equal shares of broadcasting time. Almost immediately the broadcasting authorities were in touch with the Lord President of the Council's Office which normally convenes the PPB Committee; (it is not precisely clear which side made the first contact). The Committee simply met, unilaterally as it were, asked representatives of the pro- and anti-Market compaigns to be present and proposed that they adopt the traditional format used in party and election broadcasting, which, being newcomers to the business, they instantly accepted. In retrospect several of those involved thought that a different system would have been appropriate to the Referendum; perhaps many very short sloganised broadcasts, or just one or two very long explanatory programmes, or a combination of both. In practice the Referendum campaign came to resemble in its broadcast aspect a General Election fought between two parties. The two sides drew lots in the Lord President of the Council's office to decide which would have the right to choose the order of the broadcasts. In the event the pro-Market campaign chose to have the last broadcast of all and therefore the 'antis' had the opening broadcast. Normally, in General Elections, the government has the last broadcast which takes place not the night before polling (when the nation is given an evening without politics, to enable sober reflection to take place) but two nights before, with the opposition having the penultimate broadcast. What the experience of the Referendum showed was that a new quasi-constitutional device has come into being in the era of broadcasting, the PPB Committee, self-constituted and confidential. It helps to tilt the balance of visible power towards Parliament and the existing parties. Whenever the Communist Party puts up a large group of candidates, it is normally given one small broadcast in non-peak time; it always protests vociferously at its exiguous share as does the National Front, the party from the extreme right.

The party and election broadcasts are produced under a dual editorial control. The broadcasting authorities continue to act as the publishers of the material; they reserve the right to intervene in the content of the programmes as planned and they provide the programme-makers with a producer, a studio and various other services and facilities. The producer tries to help the political group concerned make the most effective broadcast within the terms of the programme idea and the script provided by the party concerned. It is a difficult half-role for the producer. The party has to find its own means to obtain special effects or visual devices, including the cost of the actual film it uses, if any. The parties sometimes attempt whole programmes made at their own expense and simply hand them to the BBC to transmit or finish off. Usually, however, they use the time for a senior politician to address the public directly and as convincingly as possible. However the view is increasingly widely held that some kind of reform of election broadcasting is necessary in Britain, in order to render the democratic system more credible in the minds of voters, and to make it better understood. At the same time a wider circle of organised groups in society are beginning to demand broadcasting time of their own and both the BBC and IBA permit various forms of 'access' broadcasting in which groups campaigning on various grass-roots issues are allowed to broadcast in their own name, with minimal help from the institutions and at their own legal risk. The growth of 'community' broadcasting has thus helped to give fresh credibility to the concept of party time at elections and between elections. But improvements have to be made in the quality of the programmes, in the skills with which they are presented, and it is here that fresh energy is now likely to be applied.[16] Frustration with party political broadcasts is today directed more often at the fact that these programmes run simultaneously and inescapably across all three channels than at the existence of the programmes themselves. Even professional broadcasters, cynical of the results of political statements delivered *ex parte* without cross-examination, tend to accept that it may be valuable for politicians to have some opportunity to say what they like how they like to the electorate. Certainly, without this institution, there might have been more overt interference in the programmes put out under normal editorial control.

Britain has been slow to move towards the actual broadcasting of Parliament itself. The late Richard Crossman, who was Leader of the House between 1966 and 1968, made considerable efforts to persuade his parliamentary colleagues to allow television cameras, at least experimentally, into the Commons, as part of his efforts to reform the procedure of Parliament. Both Houses in 1968 permitted very limited closed-circuit experiments, but only in 1975 did the Commons agree to have a full-scale broadcast experiment, in radio only. This was judged to be a success and in 1978 radio was finally allowed permanent access to all debates, of both Houses, including certain committees. Parliament continued to insist that it retained a certain 'oversight', though both broadcasting systems are permitted to use the material, each making its own selection and commentary. Parliament's rules, however, forbid the use of material recorded in Parliament in any entertainment or 'satirical' programme; it may still be some years before politicians 'digest' the innovation and prepare themselves for the admission of television cameras.

At election times, of course, radio and television spend a great deal of time in the coverage of speeches and the debating of issues. For the political parties these are times when their attention to the broadcasting institutions is at its most hawk-like, and when post-election threats are occasionally made, in the heat of passion, when victory and defeat seem at moments to hang in the balance, at the mercy of the broadcasters. Coverage has gradually increased over the years, as new television techniques have opened up more of the countrywide campaign to live and recorded coverage. No election has occurred so far without an accusation of bias from one party or another.

Certain regular problems arise from the tension between 'journalistic' and 'political' attitudes towards elections. To the former it seems appropriate that there should be studio confrontations or debates between ministers and shadow ministers; politicians in office rarely wish to provide equivalent status for their opposite numbers and Prime Ministers rarely wish the subject of 'confrontations' even to be discussed, since the knowledge that they have refused a challenge counts against them. The broadcasters are thus denied an obvious programme format and prevented by the rules of 'fairness' even from raising the possibility of using it.

Another 'journalistic' device rejected almost always by politicians is for questions to be put to campaigning ministers and shadow ministers by audiences of voters, although this now occurs in 'phone-ins' on radio and television, and in programmes where the questions are sent in on postcards. Direct engagement live on the air between politicians and voters is firmly eschewed by the former. Nor do politicians wish to be obliged to deal with issues which have not cropped up 'naturally' in the course of the campaign. Some of the fiercest tensions between broadcasters and politicians at the hustings have occurred as a result of journalists attempting to raise issues which the major parties have wished to avoid. These three examples of divergent perspective illustrate the way in which politicians desire broadcasting to adopt a party/ parliamentary model of political communication rather than an independent/journalistic model. It is the former which has tended to prevail.

The broadcasting authorities therefore find themselves deeply involved in the minutiae of arrangements which are designed to support the parliamentary system and the parties currently represented within it. The broadcasting system emerges from Parliament and in turn provides the country with a picture of political discourse dominated by Parliament. Broadcasting is therefore not part of a 'fourth estate', if such there be, but rather operates impartial brokerage within a prevailing political system, to which new admissions are very difficult to achieve. In Scotland and Wales nationalist parties have fought their way via election struggles into the arena of regional politics, and via party political broadcasts onto the television screen. Small parties dealing in the political affairs of the whole country seldom qualify for their own broadcasting time, unless they put up a large number of candidates in a general election or make some other major manifestation of their would-be involvement in the affairs of Parliament. The 'social forces' or 'popular movements', like those of Germany or Sweden, simply have no place within day-to-day broadcasting, though they do frequently have a place in the governing bodies: there is nearly always a Governor of the BBC or Member of the IBA who is a prominent trade unionist and another who is a prominent industrialist – they appear not as the nominees of their respective constituencies (though nominations are often discussed between

Home Office and the Trades Union Congress or the Confederation of British Industry) but as individuals who are expected to take up stances on relevant issues in a manner consistent with membership of their respective groups. However, apart from the major political parties (and, in slightly different ways, the major churches) no organised group has earned for itself a *statutory* section of broadcasting time. 'Community access' time is given out randomly, and seldom to the same group twice.

Producers and Pressure Groups

Having one's own time on the air is not the only way in which to gain influence through television. Indeed, there is an argument for saying that to influence the general policies of broadcasting confers more effective power than to gain direct control of a tiny amount of broadcasting time. It is often more important to be seen by all those involved in making television programmes on a given topic as a necessary and legitimate source of *expertise* on a given subject. Imagine a group of people who wished to gain support for a proposal to make Britain leave the United Nations. If they set up an office and started to hold demonstrations they might, if events seemed to warrant it, succeed in being reported on news bulletins. Even if they managed to work up a large-scale street demonstration, they would still appear as a rather odd and eccentric group, oddballs, 'extremists'. After a time their activities would automatically gain less news coverage because their message, involving a single issue unlikely to be given platform support by a major party, would come to seem boring and repetitive to journalists and public. However, if our imaginary group succeeded in recruiting public figures already acknowledged as 'experts' on the subject they would begin to acquire a different kind of media attention; they would change status from eccentrics to plausible pressure groups. If prominent politicians started to support them publicly they would acquire considerable news value but if they acquired members of two or three parties they would acquire the unassailable status of a legitimate source of independent expertise. British political life contains many organisations which have made the complete journey from outsiders to insiders, winning the right to be consulted by ministers in the course of devising legislation. One can cite the Howard League for Penal Reform as an organisation which has made a complete transition and is seen to provide both media and government with information almost as authoritative as that of the relevant civil servants; however, the newer organisations campaigning for prisoners' rights which have sprung up in the last few years have only the status of pressure groups, sources of news information but not fully legitimate *expertise*. In the fields of health, transport, education, poverty, race relations there exist scores of organisations in a constant state of pre-recognition, attempting to redefine their public images as experts rather than protesters. Broadcasting structures and procedures of consultation follow similar patterns to other centres of power in the society. The apparatus of advisory bodies is used as part of the process of incorporation, absorbing new figures and symbolising the state of the negotiations between new pressure groups and the rest of society.

One most interesting and striking example of this process is to be found in the women's rights movements of the 1970s, where one of the key grievances was the dearth of women employed in senior positions in broadcasting. The women's movement moved rapidly inwards from the 'lunatic fringe' to full respectability – there were powerful political forces behind the transition. The consumers' movement was a slightly earlier example, and the movement dedicated to curbing the explicit presentation of sexual themes on television – the National Viewers' and Listeners' Association – provides another extremely apt example. In this last case, the organisation has yet to acquire the ultimate sense of legitimacy; its main spokesperson, Mary Whitehouse, has moved from eccentric fringe to respectability in the course of a decade, but she is still not thought of as a source of expertise, only as a reference point for a body of opinion.

A producer setting out to make a documentary on almost any contemporary issue is confronted with a phalanx of such groups, varying in status, but all with an inescapable role in the *shaping* of an issue. Television can be seen as a barometer of status for all the groups contending for a voice, as well as the arena in which they wish to be heard. The programme-maker working within the BBC or a commercial programme company is in the position of being a patron and arbiter rather than a voice on his own, and his position within the broadcasting structure is quite different in Britain from other countries where *party* and sectional influence on the governing structures is visible and taken for granted.[17]

This view of the role of the special interest group towards the media helps to explain the curious encaged position of the producer within the British broadcasting system. The obligations accepted by the broadcasting institutions towards the central political arena oblige the actual makers of broadcast material to see themselves partly as public functionaries, partly as journalists. They provide the means by which the social groups gain access to the society and there is therefore a very powerful set of constraints – indeed, prohibitions – which governs the role of the producer in both broadcasting systems. Strands of programmes cannot have political leanings, presenters and interviewers are less 'usable' the more clear cut and public their personal views on actual issues. The BBC has made it clear that each public utterance *outside television* by a programme presenter who conducts political discussions necessarily erodes his own professional position, until the point at which he casts it away altogether.[18] In 1977 a very prominent newscaster in the commercial system resigned his job after declaring his sympathies for the firemen in the course of a major strike which was then dominating the news; he had already written a book about the firemen and wished to make further public efforts to help them. On the other hand it is possible for public figures who are 'experts' to hold down politically sensitive posts (on a freelance basis) in a television programme if they take precautions to divide their public personae. Mr Peter Jay, for example, was for several years the presenter of 'Weekend World', a London Weekend Television programme which has developed an extremely high reputation for its specialised and skilful dissection of political and economic matters. Jay was simultaneously a prominent writer on economics in *The Times*. Occasionally ministers being interviewed by him would refer to influential and highly controversial articles he had written in his newspaper column and he would invariably and embarrassedly rebuke the interviewee for this reference to his activity in another place – in the context of the television programme he appeared as a neutral, with no known views. Occasionally the presenter of a programme takes a stand on a given public issue through writing or speaking and almost invariably an embarrassing situation arises. The BBC tends to keep him or her away from programmes relating to the same issue until this particular intervention passes from the centre of interest and dispute. These examples relate to freelance individuals employed to conduct political or other discussions on the air – 'neutral and self-neutred', as one of them once put it. The position of the producer who more directly represents the BBC or the programme company concerned is far more difficult. He is not in the position of a 'réalisateur' in France or a 'redakteur' in Germany; his programmes are supposed to emerge from interests and beliefs which are wholly concealed or non-existent. The closer he is involved in political television, the more serious is any divergence felt to be. In its evidence to the Annan Committee the BBC is quoted as having explained that, in its view, 'every member of the staff has a responsibility for safeguarding the BBC's reputation for impartiality'.[19] All senior staff with a role in programme-making are accordingly obliged, under contract, to refrain from engaging in political or other outside activities without prior permission (which is generally or frequently refused). Over 2000 members of the BBC staff were in this restricted category in 1976, although attempts were being made to reduce this number by several hundred. The Annan Committee were adamant in recommending that the BBC try to reduce the extent of its restrictions on the private activities of its employees. The producer within the BBC system (somewhat less so in the IBA system) is part of the *management* structure; although programme-making has evolved towards the status of a profession in Britain, it is not an autonomous profession. An Association of Directors and Producers has recently been formed, to press for further recognition (in financial as well as institutional terms) of the role of the programme-maker as an autonomous intellectual worker. However, the structures and the rubric of impartiality have not accommodated themselves to such demands, and are not likely to go very far towards them. The producer is a creative *official,* not an autonomous artist; his employers provide him with a much wider degree of freedom than in the past, but within a system which cannot find a path between individual 'authorship' and public responsibility.

The Annan Committee, however, came to the conclusion that these bonds should be loosened. Impartiality, it was suggested to them by one witness, was the enemy which outflanked the producer whenever he attempted to make a programme with an accusatory flavour on a given issue.[20] There were already programmes

– and some were cited – which had willy-nilly become identified with particular viewpoints, not closely aligned with those of any party, but none the less coherent ideological standpoints. The Committee argued that there should be committed public affairs programmes which should be appropriately labelled if they continued with the same line over a long period of time. The most problematical and more hotly debated genre is that of 'investigative reporting', where the commercial companies have long been more active than the BBC, with a record of programmes attempting to expose corruption or neglect in various public services. The BBC staff complained that the restraint against investigative documentaries stemmed directly from the wishes of the BBC Governors, who, when questioned about this by the Committee, declared that the lack of investigative reporting in BBC current affairs programmes was due to the desire of the producers to stay clear of trouble. The libel laws act as a severe constraint against investigative reporting in all media in Britain, but it could be argued that both television systems are in a better position than most newspapers to obtain legal help and sustain the costs of lost court actions. The BBC's particular approach to impartiality preconditions it towards the desire to reflect rather than to create issues: it is often bold in allowing discourse and in reporting controversy while reticent in proclaiming uncomfortable facts *ex parte,* when these are liable to have political consequences.

One example of this was the way in which the BBC held back information about the maltreatment of prisoners by British troops in Northern Ireland until this 'scoop' had been published by a Sunday newspaper, thereby providing it with a kind of 'cover' – the BBC found it easier to report a report than take the moral risk of initiating the political shock waves which inevitably followed the revelation. Investigative reporting is a matter of choosing *sources:* those who indulge in it necessarily broaden the range of sources they are prepared to take on trust or at least to take as a basis for enquiry; television is relatively chary of investigation, preferring to employ more standard and 'recognised' sources. All reporting consists in receiving information and passing it on – the more determinedly 'impartial' the reporter the more he insists on dealing only with 'reputable' sources and the greater his constraint against the investigative. It is a question of degree rather than kind.

Behind this nervousness lies the feeling that to 'create' an issue means to usurp the function of other legitimate institutions. Police, Parliament and law courts exist to perform stated functions. Broadcasting in Britain – unlike in the United States, say – is an unwilling watchdog. It is much easier to work with rather than against the recognised sources and channels of knowledge; better for the Child Poverty Action Group to expose deprivation, rather than for television to question official statistics; better for the financial press to take up arms against suspect companies; better for the Home Office to deal with 'bent' policemen. 'Investigative journalism' entails the employment of pre-legitimised sources of information and by definition these are the riskiest.

Usurpation

The most extreme institutionalised precaution against political usurpation, which, twenty years after its disappearance, leaves a legacy of symbolic fearfulness was the Fourteen Day Rule, which forbade the BBC, until 1956, to deal with any issue which was to be brought up in Parliament within a fortnight. As the *aide-mémoire* of 1947 put it (in a formula revised in 1948), 'the BBC will not have discussions or *ex parte* statements on any issues for a period of a fortnight before they are debated in either House' and that 'while matters are subjects of legislation MPs will not be used in such discussions'. The rule seems to sum up the aura of caution tinged with constitutional mystery with which the BBC approached politics for the first thirty-five years of its existence; it helped to reinforce the feeling at many levels in broadcasting management that politics was best avoided since it imposed too many risks and pitfalls. However it is difficult today even to imagine the circumstances in which such a prohibition could appear to be intelligent, still less to be in the public interest.

The rule had originated in the days towards the end of the wartime political truce when party leaders within the coalition government feared that a too rapid return to party warfare might endanger the stability of the all-party government. The BBC was pressed to 'cool' the gathering party battle, and it duly complied. The party whips were also anxious to stop individual MPs from jockeying for public acclaim. The pressure on the BBC reflected an even older and continuing fear that the forum of broadcasting tended by its nature to deprive Parliament of its due function. The Fourteen Day Rule died eventually in 1956 after a period of slow-burning protest from the broadcasters – though not before competitive television broadcasting had become established.

But the fear of usurpation continued. The main annual political 'event' in Britain is the season of party conferences which takes place every autumn in various seaside resorts just before Parliament reassembles for the new session. Until the mid-1950s the party conferences were covered only by the press. By the end of the 1960s there was gavel-to-gavel live coverage on BBC 2, as well as regular extracts and edited versions of the debates on regular news and current affairs programmes. The party conferences gradually changed their nature from private deliberative assemblies to shop windows for the parties; party leaders made ceremonial appearances. Fierce debates continue to take place, and disputes break out, and even major doctrinal splits are not avoided. Even though television coverage has become a major objective of party conference organisation, the internal political nature of the conferences has not been seriously disturbed, as many had feared. The politics of deliberation has merged with the politics of the image, and the satisfactory nature of the combination perhaps surprises those party organisers (and those broadcasters) who placed stumbling blocks in its path.

In its early days the BBC actually prided itself on *not* covering General Elections. The creation of hustings in the medium of television was pioneered by commercial broadcasters in the 1950s and only in the mid-1960s did television become established as the chief means by which rival parties and candidates contended for office. The broadcasting institutions were loaded with caveats and prohibitions which Parliament gradually lifted, and much of the pressure for change came up through the ranks of the broadcasters rather than from management. Bureaucracies come sometimes to admire the rules which cripple them. The BBC often appeared not to want to do that which it was forbidden to do.

There lingers, however, a feeling that each step taken by television into the arena of politics must be scrutinised, with a certain disdain, for fear that it will remove the functions of duly elected politicians, ministers in particular. Indeed, this inhibition has been part of the problem which has arisen in the coverage of Northern Ireland. In 1973 the BBC decided to stage a programme on Northern Ireland under the title 'A Question of Ulster', in a debating series in which, from time to time, two or three hours is given over to a debate on a single subject involving a large number of participants. This particular transmission was due to include representatives of all the groups in the Northern Ireland conflict, excluding the para-military groups (although both halves of the IRA have *legal* 'political' wings which are regularly invited to take part in radio and television discussions, including this one). The Conservative government, through the Home Secretary Reginald Maudling, exercised extreme and public pressure on the BBC to have the programme cancelled. It was very rare – perhaps unique in British broadcasting – for the Home Secretary (acting, it is true, not in his role as minister responsible for broadcasting but in his role as minister responsible for internal security) to take the step of publicly admonishing a broadcasting authority. He withdrew his own agreement to participate in the programme. Many other pressures were exerted behind the scenes. The BBC decided to proceed, so long as it succeeded in getting representatives of all groups involved, including the Ulster Unionists (in their various factions). When it succeeded in doing this, it announced that the programme would be broadcast, which it duly was. The government was defied but did not use its reserve powers. The incident was the only one in which there has been open disagreement between a government and a broadcasting authority over the handling of Northern Ireland. For the most part it has been the BBC and the IBA themselves which have imposed the controls and special systems of inspection, after receiving representations. There have been, of course, incessant expressions of disapproval by Northern Ireland politicians of specific programmes, and in both radio and television, a trail of delayed programmes, a few suppressions and a great deal of delicate compromise and self-censorship. The IRA was the first of the groups of terrorists in Europe to raise the question for broadcasters of how to cover the news of a conflict without appearing to give a platform to the users of violence.

'A Question of Ulster' was a case when, as has happened several times, the BBC, the IBA or the companies have put up a fight against intended interference or hectoring complaint by ministers and officials. But there have been instances when the institutions appeared to crumble before threats. Before 1969 there was scarcely ever any reference to the institutionalised interference in the civil rights of half a million Catholics in Northern Ireland. A commercial company made a documentary in 1965 on this subject, to the fury of the then government of Northern Ireland. Several attempts by BBC producers in the 1960s were repulsed, on some occasions even after the programme was made; the BBC's own local Controller would often see his role as that of calming the passions of the province's power elite rather than encouraging an active editorial policy. This gap in the coverage of the domestic affairs of Britain comes to seem more and more scandalous as the years pass; it is too late to wonder whether lives would have been saved if the media had brought home the injustices of the province before they erupted into inter-communal slaughter. The point is that the broadcasting authorities felt themselves *contained*, rather than constrained, within the walls of the political system which gave them birth. When Northern Ireland had its own Parliament (the Stormont), the political composition of that body (in the 1960s very heavily Protestant in religion and Ulster Unionist in politics) provided the prevailing political 'reality'. In the early 1970s Stormont's composition changed but it still represented the only political reality; spokesmen for the para-military groups were effectively kept from the air, even though they were becoming important parties to the growing conflict. The IRA was denied representation in discussions or interviews, but with the ending of Stormont the political 'realities' came to be supplied by the Parliament at Westminster rather than Belfast and a much greater flexibility became possible in the coverage of the province, although the para-military groups were still kept from frequent appearances on the air. But it is much easier for broadcasters to operate against the background of the more plural parliamentary system of the United Kingdom than that of the province alone. Both BBC and IBA have permitted programmes which dealt with the internal affairs of the IRA, for example; individuals who represented the banned organisation were permitted to be interviewed only in a context in which they were object not subject, in which they appeared to provide evidence for the reporter concerned rather than to advocate their cause (although, of course, it is difficult to separate these two functions). Despite the extreme cautiousness which has been applied in the half a dozen or so programmes in recent years which have dealt with the IRA, bellows of fury have nearly always been heard from the politicians of the province, who have continued to ignore the distinction between an interview which is conducted in order to elicit information about the IRA and an appearance in which the IRA is permitted to advocate its cause. The IBA has occasionally suppressed or delayed programmes dealing with the state of the IRA and has always 'negotiated' the scripts of such programmes with the producers.

One important and lasting effect of the Northern Ireland problem on broadcasting in Britain is the way in which the channels of internal consultation and supervision which it caused to be set up or caused to be strengthened have survived as part of the general management system of current affairs programmes. In this respect there has been a growing convergence between the practices of both systems.[21] In the case of the BBC the internal tensions created by the problem of covering Northern Ireland have led to the strengthening of the post of Editor of News and Current Affairs, a post which has been growing in importance for over a decade and which was upgraded into that of Director of News and Current Affairs (DNCA) towards the end of 1977. The evolution of this post is an apt illustration of the way in which external problems are transmuted into managerial problems in broadcasting systems.

For the BBC to deal with the barrage of political pressures to which it was subjected as soon as Northern Ireland moved into an era of violence, it had first to ensure that uniform policies were adopted and to achieve this it required a very efficient centralised system of internal information. It had to know, at the top, exactly what producers were planning to do in a wide variety of programmes, on radio and television. When Northern Ireland looms large in the news, tens of hours of programmes can take place in a single week, all of them raising ticklish questions of propriety, fairness, political risk or provocation. What happened is that, by stages, a senior official adjacent to the Director General and able to speak almost with the authority of the entire Corporation, was appointed to supervise all of the news and current affairs output. Although there is a director responsible for the whole of television, another for the whole of radio and beneath them controllers of the various channels, it became convenient for editorial authority over news and current affairs programmes to be placed more directly under a unified and separate system of control. The new DNCA has authority over content, but not over scheduling and budgeting; his authority is equal to or greater than that of the officials with responsibility for scheduling and budgeting. Every week a meeting takes place of all those with day-to-day responsibility for news and current affairs programmes throughout the Corporation and the issues of the moment are discussed and rulings made by the DNCA or by the Director General. These rulings become Corporation law and are binding on all producers. The system antedates the Northern Ireland crisis but was greatly strengthened as a result of it. The minutes of these weekly meetings circulate widely within the BBC and contain pronouncements on matters as varied as the pronunciation of the Prime Minister's name (Calla-h-an or Calla-g-an), which programme should issue an invitation to a foreign head of state and whether too little attention is being paid to the Belgrade Conference or the Common Agricultural Policy of the EEC. Scores of minor decisions, recommendations or adjudications pass down through this system. Increasingly the DNCA applies himself to the co-ordination and planning of programmes, especially in television.

The IBA has evolved along remarkably similar lines. The political pressures of the last ten years have gradually forced it to take a forward position in programme matters, exercising its editorial authority positively as well as negatively. It can argue that a programme should deal with issues it has neglected or that it should drop issues which it has been 'overdoing'. At the centre of the IBA news and current affairs system is ITN (Independent Television News) which is owned co-operatively by the programme companies and which provides the main national news bulletins of the day for the whole independent system. Individual companies supply the regular current affairs programmes but the IBA ensures that these are broadcast throughout its network of companies, as it is obliged to do under the Television Act.

The division of news and current affairs into two quite separate genres, in both systems of broadcasting, is very deeply rooted in British broadcasting and can trace its origins back to early journalistic and indeed philosophical traditions. Only in very recent years has the necessity of this separation in the broadcasting media been seriously questioned, though it does appear that in the 1980s we may begin to see the reunification of these two branches of factual broadcasting.

The rigid separation of the two categories, one dedicated to preparing an objective account of the principal events of the day, the other concerned with 'background', controversy, personalities, journalistic 'colour', has arisen in societies with deep roots in philosophical positivism. Indeed, in the nineteenth century literature on journalism, in the dicta of the great editors of the past such as J. T. Delane, C. P. Scott, R. D. Blumenfeld, one can easily discern a sediment of primitive positivism, the belief in the possibility of creating an image of the world compounded of hard facts, upon which a superstructure of speculation and opinion may be built. The concept does not occur in the journalism of Latin countries and has been strongly buttressed in the twentieth century by the way in which American journalism – and especially the schools of journalism – have seized upon the doctrine. In British journalism, the separation of fact and comment grew out of the need to escape various forms of censorship in the seventeenth and eighteenth centuries, out of the intricacies of English libel law, out of the need for the editors of the great national newspapers of the nineteenth century middle class to rationalise the system of management of their papers: correspondents were stationed in various parts of the developed and imperial world, feeding information, largely through expensive telegrams and telegraphs, to their London offices, where the editor had to make the finished product palatable to a large politically delineated audience. The better informed the editor, the better he was able to 'manage' his readership and keep them comfortably convinced of his line. But his line would change and he therefore needed his information pure. 'Telegrams are for facts', one managing editor of *The Times* used to say to his correspondents, 'appreciation and comment can come by post'. The *reporter* was a different creature; to him belonged the skills of Pitman's shorthand and he was able to recover from the flux of events a precise account of the facts – the words actually used in speeches and lectures, the events of a battle accurately perceived and reproduced. The reporter and the correspondent between them provided the newspaper with its raw material, but the editor, through his leadership of opinion, created the audience for the newspaper and sustained its historical continuity. When C. P. Scott, editor of the *Manchester Guardian*, delivered his most famous of all sayings: 'Comment is free but facts are sacred', he was echoing this ingrained belief that the medium of the newspaper somehow depended on this bifurcated system of discourse.

When radio was first organised in Britain in 1921, a prototype of the BBC was set up, of which the governing structure was largely drawn from the radio manufacturing industry. In the early years the newspaper publishers had persuaded the government that the infant broadcasting organisation should be permitted to broadcast no news at all, and in particular, no controversial material. At the end of each day a bulletin prepared by the news agencies was read over the air by a BBC announcer. In the United States the newspapers fought a similar struggle against encroachments on their preserve, only with more temporary effect. The BBC found it much easier to develop its skills in the broadcasting of talks on controversial questions when the rules forbidding broadcast controversy were slowly liberalised. Politicians and other public people were encouraged to write scripted talks for radio and a whole department grew up around the genre of the broadcast talk; in the days of rehearsed radio it was impossible for discussion formats to develop in any very lively fashion. Encroachments into broadcast news were slow to develop and the BBC thus came to institutionalise the split between largely agency-generated news bulletins (later taken over by its own staff) and more discursive speculative and polemical matter, the boundaries of which were set by problems of taste and morals. With the development of television, news came very slowly indeed: it was the 'talks' tradition on which the Lime Grove Studios – and all their pioneering of television forms – were based. The news division thought of itself as the repository of the only true tradition of journalism: Lime Grove's current affairs programmes (with early film reportage, interviews, etc.) were built out of show business, academia, the film industry, rather than in the traditions which pass from C. P. Scott. Eventually news was by-passed in terms of glamour and importance and only with the foundation of the ITN (and in particular its 'News at Ten' programme) did television really develop a news style of its own. The pace was made by the current affairs programmes in Granada, Thames and the BBC's unit at Lime Grove, and later by the feature and documentary departments of both systems. In the commercial system the separation was even greater because of the distinction between ITN and the companies (which only covered regional news). In the BBC departmental rivalries (and geographical ones, since the News department was housed in a building ten miles from the rest of television) helped to keep the two forms of factual reporting developing separately from each other.

In the middle of the 1970s, public debate about broadcasting and the evolution of several altogether new programme formats in ITV (in particular, the 'Weekend World' programme at London Weekend Television, presented by Peter Jay and produced by John Birt) forced a reconsideration of this ancient division. It proved impossible to revoke it although certain kinds of rationalisation were thought sensible. People had become tired of seeing two BBC crews at every important news event everywhere between Vietnam and Trafalgar Square, struggling over the same 'scoop'; techniques of programme-making (especially in film) meant that the visual material required for both genres was often the same. With the arrival of electronic news-gathering in England in 1977 the possibility of direct transmissions from news events and much quicker editing of material between event and transmission was evidently going to render it increasingly difficult to continue the rigid separation of news and current affairs, which were being obliged, technologically, to grow ever closer in style and format. News started to train its correspondents to report controversy and to interview in greater depth; in the past the news interview had been aimed at eliciting facts in a rather staid and often dull manner, while current affairs interviewers, drawn from academia and print journalism, were more daring in their dealings with politicians. A minister continues to expect an easier ride on news than on a current affairs programme, where he expects to be cross-questioned more searchingly. There are clear lines of expertise which will not easily transport between news and current affairs, although 'News at Ten' has evolved a great deal of the way towards a fusion of the styles. At the end of the 1970s it has become clear that the two are to merge one day or at least to reallocate their functions; the sheer extent of the discussion has made a major change inevitable; the taboos which preserved the separation have evaporated. Peter Jay and John Birt published a series of highly influential articles demanding the complete re-organisation of the news and current affairs activities of the BBC (although they worked on the rival channel) because it was at the BBC, with its larger resources and its institutional unity, that a change of the scope required could take place. They have argued that the presentation of the facts of major events should be much more closely integrated with the task of detailed explanation of the background and meaning of the events; it was senseless for news and current affairs to continue, more and more, to overlap as they grew and to shy away from the central task of public education in current events. The very division of the genres enforced an inbuilt slanting of material against the audience's clear understanding of events. For the coverage of politics, the fusion of news and current affairs would have widespread implications: hitherto audiences for the more entertaining magazine programmes in current affairs had remained high but with a greater concentration on *explanation,* would news and/or current affairs start to become something of a highbrow ghetto? The debate is taking place within a sixty-year-old broadcasting system whose very continuity seems to depend upon its ability to represent the image of the political system, as it were, to the whole of the society. In news, politicians always felt that there was somewhere they could turn for the straight and uncontroversial presentation of their arguments and actions. The centrality and factuality of their news broadcasts lies at the heart of the historic strength of the BBC and of the IBA; the pressures against change are still immense, as well as the uncertainty about the results of too complete or too speedy a change. Would a greater emphasis on analysis, as Birt and Jay demand, tend to render the political world harder of access to the mass audience? Has not political communication come to depend upon a little show business? These are among the current fears in a broadcasting system which has, by and large, acquired its independence by promising to uphold the prevailing political system and not diminish it in the eyes of society.

A Field of Forces

We have seen in the period since 1955 one important segment of the political communication of British society pass into the hands of professional television producers and managers. A considerable literature has developed, especially since 1968 when television began to play a really important role in political events, and much of it seeks to establish a working model of this new locus of media power. What has become clear is that it is no longer possible merely to ask questions about the extent of 'state control' or about the amount of 'censorship'. Political broadcasting in Britain is neither censored nor controlled invisibly from outside the institutions set up to perform the task; at least, it is no more subject to some form of habitual alien interference than is the press. But it is profoundly subject to constraints which belong peculiarly to its own institutional framework. The BBC and the IBA and all their component elements operate with a model of the political environment which is of their own making – it is a facsimile of an outer political world constructed out of precedents set in broadcasting's own history. Political television operates within a field of force, with lines of advice and pressure running right through the society. The 'controls' are built into the assumptions inside the minds of producers and management.

Professor Burns in his study of the BBC's managerial processes concludes, perhaps exaggeratedly, that if the enormous potential of the BBC as a source of political, cultural and social enlightenment is to be realised, 'some means have to be found of freeing it from its client relationship to government; above all, it has to be delivered from the paralysing threat contained in a licence which measures out its life-expectancy in ten-year doses'.[22] It is difficult to see how else the BBC could be found secure roots in British society, although the prescription is no doubt correct. An institution requires to hold some form of title deeds to its monopoly or hegemony over an area of social activity; the BBC operates according to a Tudor-style 'royal privilege' and the entire world picture which it contains and which it passes on to the society is shaped by that central fact. There is no other sector within economy or society available for a non-commercial organisation wielding so much power. As is illustrated in the other chapters of this book, the sovereignty of broadcasting has to rest somewhere within political parties or industry or a national constitution. It has in practice to be held accountable to that source of sovereignty either at prescribed times, or according to statute or custom, otherwise it becomes subject to permanent demands for reorganisation and reconstruction. New proposals exist in Britain for different forms of organisation for the control of broadcasting, but they are all based upon the idea of a public 'authority', its controls resting upon the bedrock of 'public' individuals tested in 'public' life and representative in a general way of different segments of the society. These are held to mediate and diversify the power of the state (or, rather, the government of the day) but they are not a substitute for it.

Professor Burns' study has opened up a variety of wholly new considerations concerning the operations of British broadcasting, perhaps more profoundly than those of any of the three post-war official committees of enquiry. He shows how the BBC's original set of high purposes, the public service mission of its founder John Reith, have been supplanted by a 'miscellany of values and purposes compounded of individual commitments to professionalism, to careers, to managerial efficiency, to saving money or making money, which are the prevailing currency'.[23] Successive attempts to 'modernise' the operations of the BBC, in particular in response to the rise of its powerful rival and companion, the IBA, have amounted to the imposition of different managerial 'atmospheres' in which producers develop (partly illusory) loyalties to topical ideas of perfection, which tend to shift their attention from the central historic ideals of the BBC. In the 1970s, however, this dedication to efficient managerialism and professionalism has pervaded the whole of British broadcasting; the institutional worlds of the BBC and the commercial system have grown more and more alike, their personnel interchangeable, at the humblest production levels, at technical levels, and at the highest levels of management. One Chairman of the IBA has become Chairman of the BBC; one Vice-Chairman of the BBC has become Chairman of the IBA. The Chief Secretary of the BBC has become Director of Television at the IBA. Three BBC Channel Controllers since 1967 have accepted posts in senior management in various commercial programme companies. Managerial miscegenation has become almost complete and it is inevitable, therefore, that one convergent set of ideals and cultural purposes will come to be expressed by British broadcasting, despite the differences of structure and constitution within the double system. The commercial system, less deeply embedded in political life than the BBC, has always tended to be slightly more detached from politics, enjoying what appear to be better relationships with senior politicians while worrying less at times about offending them. Commercial television, in its documentary output in particular, has demonstrated a greater willingness to allow its producers individual independence, not appearing to mind when programmes have been publicly labelled as partisan. The difference is one of degree, and the BBC would argue that in the field of drama it has allowed producers to take a far more forward stand than their counterparts in commercial broadcasting. Certainly, each institution has areas of programmes which are less worried over, less picked at.

The paradox is that this loosening of the system has resulted partly from the growing convergence of its two halves; producers must be treated in one institution as well as they have come to expect from the other. Vexations produced by over-management have made producers increasingly aware of their own professionalism and its marketability. There is a growing tension, which is almost certain to become one of the main themes of the 1980s throughout the world of the electronic media, between institutions and creative workers, who more and more find themselves ready to face the open market-place, or who wish to work only for brief periods at a time, on stated projects, with one organisation or another. This is not the place to examine all of the ramifications of the move towards freelance employment, and the pressures it generates within trade unions as well as employing bodies, but it is extremely relevant to our theme to point out that any significant increase in the number of producers who turn freelance will have considerable repercussions on institutional ability to control output *ideologically*. Freelance workers are far less susceptible to the conditioning of the 'private world', less accessible to the flow of unstated inhibitions, less manipulable by the promise of a place in a large and secure career structure. The growing power of freelance producers will also increase the power of staff producers, through the processes of convergence and compatibility. A profession can survive half staff and half freelance but the rights earned by the latter will affect the attitudes of the former. One must expect a new mood of independence on the part of producers towards management, as well as a growing *dependence* as producers compete piecemeal for jobs.

The BBC and the IBA both face the 1980s in a mood of great nervousness. It is inevitable that before another decade is out there will be some kind of major reorganisation within broadcasting or perhaps in the shape of a third or fourth broadcasting authority (as proposed by the Annan Committee). No one expects the issue to be quickly resolved. It is more than forty years since Reith left the BBC which he had created to be a keeper of the nation's conscience, above the buzz of political parties and factions. Yet Britain has never been able to lose track of the idea that broadcasting was to operate according to the principle of a second Established Church, even though both parties have undermined the ideal. The Labour Party treated it as another large nationalised utility; the Conservatives have looked for appropriate bits of broadcasting to hand over to commercial operators. The system seems more and more riven. The broadcasting institutions themselves demand only more of what they have already, more channels, less change. For some observers – including the present writer – the only route back towards a dedicated broadcasting is through a plurality of institutions, some large, some small, each with its own safe form of finance and its own section of electronic media. A low-key competition between parallel institutions should maintain whatever level of independence is possible from political interference in a society where politics has come to depend upon broadcasting. Caution has grown over broadcasting slowly like lichen over standing stones; it has also perhaps attacked British society as a whole. The BBC and IBA are hemmed in by their own accumulated rulings and procedures and need the helpful competition of a newly-founded broadcasting authority concerned with a new channel, or with cable or local sound radio or another of the new electronic media which are destined to arrive in the decade of the 1980s. Fresh impetus can come only from a new enterprise which has not yet acquired the accumulated inhibitions which accrue from operating over the course of decades within British society. That would perhaps dispel one real danger built into the system: broadcasting in Britain needs to be fearful of its own proneness to fear itself.

2 France

The Monopoly that Won't Divide

Antoine de Tarlé

The relationship between the world of politics and television in France is looked upon by observers in other European countries with a certain puzzlement. It has various characteristics which are particularly difficult to understand, though they are really nothing more than the reflection in television of certain recurring features of French political life which one may define, without pushing the paradox too far, as a 'manichean consensus'. In fact, since the end of the nineteenth century, French political leaders have always held a manichean view of society. Those who accepted the system, or in the words of the political scientist, Stanley Hoffman, those who supported the 'republican synthesis', were considered as 'good'; the others, the anti-republicans, represented the opposition, but were also thought ready to overthrow the regime; they formed a kind of band of delinquents and outlaws who had to be kept away from the centres of power at all costs. At the same time there has developed a conception of the state and of government in which there is similarly no room for compromise. The state is the incarnation of the public interest, and it employs civil servants to execute it. Yet, in as much as this public interest has merged with that of the regime and the Republic, it seems only natural that the state should be at the service of the parties in power and that it should mobilise its forces against their enemies.

Power and the Groups of Delinquents

This overall view of society has affected the attitudes of French
politicians all the more easily, since all three republics which have
followed each other in recent times have been challenged by
strong political movements whose aim it has been to change the
regime. It applies equally to right-wing parties, Socialists and
Communists. Indeed, the upheaval of the Second World War,
which brought to a head the struggle between democracy and
fascism and considerably strengthened the role of the state, only
served to reinforce this way of thinking.

After the Second World War, the parties which had grown out
of the resistance movements thought it logical to increase the
strength of the administration, which enjoyed a reputation for
competence, independence and integrity, in order to reduce the
influence of the large financial interests which had proved so
harmful during the 1930s. It was therefore quite natural that in a
period of governmental reconstruction, and with the need to
rebuild a shattered economy, broadcasting should be brought
under the control of a public administration. It also seemed quite
natural that it should be used to defend the regime against the
threat posed by the two groups of 'delinquents', consisting, after
1947, of the Gaullists on the one hand and the Communists on the
other. These two groups were therefore denied access to radio and
television under the instructions of successive Ministers of Information. When questioned in Parliament by the Communists, a
Minister of Information under the Fourth Republic declared that
'The French broadcasting system is continuously involved in
politics, in defending the national interest of France . . . The
Government believes that it is the true representative of the
nation, since it is supported by a majority of the National
Assembly, and that it has the duty to express the wishes of the
nation.'[1]

These ideas are echoed in a declaration made by Roger Frey,
the Gaullist Minister of Information, in 1959: 'The State has at its
disposal a means of communication which links it to public
opinion. It would be absurd for the State to hand it over to those
who, in the press or elsewhere, seek only to vilify its actions.'[2]
Thus, in reality, the Gaullists who came to power in 1958 shared
the views of their opponents. For them too, the state, the regime

and public service were one and the same thing. The public interest was identified with the interests of Gaullism, which was the main safeguard against the ruin of the state and hence of France itself. In order to save the nation, the state had to use all the means at its disposal; such a step could not be illegitimate since the government had received a majority of votes under the system of universal suffrage.

The establishment of the Fifth Republic could not possibly have brought with it a change in the political status of the public television service. On the contrary; because of its importance, it became a principal weapon in the fight against the new delinquent group made up of the old leaders under the Fourth Republic who now posed a threat to the new regime. Under these conditions, the notion of objectivity lost all its meaning and even came to constitute a threat to the national interest. The main object was to defend the government. Senior civil servants in charge of the RTF, who had, so to speak, 'a sense of [the] State', applied themselves to this task with the same zeal as their predecessors, by different means but in the same spirit, had worked for a secular society and for the Republic at the end of the nineteenth century.

During the first years of the Fifth Republic the Opposition was in a poor position to counter-attack. The former Ministers of Information among its ranks (including important left-wing leaders such as Gaston Defferre and Francois Mitterrand) had proved no less intolerant in their time. Furthermore, the Opposition shared with the government the conviction that the monopoly should be in the hands of the state as guardian of the public interest, a concept constantly being invoked by politicians and administrators alike, without ever being defined.

The Communists, despite employing their own terms in expressing their point of view, did not differ fundamentally from the rest of the opposition on this question. Their Jacobin conception of the state and their confidence in their role as guardians of the truth showed them to have a mentality closely akin to that of the Gaullists, with whom they agreed that broadcasting should not be in private hands and that the monopoly should be defended at all costs. They sincerely believed that they alone were capable of giving the state its true role as the incarnation and defender of the democratic public interest – which happened to coincide with that of their party.

When Georges Pompidou succeeded General de Gaulle as President of the Republic in 1969, there was, contrary to all appearances, no change in the doctrine of power. The new President had exactly the same outlook as his predecessor. He declared: 'History has demonstrated that our people, who by nature are given to division and the most extreme individualism, has only been moulded into the French nation by means of the State . . . Today it seems necessary to recall that France must be identified with the State.'[3] He applied these principles to the particular case of television, which he considered as part of the state, when he stressed in a widely quoted statement:

> Whether one likes it or not . . . a television journalist is unlike any other journalist. He has additional responsibilities. Whether one likes it or not, television is regarded as the Voice of France both by the people of France and abroad. This fact demands a certain reserve for two obvious reasons: the first is that the responsibilities of an informant are in direct relation to the means at his disposal and there can be no comparison between those of television and any others, and the second is that at the present moment they exercise a monopoly.[4]

As Jacques Thibau, a former senior official of French television, points out:

> The doctrine of the Voice of France encourages and justifies the liberties taken concerning the governing principle of liberal democracy: equality in the question of electoral propaganda . . . The most powerful means of information has been established by the highest authorities of the State according to the rules and criteria of political authoritarianism. Therein lies the serious fault of a doctrine which makes it difficult, if not impossible, for television to carry out the important tasks which belong to an information service in a modern society.[5]

Nevertheless, after 1968 the ideological climate in French political circles began to change, very slowly at first, but thereafter with increasing rapidity. Belief in the infallibility of the administration and confidence in the state began to crumble. The technocratic conception of the state sustained by the Gaullists came under criticism from both left and right.

According to the neo-liberal forces whose voice began to be heard again, thanks to the economic expansion during the 1960s, the state could not do everything or exercise a complete monopoly. Liberty was equated with pluralism. As Olivier Giscard d'Estaing, brother of the present President of the Republic, pointed out during the parliamentary debate on the status of the ORTF in June 1972: 'The greatness, and I would say the originality of our institutions is the creation of a society in which the state and private enterprise can exist side by side and combine to provide a public service . . . Would there be any freedom of the press if there were a state monopoly of the press? Whatever form this might take, it would be to the detriment of liberty.'[6]

It is not surprising that when M Giscard d'Estaing, who is a neo-liberal, became President of the Republic in 1974, there was a change in the official doctrine of power. M Giscard d'Estaing was publicly contradicting his predecessor when he stated on several occasions that television was not the 'Voice of France' and advocated a pluralistic organisation of channels while keeping them within the framework of a public monopoly. These opinions corresponded very closely to his conception of the state, which again was very different from that of the Gaullists. Shortly after coming to power, the President declared that 'The state and its representatives are the servants of the people of the country . . . The state is an important instrument placed at the service of the nation, but what we must have most at heart, is the destiny of the nation. The role of the state is not to protect the French nation but to guide it.'[7] Two years later, he took up this idea again when he declared: 'Let us banish from our minds the idolatry of the state . . . The state is not an end in itself, it is an instrument.'[8]

An increasing proportion of the left wing also came to share this distrust of the ideas of 'statism' and monopoly, but obviously for different reasons. Undoubtedly, the origins of this change can be traced back to the revival of liberal sentiments which spread in May 1968, and which for many left-wing militants were crystallised in the idea of 'autogestion' – a vague idea, impossible to define, which reflects a rejection of bureaucracy, excessive restraint and an overwhelming technocracy. The idea was first put forward by the PSU, a small, extreme left-wing party and by certain members of the CFDT trade union, and spread through the higher echelons of the left, the Socialist Party and even of the Communist Party, despite its tendency toward statism. Such a change in attitudes has already produced certain results. It has helped the word 'monopoly' to lose much of its meaning, the opposition parties being ever more reluctant to use it, and it has attenuated a little the simplistic manicheism which these parties tend to share with the majority.

The Communists too have tried to revise their ideas somewhat. Their General Secretary, M Marchais, has declared that it is not normal for 'a public monopoly to become a government monopoly. We therefore propose to reorganise the monopoly of television in a democratic way, so that it constitutes a real public service, without a philosophy or a public and obligatory political doctrine . . . No party will be able to dominate the state or be identified with it.'[9]

One can certainly reply that such declarations are not binding on a party in opposition, yet they do represent a change in language compared with previous policy.

1974 saw the establishment in France of a new system of organisation for television, which constituted a departure from that which had existed for fifteen years. Of course, the state preserved its monopoly over broadcasting and planning, but it delegated its powers over programmes to three public television companies who were given a large measure of autonomy in relation to each other.

At least on the surface, this appeared to constitute a radical upheaval in the monolith which was the old ORTF. It was therefore legitimate to believe that the pluralism established by the reform would lead to a change in the nature of the relationship between television and the world of politics. It would appear that this has not been quite the case. Indeed, one can see re-emerging the old conflicts which for decades kept alive the spirit of contention between broadcasting, government and opposition.

One must employ several methods of analysis in order to explain this situation. The role of television in French public life should be looked at under three headings: the weight of the administrative burden which arose in the early years of its existence; the particular characteristics of French political life and the functioning of its institutions; and finally, the antagonisms which can be observed in any country where television exists side by side with a democratic pluralist system.

Broadcasting: An Administration Like Any Other

In 1944, after the liberation, French broadcasting became a state administration, a branch of the Ministry of Information managed by civil servants. This important reform was approved by politicians as a whole and was generally considered as a step forward. Before the Second World War, in fact, there was great confusion in broadcasting. Private stations, financed by advertising revenue, existed side by side with public stations financed by taxes and placed under the authority of the Ministry of Posts and Telecommunications. For the leaders who had grown out of the resistance, it was essential to put an end to the power of wealth and private interests in the information sector. In this situation, and according to the prevailing ideas of the period, the state appeared to be the guardian of the common interest and of public services. It was therefore perfectly natural to entrust it with this medium whose importance had been revealed during the course of the war.

Television made its appearance shortly afterwards, the first regular transmissions beginning in 1948.[10] All the same, it fitted quite naturally into the system, becoming one of the two branches of a strictly hierarchical and closely supervised public broadcasting administration, watched over by the Minister of Information. Clearly, the information services of the 'Radiodiffusion-télévision francaise' (RTF) came under strict political control. Thus, for example, when François Mitterrand was Minister of Information in 1948, 'Every day, at midday, his principal private secretary, Georges Dayan would preside over a meeting with the private secretaries of Jules Moch (Minister of the Interior) and Robert Lacoste (Minister for Industry), to discuss the latest events with Vital Gayman, the head of news broadcasting. It was during these meetings, in fact, that Gayman received his instructions.'[11] The Ministers of Information who succeeded Mitterrand followed the same procedure, and became increasingly interested in television.

All the same, this arrangement came in for less criticism than one might have expected, for two reasons. On the one hand, the political system under the Fourth Republic was marked by the absence of bipolarisation. Between 1945 and 1958 every party, including the Communists, had from time to time a share of power which allowed them to control and therefore to mould the media. Thus the RTF was never the instrument of one single party for any length of time. On the other hand, there was a kind of consensus in political circles in favour of 'statism' and governmental control. State control of the audiovisual media seemed the best way to protect them from commercial interests, and it appeared quite normal for the government to use radio and television to protect what it considered to be the interests of France. Towards the end of the Fourth Republic, however, the system became more and more difficult to control. The war in Algeria, which broke out in 1954, created serious tensions in the news media. From that moment on, the criticism and disenchantment which had hitherto been very limited began to spread and was increasingly voiced in the press.

Georges Hourdin, director of *La Vie Catholique*, summed up these criticisms when he wrote:

Dependence on power, and especially on the government of the moment, is one of the drawbacks of the present regime, which considers these new techniques as a public service. The formula which sets up the RTF as a straightforward specialised administration . . . increases the risk . . . News broadcasts are being infected by a form of censorship which is unacceptable because it is unacknowledged.[12]

Furthermore, the RTF was suffering from severe administrative problems, since the growth of television had forced it to call increasingly on technicians and producers whose habits and activities were more akin to those of the cinema than of an ordinary administration.

A reform was therefore essential in order to administer properly an organisation which was being suffocated by its bureaucratic structure. This reform was carried through under the Fifth Republic, in 1959, and for the first time it gave the RTF a statute. It became an autonomous public institution, but it remained under complete government control. The government was to nominate its Director General, and it refused to allow it to have a board of directors. Thus it was not for reasons of liberalism that the RTF was reformed, but in order to adapt a heavy, rigid machinery to the rapid development of technology. It is worth keeping in mind, for the process was to be repeated on several occasions in the following twenty years.

Two very important phenomena coincided with the birth of this public institution. First of all, there was the enormous political upheaval which resulted from the establishment of the Fifth Republic. A much more rigid system took the place of the ministerial instability and the fluctuating majorities of the preceding regime. A majority coalition established itself in power in 1958, and has remained there ever since. The opposition organised itself and became ever more identified with the left, thus creating the bipolar system which is still in existence. Secondly, television, which had been stagnating for about ten years, witnessed a very rapid growth. There were one million television sets in 1958, ten million in 1968. Television, which had been aimed at a minority of the population, and which had been the poor relation of the RTF, suddenly became the main and often the only source of information and entertainment for the people of France.

The new majority could not avoid the temptation of employing this rapidly expanding medium for its own ends, and it did so all the more willingly as previous governments had shown it the way. Yet the facts of the matter were quite different since television was now reaching the whole population, and since it was now the same group of parties always at the helm.

This change was so great and so unexpected that politicians found it difficult to adapt. At the beginning of the Fifth Republic, the opposition parties, trapped in their old ways, believed that their absence from power was merely temporary. They saw no need to question the organisation of the RTF – which was based on a state monopoly – or to propose a truly pluralist system. On the whole, they limited themselves to criticising government methods and demanding access to broadcasting for all the political parties, without, however, showing much imagination when it came to proposing alternative solutions.[13] Clearly, the administrative system established after the liberation weighed heavily on everyone's mind.

The Birth of the ORTF

In 1964, Parliament accepted a government proposal for a new statute for radio and television. This was the Law of 27 June 1964 which created the 'Office de radio-télévision francaise' (ORTF).

In presenting it to Parliament, the Minister of Information, Alain Peyrefitte, said that the aim of the bill was to 'put the RTF in order, to overcome the inefficiency of an organisation imprisoned by its old structure, to inject a spirit of responsibility and competition, to eliminate particular interests in favour of the common interest and to protect it from the abuses of power and impotence'.[14] These ideas are a *résumé* of the doctrine of all post-war governments anxious to reform the broadcasting service. One can recognise the familiar concepts of a common interest, the desire to improve management and the promise of greater freedom in relation to government.

The new service was a public institution with a board of directors whose employees enjoyed a status quite different from that of civil servants. It was placed under the authority of a Chairman and a Managing Director. Yet the occupants of these two posts as well as the majority of the Board of Directors were appointed by the government, which in a French context left them with very little independence. What is more, M Peyrefitte refused to accept any of the modifications proposed by the opposition during the parliamentary debate, most of which were aimed at liberalising the organisation.

The left was also paralysed by its own intellectual contradictions. It remained faithful to the concept of the state which it shared with the Gaullists, with the result that it was fighting simultaneously both for the liberalisation and the maintenance of the monopoly. In other words, it criticised the government for its persistent interventions, but it continued to believe that only the state could possibly hold the monopoly. Thus it trapped itself in a political dilemma from which it has yet to emerge.

Between 1964 and 1968, the ORTF worked under very difficult conditions. The loosening of the administrative stranglehold was not great enough for it to adapt to a very rapid rate of expansion, and its management problems continued to worsen. At the same time, the government retained a firm control over information and this led to continuous criticism and to a growing unease. It would be tedious to list all the cases of journalists silenced or sacked for their lack of submissiveness or of those dismissed for not conforming to the wishes of the government.[15] Let us simply recall one statement and one important fact.

The statement was made by M Peyrefitte, the then Minister of

Information, when he asserted before the National Assembly that television ought to counterbalance the influence of the regional press which was to a large extent hostile to the government.[16]

The fact is the shock felt by the public when it was able to see on television a certain number of opposition leaders who had not been seen on it for years, on the occasion of the Presidential Elections of 1965.

The rules governing Presidential Elections, established under the Law of 6 November 1962 and the Decree of 14 March 1964, actually offered the candidates wide possibilities to express themselves. They were allowed two hours radio time and two hours of television time before the first round of voting, and the same number of hours were allocated to the two remaining candidates before the second round. A national commission for the supervision of the use of the ORTF channels, made up of senior magistrates, was entrusted with the task of seeing that the principle of equality between the candidates was respected.

This system was applied for the first time in 1965, was much appreciated, and was used again in 1969 and 1974. Given its results, some observers believe that, with certain modifications, it could become permanent. It is worth noting that the supervision of the national commission extended, during the electoral period, to all broadcasts, since they too had to respect the principle of equality between the candidates.

Many observers consider that this sudden opposition appearance on television caused General de Gaulle to lose votes in 1965. Michel Debré, a former Gaullist Prime Minister, wrote: 'Opening radio and television to different opinions, in other words those most opposed to government policy, can further the cause of the government and of the state.'[17] During this period, television news was controlled by a new body, the 'Service de liaison interministerielle pour l'information' (SLII), under the authority of the Minister of Information. The workings of this body have been described by Jacques Thibau, who at the time was assistant director of television: 'Each morning, about 11 a.m., ten or so civil servants would meet to determine: (1) What television should not deal with; (2) The official inaugurations and ceremonies which had to be given maximum coverage.'[18] In the same article, Jacques Thibau notes 'that one must go right back into the past, to the Third and Fourth Republics to discover the origins of certain forms of political behaviour'. This remark doubtless goes some way towards explaining the situation which the national television network found itself in. It inherited the destiny mapped out for radio since 1944. It remained part of an administrative hierarchy, in practice if not in theory. Like his predecessors under the Fourth Republic, M Peyrefitte considered himself to be a kind of super-director of broadcasting, with the job of maintaining order and safeguarding a certain conception of the common interest within the services entrusted to him. His behaviour with respect to these services was not unlike that of a minister of agriculture or industry in their particular fields. While television increasingly acquired a strong character of its own, politicians were more inclined to consider it as a branch of the civil service than as an element of public freedom. Under the influence of the press, public opinion evolved rapidly on this question, with a resulting gap developing between its views and those of the government.

The Crisis Years: 1968 – 74

The events of May 1968, which were so dangerous for the state, clearly put this fragile edifice to the test. Those in charge of television news broadcasts, faithful to government instructions, made the mistake of not transmitting reports of the riots, while public opinion was kept well informed by the press and by stations broadcasting from abroad. This escapist policy irritated viewers, made television journalists ill at ease and caused television to lose much of its credibility. The position soon proved to be untenable, and the ORTF authorities were obliged to organise debates on television, though this did not prevent journalists from going out on strike until the end of June.

In July 1968, the majority won a sweeping victory in the General Elections. The ORTF was brought to heel and many of the journalists found guilty of having taken part in the strike were either sacked or transferred – to the provinces or abroad. They were accused of not having carried out their duties during a period of crisis, and in some sense of having betrayed the state and the government. Thus, though they had not held the status of civil servants since 1964, the employees of the ORTF were still considered as such, indeed they were thought of as civil servants with special responsibilities, since they worked in a strategically important sector.

However, the *status quo* was only re-established in a superficial sense. In retrospect, 1968 appears to have been a turning point in the relationship between government and television. The ORTF, in common with all institutions, was profoundly shaken by the spirit of dispute and criticism which blossomed during the month of May. It finally lost the authority which had already been weakened by the revelations made by Jacques Thibau in December 1967 of the workings of the SLII (Service de liaison de l'information interministerielle). All of a sudden, the government's authoritarian off-hand treatment of the media became unacceptable. A poll organised by the popular weekly magazine *Télé 7 Jours* after the events of May 1968, showed that 87.9 per cent of those who answered were in favour of a reform of the statute of the ORTF, while 85.7 per cent thought that television news should be free of government control.[19]

Between 1968 and 1974, the ORTF was regularly shaken by crises: strikes, political and financial scandals, frequent changes of officials, and parliamentary enquiries. Such were the symptoms of the gradual degradation of the ORTF which finally led to its demise.

The Presidential Elections of 1969, which followed the departure of de Gaulle, offered the candidates an opportunity to express their views on the organisation of the ORTF. In an interview in *Télé 7 Jours*, Georges Pompidou, who had been Prime Minister between 1962 and 1968 and who was to be elected President of the Republic, declared:

When I had the statute of the ORTF drawn up, I believed it to be liberal. I am now told that it is no longer liberal enough. I quite agree that a more liberal one is needed . . . As to my position as regards the journalists who were dismissed . . . if they really believe that they were honest with themselves and with the viewers in their reporting of the events of May 1968, then I do not see on what grounds they can be reproached.[20]

Measures to liberate the television service were announced by the new Prime Minister, Jacques Chaban Delmas, during the course of his policy statement on 16 September 1969. An autonomous information unit was set up for each of the two channels, and these were entrusted to two excellent professional journalists: Pierre Desgraupes, who was considered something of a left winger, for the first channel, and Jacqueline Baudrier, a known Gaullist, for the second channel. In addition, the Ministry of Information was abolished.

M Chaban Delmas' experiment lasted three years and came to an end in 1972, but it is nevertheless worth studying for several reasons. It provoked extremely violent reactions among members of the majority who were unable to adapt to the development of the broadcasting media. Important figures in the Gaullist party such as Arthur Conte and M Tomasini publicly attacked the television service, accusing it of bias toward opposition. The whole Chaban Delmas government was weakened by this incessant criticism, which helped to lead to the dismissal of the Prime Minister in July 1972.

It was the first time in the history of France that a government had been put in question by its own majority because of its policy on television. But the blame for this situation lies deeper than the intolerance of the political world. At the beginning M Chaban Delmas had committed a fatal error. He had put television current affairs on a political footing when he appointed two personalities of different political convictions to be in charge of the information units. Instead of playing the problem down, he made television current affairs broadcasts the scene of continuous confrontation, and he made M Desgraupes the scapegoat of the majority by placing him in artificial opposition to Mme Baudrier. As Denise Bombardier, a Quebec sociologist, has written: 'How can one possibly find acceptable a formula which links the Director of Information so closely to government, in this case the Prime Minister himself! . . . The personal intervention of the Prime Minister in the appointment of M Desgraupes inevitably linked the fate of the two.'[21]

M Chaban Delmas' government might have been able to adjust the balance in the relationship between television and the political world if it had implemented the recommendations of a distinguished commission (under the chairmanship of M Paye) which had been set up by the Prime Minister. In its report, published on 30 June 1970, the Paye Commission asserted that the news on radio and television should be: 'complete, correct, balanced, impartial and free'. As regards the actual organisation of the information service, it recommended that the board of directors should be given special responsibilities in this field, to maintain the plurality of the information units and to provide a clear definition of their relationship with government.[22] These recommendations were never put into practice. The Paye Report was shelved and was never discussed by the government or in Parliament.

Furthermore, management problems again engulfed the ORTF. In November 1971 a scandal over 'clandestine advertising' came to light. Both the National Assembly and the Senate set up commissions of enquiry whose reports revealed the malfunctioning of the ORTF. A familiar pattern was thus repeated: political discontent together with the difficulties involved in running an increasingly unmanageable organisation led to a crisis and pointed to the need for reform. In May 1972 the President re-established the Ministry of Information and pushed a new statute through Parliament. The Law of 3 July 1972 retained the principle of monopoly and the 'uniqueness' of the ORTF and contained no change in the make-up of the board of directors, the majority of whom were still to be appointed by the state. On the other hand, the direction of the ORTF was entrusted to an Executive Chairman appointed for a period of three years, which in theory was intended to increase his authority. The law also made it possible to give certain branches of the ORTF an independent status in order to bring about the demonstrably necessary decentralisation. A Higher Broadcasting Council was established which was intended to play a consultative role for the government.

The opinion of politicians as a group, as expressed during the parliamentary debate preceding the division, revealed disappointment with a limited reform which appeared to avoid the really fundamental problems. It must be added that for the first time since the beginning of the Fifth Republic, a number of Deputies and Senators who had been involved in the various commissions of enquiry knew the issues better than, or as well as the government. A discussion began, but was soon exhausted because of the inadequacy of the material laid before the Chamber. A long debate on the question of the monopoly was initiated by Olivier Giscard d'Estaing, but his proposals were rejected by the Deputies. Besides, the general opinion seems to have been summed up by a majority spokesman, Griotteray, who believed that 'the bill that we are about to vote on, represents the timid betrothal of the ORTF and the modern world' and regretted 'the perhaps excessive prudence of this attempt at renewal'.[23]

M Pompidou then appointed Arthur Conte, a Gaullist Deputy who has distinguished himself in the past for his attacks on television, to the Executive Chairmanship of the ORTF. This appointment represented an interesting innovation, because it made a politician from the ranks of the majority Director of the public broadcasting service. Having experimented with two solutions, the first involving a senior civil servant as Director General under the Minister of Information, the second appointing two civil servants as Chairman and Managing Director under the distant tutelage of the Prime Minister, the government was now trying a third solution: a Minister of Information and an Executive Chairman who were both politicians.

At the time, many observers considered the appointment of M Conte as an unprecedented subjection of the ORTF to the majority. Furthermore, the decision of the new Chairman to abolish the two independent information departments and to dismiss M Desgraupes appeared to confirm this judgement.

In practice, Arthur Conte was not a man who submitted to authority like a civil servant merely because he was a politician. His strong personality created serious tensions within the administrative organisation which predominated at the ORTF. It would seem that President Pompidou had been only too successful in his wager on the autonomy of the ORTF, since the methods he employed slipped out of his control. This in fact became evident in the early months of 1973 and greatly worried the politicians of the majority, who were afraid of loosing their hold on an instrument which was of such crucial importance to them. The antagonism between M Malaud, the Minister of Information, and M Conte grew steadily worse. Following a now well established pattern within the ORTF, management problems were closely linked to political dissension. The 1972 law and the internal reorganisations did nothing to improve the administrative and financial functioning of the ORTF. It was threatened with paralysis because of administrative deficiencies and trade union conflicts, all of which made it more vulnerable in the face of government pressure.

The decisive shock came in October 1973, when M Conte produced before Parliament a letter from M Malaud to his assistant, which accused several radio service executives of being Communists. About the same time, the National Assembly's Finance Commission noticed that the accounts of the ORTF were in the red, and refused to authorise payment of the licence revenue. The conflict was resolved by the simultaneous departure of Conte and Malaud.[24] Conte was replaced by a senior civil servant, Marceau Long, and the National Assembly set up a new commission of enquiry to look into the management of the ORTF.

What is most striking in this affair, is the shift it reveals in the locus of decision-making on broadcasting affairs. M Malaud's methods were very similar to those of other Ministers of Information in the Fourth Republic and in the early years of the Fifth Republic. Yet they profoundly shocked both politicians and public, with the result that M Pompidou was forced to dismiss him. In practice (and M Conte's book was to show this very clearly), the Minister of Information no longer had any formal validity after 1968, and had lost his powers of political control. The disappearance of the Ministry between 1969 and 1972 had created new habits from which it was difficult to retreat. The role of political supervision was taken up by the President and the Prime Minister. What is more, the press service of the Elysée had been greatly expanded since 1969. One of its members, Guillaud, was a former director of the television service, and was to return there in 1973 (as director of the third channel).

This apparently irreversible development showed that the concept of a television service forming part of the administrative hierarchy, with a minister naturally at its head, was losing ground. The ORTF had become such a large and complex instrument that it had to be handled with care, by specialists directly vetted by the President of the Republic. Marceau Long prepared a new reform of the ORTF, but this project was interrupted by the death of President Pompidou in April 1974.

The 1974 Reform and the Break-up of the ORTF

As soon as he had taken office the new President of the Republic, Valéry Giscard d'Estaing, showed himself to be in favour of a radical reorganisation of the public broadcasting service. He rejected all proposals for putting broadcasting into private hands since 'The President of the Republic, cannot expose himself, any more than could his predecessors, to the risk of losing control of an essential political instrument'.[25] On the other hand, the recommendations submitted to Parliament in July 1974 represented a radical change compared with the previous organisation, because they proposed the breaking up of the ORTF into seven separate organisations: three television companies, TF 1, Antenne 2 and FR 3, the last of which was to run the regional stations; one radio company, 'Radio France'; the 'Société française de production' (SFP), which was to take charge of film and video installations; the 'Institut national de l'audiovisuel' for research, archives and professional training; and finally the transmitter network, which was assigned to the TDF, the public transmission institution.

Each company is run by a Board made up of six Directors, of whom only two are representatives of the state, and by a Chairman appointed by the government for a period of three years. All seven companies are independent, but they have to abide by the conditions set out in a very detailed dossier of directives established by the government after consultation with Parliament. The dossier contained in particular very precise directives on programme content and on the administrative and financial relationships between the companies and the other organisations which have grown out of the ORTF.

The Financing of Television

On the question of finance, the law sets out a complex system for the division of revenue among the different organisations. It should be remembered that French television has two sources of revenue: a tax paid by the owners of television sets which represents about two-thirds of its income, the rest being supplied through advertising. Advertising is only allowed on two of the channels, TF 1 and Antenne 2, who share the revenue. The income from taxes is shared out among the companies by a commission of senior civil servants, chaired by a magistrate. This commission takes into account the needs of the companies, but also their performance measured in audience and quality ratings. The total sum to be shared out is determined each year by the authorities. The government fixes the rate of tax imposed on television sets (the rate being different for colour and black and white sets), while Parliament has to authorise the payment of the revenue when it examines the budget. Without the authorisation of Parliament, this payment – which is carried out by the Ministry of Finance – cannot take place.

What were the reasons for such a radical change in the public broadcasting sector? It is unlikely that the authorities were particularly interested in raising the standard of programmes. Their main preoccupation seems to have been to put an end to an endemic crisis which had serious political repercussions, and to smash the troublesome trade unions within the ORTF by obliging them to divide themselves up among seven new organisations.

At the time, the reform appeared to be an undoubted liberalisation. The authorities no longer had to deal with one single organisation which still worked along administrative lines, but with a number of organisations, to some extent in competition with each other, and run by teams in which the representatives of the state were in a minority. It still remained true that the executives of the three television channels were appointed by the authorities, but this is the case in most European systems.

Television and Parliament

These changes marked an increase in the overall role of Parliament in the affairs of television. Henceforth, there was to be a member of Parliament on each Board of Directors (a Deputy for TF 1 and A 2, and a Senator for FR 3). It is worth noting that all three come from the ranks of the majority. Furthermore, the law considerably increased the powers of the parliamentary delegation for French television. This body, quite unprecedented under French law, was set up under the Law of 3 July 1972. It is made up of eight Deputies and six Senators representing all the political groupings. Whereas previously it enjoyed only limited consultative powers, it is now consulted on all the fundamental problems of broadcasting, and it has the right to give advice on its own initiative on these problems. Finally, Parliament retains considerable powers over the financing of the public broadcasting service. Each autumn, when discussing the budget, the two assemblies examine the accounts of radio and television, and vote on the authorisation of payment of revenues, and the way they are to be shared out among the organisations concerned. This is not a purely formal operation. The National Assembly, which was unhappy with television, almost unanimously rejected the authorisation of payment of revenues in November 1975, and it only went back on its decision after difficult negotiations with the government.

From this point of view, the 1974 law marks the conclusion of a process begun in 1964, which began to involve Parliament more and more in the organisation of television. It would appear that successive governments, after being constantly accused of censoring this medium, tried to avoid dealing directly and exclusively with it by making the assemblies act as intermediaries or mediators. Parliament has always been happy to accept these new functions, though they often put it in the uncomfortable position of having to arbitrate between two conflicting interests.

The directives governing the television companies also contain precise instructions about the transmission of parliamentary debates and of the opinions of the political parties. Thus TF 1 and Antenne 2, which both have a national network, are obliged to broadcast the main debates in the National Assembly and the Senate. The choice of debates is made in consultation with the office of the Chamber concerned. The meetings of parliamentary commissions, despite forming an important part of the work of the French Parliament, are not televised. Furthermore, those political parties represented in Parliament by at least twenty members have the right to regular programmes financed by the television companies up to a limit of 60,000 francs.[26] These party political programmes each last about a quarter of an hour, and are put on the air just before the news at 8.00 p.m. – in other words, at peak viewing time. Each party may express itself in this way five or six times a year.

The political organisations have tried very hard in the last three years to make party political broadcasts lively and attractive. For this reason, television experts have the greatest say in planning the programmes, and all the large parties, PS, PC, and RPR (socialists, communists and Gaullists), have set up teams of specialists to help in General, or Presidential Election campaigns.

When allowing the political parties to express themselves in this way, no allowance was made for the smaller groups such as the ecological pressure groups, and the extreme right or the extreme left, who are excluded from the media because they do not have enough votes to be represented in Parliament. These have only one opportunity: the FR 3 Channel gives over a quarter of an hour each day from Monday to Friday between 7.45 and 8.00 p.m. to 'free expression'. A great variety of individuals and organisations have had access to this series since 1975, a certain number of small parties included, although they still complain of being the victims of a scandalous form of discrimination.

A Different Form of Tutelage

The reform was accompanied by a reorganisation of the information service at government level. The Ministry of Information, which had been re-established in 1972, was once again abolished. The task of supervising television was entrusted to the Prime Minister, who delegated this responsibility to a Secretary of State, André Rossi. The latter combined this with the job of Chief Government Spokesman. When M Barre replaced M Chirac as Prime Minister in August 1976, M Rossi's post was abolished. Thus there was a return to the situation when M Chaban Delmas was Prime Minister, but with one important difference: the team working under the President of the Republic on broadcasting matters was considerably stronger. In charge of it was M Lecat, who had been the last Minister of Information under M Pompidou. Thus the transfer of responsibility within the executive, already discernible before 1974, now became quite evident. The supervision of television, which had been the responsibility of the Minister of Information under de Gaulle and of the Prime Minister under M Pompidou, became the exclusive responsibility of the President of the Republic under M Giscard d'Estaing.

However, the way in which the law has been applied justifies the fears expressed by those who believe that old habits have not had enough time to change. If the nomination of the Chairmen of the new companies did not provoke many objections, the constitution of the teams to be in charge of television current affairs at the end of 1974 gave rise to negotiations worthy of the sacred traditions of the ORTF. Jean Diwo explains:

In fact, everything is decided by the Minister of State [for the Interior], and by his principal private secretary, André Mousset.

It forms part of the policy of the Elysée and the government to intervene as little as possible in the activities of the companies once they have started operations. No doubt this is all the more reason for choosing the directors of the information services with care. Every name, down to the heads of department, has been carefully scrutinised. It is most unfortunate for anyone whose past record is not entirely reassuring ... Never in the history of television have the authorities been so closely involved in the appointment of those in charge of current affairs.[27]

The author adds, however, that after the constitution of the teams, 'journalists are perfectly free to carry out their professional duties'.

However, during the course of 1975, the companies appeared to take their new independence seriously. Television current affairs programmes, news bulletins and commentaries had a freer tone. In any case, one thing was definitely achieved: the participation of opposition politicians in all current affairs programmes. There is no example of an important figure being denied access to television, and the leaders of the opposition, Marchais and Mitterrand, have had a greater opportunity of expressing themselves on the screen than before 1974.

The Persistence of Incomprehension in the Political World

Unfortunately, this liberalisation provoked a negative reaction among politicians of the majority, in a way which recalled that witnessed at the time of the Chaban Delmas government. A wave of hostility, mainly aimed at Antenne 2, began and swelled when the National Assembly examined the budget of the RTF in November 1975, and the debate on this occasion shows the extent of the breach between politicians and broadcasters.

Thus, M Donnez, speaking for the centrist group of the majority (that is, the reformers) declared that: 'We reformers ... complained before the Law of August 7th 1974 of a closed broadcasting service which was supervised and which ignored us completely. We notice that today we are no better off ... if politics has taken over certain television channels, it has certainly not been to the benefit of my political friends.'[28] A Communist, Roland Leroy, asked whether 'any record has been kept of the anti-communist commentaries on television. Why has the position of the Communist Party on civil liberties, on respect for the principles of democracy, been passed over in silence, or at least been seriously distorted in commentary.'[29] Jean Pierre Chevénement, speaking for the Socialists, declared that: 'In practice, about half a dozen men are in charge of the whole of current affairs at peak viewing times. Since they are chosen by M Mousset, M Poniatowski's personal private secretary, when assigning journalists to the different companies, how can they avoid being indebted to him?' Finally, M Aubert, for the Gaullists of the RPR, said that: 'One cannot say everything, no matter what it is, in a current affairs broadcast, but one can say everything which permits the listener to choose freely . . . We do not believe that the present conditions of balance, diversity and confrontation in programmes allow this to be so.'

After all this criticism from majority and opposition alike, only one speaker appealed to the common sense of the orators. This was R. A. Vivien, an RPR deputy, who was the parliamentary representative on the Board of Antenne 2. He reminded the house that if certain of his colleagues had the impression that M Marchais or some other opposition leader were seen too often on television, the opposition could equally be accused of seeing members of the government or the majority on it far too often, for 'one always sees one's opponent and never one's partner' and he emphasised 'that it is very difficult to be a good television journalist'. In conclusion, he quoted figures to prove that political parties had the benefit of more television time during the course of the year than they claimed to have had.

It is worth recounting this debate because it summed up fifteen years of controversy between politicians and television, and betrays the former's fundamental incomprehension of the latter. For politicians, television is merely a prop to be used to express their opinions and convey their messages. For them, their time on the air is of the utmost importance. For professional broadcasters, the main task is to run a complex instrument with very varied functions, and current affairs is just one branch among many. The discontent of professional broadcasters in the face of such criticism is forcefully expressed by J. P. Elkabbach, Director of Current Affairs on Antenne 2: 'I hope no one will go in for the luxury of counting up the time politicians spend on the air. I am a journalist, not a propagandist, nor a wrestling referee either.'[30]

Thus the division of the ORTF did not put an end to the manoeuvring and rumours which had plagued it from time to time during its short history. For some obscure reason, Antenne 2 seems to monopolise the discontent. Between 1975 and 1977, four men have succeeded each other as Director of Current Affairs: Sallebert, Georges Leroy, Baudinat and Elkabbach. It would appear that the Elysée has intervened each time to designate a successor, and that it was successful in all but the case of Baudinat.

On the other hand, it must be said that the television companies have reacted much more vigorously against such pressures than the ORTF would have done. An example of this is the case of Christian Guy: while he was head of the political department of Antenne 2, he was accused by two radio journalists, Péricard and Elkabbach, of wanting to organise a demonstration against M Giscard d'Estaing in Red Square in Moscow, while the President was on a visit to the USSR. The case was taken seriously by officials and even came before the President. It is quite likely that Guy would have been dismissed in the days of the ORTF, but the management and Board of Directors of Antenne 2 counter-attacked, and refuted the accusations by calling on 'precise facts which are verifiable and *grandguignolesque*' as *Le Monde* put it. M Guy kept his job.[31]

In the same way, Antenne 2 has found itself in conflict with the government over a very popular programme called 'Les Dossiers de l'Écran'. This programme uses a film to introduce a live televised debate on a more or less burning topical issue. Twice, Antenne 2 has been prevented from organising 'dossiers', one on the Army, the other on crime, following public interventions by the Ministers of Defence and the Interior. In both instances, the Chairman of Antenne 2, M Jullian, had no hesitation in making a public reply with the support of his Board of Directors. What is more, the joint parliamentary broadcasting committee entered into the affair. Its Chairman Dominique Pado, asked himself whether these government interventions were not 'difficult to reconcile with the independence accorded to the broadcasting companies',[32] a view shared by another member of the committee, Le Tac (RPR), who observed that 'the spirit of the law was put in question' and that 'the Chairmen of the companies were in some sense on parole'.[33] The parliamentary delegation heard Jullian draw his conclusions from these events, when he declared that 'There is a danger that the suppression of a programme may be interpreted as a step backward or as a form of censorship. To avoid this danger, the board has prepared an emergency procedure for deciding on the postponement of debates and explaining the reasons for such alterations.'[34]

Thus the company took up a firm yet cautious position. It had no hesitation in explaining its motives to the press nor to a parliamentary tribunal, though it did not openly oppose the government, which could still exert strong administrative and financial pressure.

The municipal elections of March 1977 caused renewed tension between television and politics. The Gaullist Party (RPR) joined with the Socialists and Communists in demanding the setting up of a parliamentary commission of enquiry into the supposed bias of current affairs on television[35].

Television has not, therefore, entirely rid itself of the administrative context in which it has been imprisoned from the start. Its links with the authorities surveilling it have certainly been loosened since the period immediately after the Second World War, when the officials of the RTF were simply civil servants. The reforms of 1959, 1964, 1972 and 1974 all contributed to the gradual emancipation demanded by the more immediate necessities of management. Over the years there have also been some changes among directors, and journalists have come to television from the press and from private radio stations where they were used to a greater freedom.

The Development of Political Programmes

In this way, television was opened up stage by stage to political pluralism. In 1966, after the shock caused by the Presidential Elections in which de Gaulle had to go to a second round before being elected, a political programme was allowed on television. It was called 'Face à Face' and in it politicians were directly confronted by journalists of differing opinions; on the new second channel, two young journalists, André Harris and Alain de Sédouy launched a very lively current affairs programme called 'Zoom'. Both of these programmes were removed in the storm of 1968.

In 1969, television transmitted another type of programme: 'À

Armes Égales', in which two politicians, one from the majority and one from the opposition, discussed a precise problem under the guidance of two journalists. This formula was extremely successful and offered the public lively and interesting discussions. Nevertheless, it ran out of steam and was abandoned in 1974. 'Face à Face' and 'À Armes Égales' have disappeared, but they had the merit of accustoming public opinion and especially the government to a more controversial tone on television. Thanks to the lessons learnt from these programmes the medium was able to begin to transform itself a little.

Since the 1974 reform, solemn debates between political figures have become very rare. The most important was the one in May 1977 in which François Mitterrand confronted the Prime Minister Raymond Barre. On the other hand, the three channels, under the stimulus of competition and a greater autonomy, have organised many round-table discussions and debates involving ministers, deputies and leaders of the majority and of the opposition. These tend to draw inspiration from the techniques of the radio stations operating from foreign territory: Europe N.1 and RTL. What is more, several joint operations have been mounted with these stations at election time. The large number of such political programmes has made them rather commonplace. Their impact on the public has been considerably reduced, and people will hardly go out of their way to watch anything except duels between the most eminent figures, where the political content is largely overshadowed by the theatricality of the event; because of this, the authorities have proved more tolerant of this form of programme.

For its part, the opposition has practically given up complaining about being excluded from television. Such a complaint, which was justified during the 1960s would no longer be credible today. At the same time, the left insists much less on the problem of the time available to express itself. Its experts have realised that this sort of calculation can be challenged and is rarely significant. It is obvious, for instance, that one minute on the air is much more valuable at 8.00 p.m., with a large audience than at 5.00 p.m., when the audience is one tenth of the size. For this very reason, a commission set up in 1975 to examine the problem of air time under the patronage of the left-wing parties, and chaired by the novelist Edmond Charles Roux, had to be rapidly suppressed.

On the other hand, the left insists on being given the right of reply to the television appearances of the President of the Republic. It is true that M Giscard d'Estaing uses television in a very different way from his predecessors. For him, as for President Carter, television is a flexible and effective way of communicating with his countrymen. His appearances are therefore quite frequent and lacking in excessive solemnity. Thus the President has not hesitated to hold direct discussions with a cross-section of French people and with a class of secondary-school children, something quite inconceivable with de Gaulle or Pompidou.

This type of programme allows the President to appear quite often on television to express his opinion on a variety of subjects, without offering the left the opportunity of criticising or refuting his arguments. The right of reply on television is governed by a decree of 13 May 1975, and is available only to particular individuals who might have been accused. Corporate bodies such as minority political parties or trade unions, do not have the right of reply to accusations made against them on television by a politician or *a fortiori* by the President of the Republic. The latter can always claim that he is acting in his capacity as Head of State and not as the leader of a party. This is a problem well known in America, but neither in the USA nor in France have criteria yet been devised for distinguishing between the governmental and political functions of the President. The Socialist Party is the only one to have sought a solution to this problem; in 1976 it proposed a law giving the right of reply to trade unions and political parties, though their proposals were never adopted. (M Schwartzenburg, a representative of the 'Radicaux de Gauche' has also put forward some proposals published in *Le Monde* on 4 July 1977.)

In the regions, the conflict between the authorities and television has been much less spectacular, but is nevertheless extremely important. In 1974 the eleven regional television stations set up by the ORTF during the previous decade were attached to FR 3. They have continued to provide the material for a twenty-minute regional news programme, which has the distinction of being broadcast every evening except Sunday on all three television channels. In other words, TF 1 and Antenne 2 are obliged to transmit a news bulletin prepared by the third company at peak viewing time between 7.20 and 7.40 p.m. It is the only moment of the day when viewers do not have a choice of programmes.

In the past, the directors of the regional stations and those in charge of the regional information bureaux (BRI) attached to them, were frequently accused of submitting too easily to pressure from 'préfets' and members of Parliament. It is also significant that before every important election, the government has made changes among these officials to ensure that crucial regions are under control. Since the 1974 reform, however, there has been some measure of liberalisation in this sector. Enquiries conducted, region by region, by *Télé 7 Jours* in 1976 and by *Le Monde* in 1977 seem to show that the BRIs do respect a certain balance between regional political forces.

Nevertheless, it remains true that French television does not yet possess a regional information network worthy of the name. Contrary to expectations, the suppression of the ORTF did not lead to a real decentralisation. Regional stations remain strictly under the control of the Head Office of FR 3 in Paris, and they have little scope for individual initiative. Before elections, they are advised to be cautious and to avoid controversial topics. All this often makes the regional news programmes rather dull and characterless, and they avoid dealing with the most important issues. The information has become more objective but also more sterile.

Governmental practice regarding television has therefore not always been compatible with declared public policy. There has been no shortage of interference in current affairs and in individual programmes, as is pointed out in Jean Diwo's book; witness M Chevenement's statement to the National Assembly, the reaction of the RPR group in February 1977, the cancelling of the 'Dossiers de l'Ecran' in November 1975 and February 1976, and the frequent changes in the staff on Antenne 2.

All the same, in order to make a fair assessment of the gap separating theory and practice, one must also take into account another phenomenon which is not peculiar to France, that is, the permanent antagonism between the politicians and television which can be recognised to varying degrees in all pluralistic democracies. This antagonism came to the surface with particular intensity during the parliamentary debate in November 1975 discussed above, but there are many deep-seated reasons for it. For the politician, television is at the same time a distorting mirror, a threat and an extraordinarily powerful instrument; three apprehensions which are to a large extent contradictory, but which lead to a widespread feeling of frustration, constant tension and to an attitude of animosity in political circles towards television.

Television as an Actor in Political Life

Television is a distorting mirror in as much as it deals with a few aspects of a few personalities. It creates a rigid hierarchy among politicians. Only a few of the most important figures have easy access to television and it is always the same ones who tend to be invited. The vast majority of parliamentarians must be content with watching and listening. The effect of this has been such that even the organisation of important parliamentary debates has been affected. The leading spokesmen of the parties now speak during the afternoon sessions so that they can appear on the 8 p.m. news broadcasts on television, while the other members have to be content with speaking during the evening sessions which are not televised.[36] This permanent form of discrimination also has a cumulative effect. One can see a widening of the gulf between the few men in each party who, thanks to having plenty of practice, have acquired the necessary ease in front of the camera, and those who do not usually appear on television. The former become studio regulars; they are the first to be considered for round-table discussions and to lead discussions which are often on subjects quite outside their normal interests. Indeed, since they are often thought of as show business stars, it seems only natural for them to take part in literary or variety programmes as well. On the other hand the rest are so uncomfortable in front of the camera that professional broadcasters tend to overshadow them.

Television also distorts political realities in the way it always seeks to present them dramatically in terms of spectacular confrontations. This tendency, which is to some extent due to American influence, appeared rather late in France. This may be explained by the negative influence of the authorities, but the methods of French journalists have also had something to do with it. While Anglo-Saxons are careful to report straight facts, and to make rigorous separation between news and editorial comment, the French frequently mix facts and commentary. Furthermore, unlike their British and American counterparts, French daily newspapers do not have editorial pages. The methods of the French press were thus naturally transferred to television when it began.

Thus the dramatisation of news has only appeared quite recently, and in certain respects it may seem beneficial. Everyone has grown used to seeing representatives of the opposition participating regularly in debates or replying to questions put by journalists, yet the replacement of the cautious words of commentators by the deafening din of present-day discussions has not really improved the quality of televised information. It is often treated hastily and superficially. Discourse often occupies an exaggerated position beside the search for facts, thorough enquiry and the examination of important social problems. Finally, certain topics are more or less taboo, under a tacit agreement between all the major political groups. This is the case with historical problems like collaboration with the Germans during the Second World War or the Algerian War, or with current problems such as police methods or racism in France.

The threat posed by television is conceived by French politicians in a more general but perhaps more serious way. They firmly believe that it has a harmful influence on their supporters and that it strengthens their opponents. For them, it is a powerful machine for indoctrinating a versatile and malleable public with views opposed to their own. Furthermore, because of its way of favouring certain figures to the detriment of others, television is considered as a means of calling into question the procedures for selecting leaders which are so dear to the parties. This is very important in France, where the election of the President of the Republic by universal suffrage is the essential factor in the political game. To maintain their credibility, the major groups must each have at least one potential presidential candidate, that is to say, someone who is sufficiently well known to be able to assert himself rapidly during the brief weeks of an electoral campaign. Nowadays, the only way to attain this position is to appear frequently on television, and the question arises whether it is the parties who impose their candidates on the media, or the media who choose the personalities by their own criteria.

Two recent cases illustrate the fact that this is not merely an academic hypothesis. It is quite probable that a skilful and persevering use of television helped M Giscard d'Estaing in 1974 to appear as the best majority candidate. Observers noted that in the three months preceding the death of President Pompidou, M Giscard d'Estaing, who was then Minister of Finance, appeared rather more frequently on television. Officially, his purpose was to explain the government's financial policy, but in reality his main objective was to make an impression on the electorate before the elections which were known to be imminent.

On the left, Michel Rocard has for several years been a favourite on television. This situation causes serious discontent in the Socialist Party to which he belongs. Many members of the Socialist Party fear that they will have to elect him as the successor to Mitterrand simply because he is so well known. This is particularly frustrating for a left-wing party which traditionally believes in leaving considerable powers of decision in the hands of its activists.

The Communist Party, whose leader does not appear well on television, has tried, with its characteristic earnestness, to compensate for this handicap by taking the maximum advantage of each television appearance. Marchais had no hesitation in announcing the abandonment of the idea of the proletarian dictatorship for the first time on television, thus giving more importance to a television broadcast than to communication with his activists, some of whom felt frustrated by such irregular methods.

Can this medium be mastered and put at the service of one particular movement or ideology? Many politicians believe it is possible, though they are convinced that television is used, indeed monopolised by their opponents, whom they consider much more adept in the techniques of manipulation. To redress the balance they believe it necessary to exercise an influence over the staff and journalists most in the public eye. In 1968 and 1974, the majority did not hesitate to carry out widespread purges in the television current affairs departments, but the result of such action is often questionable as the criteria for judging technical competence do not always coincide with political allegiances.

At the present moment there is a kind of pool of qualified journalists who, according to the circumstances, work either for television, Radio France, or the radio stations operating from abroad: Europe No. 1 and RTL. When a talented journalist working for television is in political disgrace, he goes to one of the radio stations abroad, and comes back to one of the three television companies when it wants to improve its image by the use of prominent personalities. Thus there is a kind of 'Brownian' movement within broadcasting. Journalists from the press are called on less often. Henry Marque, for example, who is now the Head of Current Affairs at TF 1 comes from RTL. Jean-Pierre Elkabbach, his counterpart at Antenne 2, worked on the second television channel until 1974; forced to leave for political reasons, he went to Radio France, which he left in 1977 to return to television. He appointed Noel Copin, who used to work on the daily newspaper *La Croix*, as head of the Political Department, and Jean-François Kahn, who had first worked on Europe No.1, then on the *Quotidien de Paris* and then on FR 3, as Head of the Cultural Department.

The fact that the number of men with a sufficient command of broadcasting methods is rather limited tends to reduce the effect of political exclusiveness. A journalist who has been disgraced by the authorities acquires a new virginity by working in another sector of current affairs, only to return a few years later as a saviour. For the best professional broadcasters, the problem consists in choosing between a job in the national television service, where they become very well known but are badly paid, and one with private radio which is more anonymous but more financially rewarding.

Nevertheless it remains easier to control current affairs on television through men whose loyalty is assured, than by constantly issuing instructions which run the risk of being only partially respected. It is quite significant that one of the central parts of the Communist Party's campaign in the field of information during the last two years has been the placing of Communist journalists in television. Without a doubt, the Communist Party is afraid that if the left comes to power, the editorial staff of television news will consist largely of Socialists or their sympathisers, while the Communists will suffer from the fact of having no qualified people on the spot at the beginning.

Thus many factors intervene to poison the relationship between television and the French political system. First, there is the overriding importance of the concept of broadcasting as a public service institution. Unlike other Western European countries, television in France remained a centralised, hierarchical administration under the direct authority of a minister for far too long. This state of affairs formed certain habits and a pattern of work and authority which were particularly marked in the provinces, but above all it formed a conception of television which made it thought of as the voice of France and in practice as the voice of the government.

Secondly, the media, and television in particular, are profoundly influenced by the concept of power which predominates in the French ruling classes, according to which, the state, the interests of the regime and the majority in power are one and the same, and must be defended together. This is a historical tradition which goes back to the Third Republic but which was revived by the political crises and the growth of state control which followed the Second World War. Since 1968, the state and the higher administration have lost some of their credibility, and certain politicians are more willing to accept the idea that television is not simply a branch of the state. Nevertheless, the French political world is still dominated by a manicheism which is partly upheld by the current bipolarisation between right and left, but which is also a much older, deeper phenomenon. Most French political leaders are still convinced that when they are in power, they are the incarnation of truths which must be defended at all costs. In such circumstances the use of the instrument of broadcasting becomes perfectly justified. One may therefore wonder whether the independence of television will only be assured when French politicians admit that they have no absolute rights over it.

These peculiarly French characteristics only aggravate the friction which exists between politicians and the broadcasting media in every democratic society. The brutal eruption of television into a system which had managed to accommodate the written press caused a disturbance, the extent of which is difficult to calculate. The parties themselves were put in question by this new instrument, which influenced their internal hierarchy, their methods of choosing their leaders and the ways of reaching the electorate. Under such conditions it is not surprising that the machinery of the parties reacted passionately and sometimes violently against these new constraints, while trying all the same to adapt themselves, most notably at the time of the Presidential Elections.

An Assessment of the 1974 Reform

The 1974 reform was an interesting attempt to break away from the habits of the past, since it broke up the single, administrative institution which was constituted by the ORTF. This break-up was followed, on a political level, by the abolition of the Ministry of Information, by a strengthening of parliamentary influence over television, and by the transfer of effective powers of control over broadcasting from the Prime Minister to the President of the Republic. It was therefore an ambitious experiment which tried to put in practice the President's neo-liberal ideas.

However the reform has also been a partial failure.[37] It has suffered right from the start from the fact that it was not established as a result of co-operation between the majority and the opposition, a circumstance which has placed it in a rather precarious position. Furthermore, the television companies have not managed to acquire a true freedom to manoeuvre or a credible political independence, owing to the financial constraints upon them and to the fact that, directly or indirectly, their officials are appointed by the President of the Republic on the basis of political criteria.

Finally, it would appear that during the debates on the ORTF and the RTF, the authorities as well as the opposition have always considered television from the very restricted viewpoint of information, their policy on this question all too often being limited to the arrangements for news bulletins and the time allowed for each party to appear on television.

This attitude is shown by the importance which the parties attach to the granting of free and equal access to television for all groups. The opinion commonly held by politicians is that there will only be objectivity on television when each party has a regular and significant amount of television time at its disposal to express its views; the system applied during the Presidential Election campaign constitutes a kind of ideal. Thus, proposals submitted by the Communist group in 1973, for example, put forward as one of the principal objectives of the national broadcasting company which they outline: 'the granting to the political parties and major trade union confederations of a regular time on the air governed by rules defined by the law'. Similarly, a Socialist Party leader, M Defferre, proclaimed that if the left came to power: 'The expression and confrontation of thoughts and opinions will be guaranteed by the allocation of time on the air, not only to the government, political parties, trade unions and representative organisations, but also to religious faiths.' There is a lack of awareness of the fact that certain programmes cannot be artificially isolated from the rest; whether they be variety programmes, detective stories or drama series they often have an ideological content and impact which is much greater than that of straightforward political broadcasts to which viewers pay relatively little attention.

On the other hand, there is never any serious or thorough discussion of the overall organisation of programmes or of the educational and cultural functions of television. In the words of a leader writer in *Télé 7 Jours*, 'For majority members of Parliament, television current affairs is a den of leftists; for the opposition, television is under the thumb of the authorities more than ever before . . . There is naturally no discussion of programmes, nor of the savage competition between the channels, nor of the sinking of TF 1 and A 2 into the morass of ratings.'[38]

This absence of an overall view of the problem, the indifference of politicians to the cultural role of television, is in sharp contrast to the active and liberal cultural policy of governments under the Fifth Republic in other sectors of artistic life: music, cinema, theatre and the plastic arts. Neither has it allowed the creative aspects of television to develop in the no-man's land which was left to it. The fact that the four reforms which French broadcasting has undergone since 1959 have all aimed at settling the problem of current affairs and overcoming management difficulties, has had the effect of somehow sterilising the other functions of television. The 1974 reform helped to speed up the process of debasement which was already noticeable before. Thus, French television has suffered from a faulty definition of its function and from the ambiguity of its role.[39]

The development of new means of communication such as cable television, local stations and broadcasts via satellite, will once more force the public broadcasting sector to change. Once again, the choice is in the hands of the political authorities, who will be obliged to evolve a new doctrine for broadcasting.

3 Italy

From Party Occupation to Party Partition

Fabio Luca Cavazza

The Political Setting

The first regular Italian television broadcasts began in 1954, watched by just 88,000 subscribers. Four years later, in 1958, the number of subscribers had risen to over one million. At that stage television was not yet a form of mass entertainment, nor had it become a habit, and to possess a television was still a status symbol beyond the means of many Italians. In 1964, ten years after the first broadcasts, the number of subscribers passed the five million mark, and television was established as an important phenomenon in Italian society. By 1971 there were ten million subscribers, but thereafter the rate of increase became less spectacular; the market was reaching saturation point.

Since 1975 the number of subscribers has settled around twelve million: the number of subscribers to the 'RAI – Radiotelevisione Italiana – Società per Azioni', represents about 72 per cent of Italian families. To be more precise: 77.9 per cent in northern and central Italy, and 61.5 per cent in the south and in the islands.

Until recently Italian viewers were only able to watch the programmes broadcast by RAI, which operated a monopoly thanks to an exclusive state concession. Today, however, Italian viewers can receive a great number of television programmes as well as those broadcast by RAI on its two channels. There are those broadcast by the stations at Monte Carlo in the Principality of Monaco, at Lugano in Switzerland and at Capodistria in Yugoslavia; even French television broadcasts can be received.

But in addition, there are the multitude of small private television stations now operating all over Italy. The exact number is uncertain, but it is probably just over 250 in all. Nor is it clear how many television sets belonging to viewers of RAI are actually capable of picking up either foreign or private Italian television stations. Of the RAI's 12 million subscribers, 6.6 million live in northern Italy, and 2.5 million in central Italy, the areas most easily reached and most extensively covered by the various foreign television services. A good two-thirds of the subscribers to the RAI are in a position to receive at least one of the foreign television services, and it is likely that at least one third of those, some four million in all, do in fact receive them.

There are also a large number of radio stations. According to one source, in 1977 there were about 900 private stations in competition with the radio programmes broadcast by the RAI.[1] Like the private television stations, these radio stations operate on a local basis.

The comparison that can be made between the situation in the past and that prevailing today is merely the most conspicuous result of a long and complex series of political events which, as we shall see, has not yet been finally resolved.

As a legal entity the RAI is an ordinary limited liability company, but in practice it functions as a public institution subject to the control of various political forces. The state, through various intermediaries, owns all of the shares and forbids any transfer of them. The events – politically motivated events – which have led to the reform of the RAI and to the ending of the position of absolute monopoly which it once enjoyed began with the issue of the whole political and cultural control of this institution. In fact, when one talks of 'reform' of the RAI, one is really talking about a political struggle for control of what is in fact a public institution. After much debate and after complex negotiations involving the main Italian political parties, lasting almost five years, the law (No. 103 of 14 April 1975) concerning 'reform' of RAI was passed. The final status of RAI is still not resolved: in referring to a 'monopoly' one is referring to a definition of Italian radio and television services which has yet to be finally established. Indeed the Constitutional Court, in its decision No. 202 of 15 July 1976, declared that part of Law 103 concerning the range of RAI's monopoly was illegal. At the time of writing this ball remains in the government's court, and new proposals must be put before Parliament. The last chapter has yet to be written but the authors will clearly be those same political forces, which, after having fought for the reform (or, as we shall see, the control) of RAI, agreed on the text of Law 103.

Despite foreign and private competition, RAI remains the most important and almost the only source of televised information and entertainment for most Italians. Even among those who are in a position to receive other, foreign or private programmes, most end up, almost involuntarily, watching their own national television. Many factors have tended to confirm this pattern and to reinforce the lasting preference for the RAI and its programmes. Firstly, there is the question of habit; secondly, the fact that no other television service is in a position to supply as much news about Italy to Italian viewers; thirdly, there is practical difficulty in finding out about other stations.

RAI is undeniably in competition with other services, but they are in no position to threaten its primacy, nor deprive it of its audience and its advertising. However tough the competition the lack of financial means and of production capacity prevents it from meeting the RAI on equal terms; and it is not likely that the present situation will change radically in the near future. A reversal would entail a radical change in the views shared by the majority of the Italian political forces, and that is extremely unlikely. The battle waged over RAI has not been so much financial or industrial as political, though one cannot disregard entirely the existence and the activity of financial groupings hoping to make a profit and obtain some political influence should the RAI monopoly be broken up. These interests have never been openly declared and have not played a decisive role; business interests have been of considerably less importance than the interests of purely political forces. There are certain features of the Italian political situation which have influenced and to some extent predetermined the behaviour of the political groups which have crossed swords over the control of RAI. These must be described and the relative strength of the protagonists in this political battle assessed.

At the centre of the Italian political structure stand the parties, in particular the two largest, the Christian Democratic Party (DC) and the Italian Communist Party (PCI), with the so-called minor parties existing as satellites in orbit around these two major planets. The Movimento Sociale Italiano (MSI), the perpetuation of the fascist tradition, exists in its own sterile sphere outside this bipolar political system.

The minor parties are, from right to left: the Italian Liberal Party (PLI), the Italian Republican Party (PRI), the Italian Social–Democratic Party (PSDI) and the Italian Socialist Party (PSI). The multi-party scene is completed by a number of tiny groups with very small parliamentary representation which stand either to the left of the Communist Party or in opposition to the invisible Holy Alliance which binds the large and small parties together.

Naturally enough, no one likes to be a satellite, and as a result the minor parties are continually looking for ways to increase their bargaining power and hence reduce their level of dependence on the larger parties. They do, however, carry out a useful function in relation to the two large parties, absorbing and lessening the intensity of much of the conflict and friction that would arise if the two political giants were to meet at close quarters, and be subject to the usual pattern of a two- or three-party system: alternation between government and opposition. The two large parties are not ready for that: there are too many pressures from both international and internal political forces preventing the establishment of such a system. The two parties prefer the disadvantages (and the complexities) of a multi-party system which works exasperatingly slowly – involving as it does an exhausting system of mediation – to the advantage (and the simplicity) of a straightforward two-party competition or one weakened by the presence of a third party. From this awareness is derived the Communist proposal for an 'historic compromise' as a substitute for alternation.

Italian politics moves forward very slowly because of its main protagonists' caution – a sign not of uncertainty so much as mere prudence. The two major parties, observing their more immediate interests, are wisely in no hurry to hasten the demise of the minor parties.

In a multi-party system it is rare for any one party to receive 51 per cent of the votes at an election, and therefore be able to govern alone. On the contrary, the votes are normally divided between the parties and then a coalition is formed led by the party which has obtained a plurality.

Roughly speaking, Italy has witnessed three distinct political phases. The first, beginning in 1948, can be defined as the period of government by the centre parties, with the DC in coalition with the PLI, the PRI and the PSDI. The second phase officially began in 1963 when the PSI joined the coalition and the PLI went into opposition (though not the PRI nor the PSDI). It can therefore be defined as the period of the centre–left formula. This phase, marked by the intermittent collaboration in government of the PSI and the failure of a proposed unification of the two Socialist parties, continued until 1975. The third phase began with an abrupt change in the strengths of the DC and the PCI in relation to one another. The DC remains the largest single party, but the PCI, thanks to a more favourable balance of power, finds itself in a position to be able to make a bid to join the government.

If we compare the percentage of votes obtained by the three minor parties (PLI, PRI and PSI) during the course of the first phase with that obtained by the DC, we can see that the distance between them varied from 35 points in 1948 to 24 points in 1963. In 1963, at the beginning of the second phase, there was a difference of 24 points between the DC and the PSI. If we add the PSDI percentage to the percentage obtained by the PSI, the difference in respect of the DC is 18 points. In the election of 1968, the two Socialist parties presented a united front, but lost votes instead of gaining them, while the DC gained slightly. Therefore the difference between the Socialist block and the DC increased from 18 to 24 points.

The extent of the DC's electoral superiority over its allies during the first two phases allowed it to remain the dominant party, and naturally the DC behaved accordingly. But during these phases, when the PCI remained firmly in opposition, the distance between the DC and the PCI was always less than that between the DC and the other parties, even, as we have seen, when taken together. This figure, in years of national elections, was as follows: 1948, 17.4 points (the year when the PCI and the PSI joined to form the 'Fronte Popolare'); 1953, 17.4; 1958, 19.6; 1963, 12.9 (on that occasion the DC dropped 4 per cent while the PCI gained 3); 1968, 12.1; 1972, 11.5, when there occurred the great change which opens the third phase; 15 June 1975 (on the occasion of local elections held all over Italy), 3.2; and in the general elections of 20 June 1976, 4.3. Since 1975, DC and PCI between them monopolise the votes of almost three-quarters of the entire electorate.

The real cornerstone of a multi-party country is an electoral system based on proportional representation. However, proportional representation is not only a method of conducting elections, it may also be a system rendered necessary by a prevailing political climate. This is the case in Italy, where it also characterises the way Italian political leaders think, their concept of politics and the way they act. Proportional representation is a translation into political terms of a spirit which governs all Italian social life. It is a method which in all spheres conditions the actions of the Italian ruling classes, to whom it is second nature. It can be defined as a reluctance, be it in business or politics, in cultural or social institutions, to entrust anyone with a clearly defined task or responsibility, or alternatively as a desire or a greater willingness to assume such tasks jointly and to share responsibility for them.

Proportional representation teaches the subtle and sophisticated art of government through the search for a consensus of opinion within the group to which one belongs. The more able politician widens the area of agreement to include groups outside his own – like the ripples which expand in concentric circles when a stone is dropped in a pond – and then tries to dominate the groupings which emerge. Viewed in this fashion, proportional representation is an excellent school for learning many of the skills demanded by politics and diplomacy. However, from another point of view, it can easily make politics degenerate into mechanical group exercises which tend to isolate the participants within four walls like a group of conspirators. Indeed, when collective responsibility shared by a group (and, in the final analysis, by a party), always takes the place of individual responsibility, there arises a tendency to eliminate from the group anyone who does not belong or who does not seem willing to abide by all its rules.

How can one trust someone who does not accept the rules of the game? The parties divide the control of sectors of public life and of society proportionally among themselves. The benefits must not be lost or dispersed, so the parties need men of proven obedience to run the institutions which they control. The spirit and the machinery of proportional representation together engender a method of running public life which can be quite accurately and realistically described as a political system developing through endless adaptation. It is characterised not by the exercise of leadership, but by the search for agreements and distributions of responsibility which reflect the relative strengths of the parties concerned. Every agreement involves adaptation.

The DC has always proved basically faithful to these principles and practices of proportional representation. They have been accepted by the PCI, conditioning its behaviour during its political quarantine. Thanks to the machinery and spirit of the system the PCI has managed to carve out a sphere of political activity of its own. This has been on a local rather than on a national level, as a result of the isolation in which it found itself. The PCI has thus exercised power in many urban and provincial administrations, in sectors such as the co-operative and trade union movement, and also among groups within society itself, principally among the intellectuals, who regard it as a dynamic political force and a promoter of cultural activity, spreading, with a remarkable liberality, the satisfactions of being left wing and keeping in step with the march of progress. The DC, on the other hand, has spread its influence through the many institutions controlled by national government, and has established itself, in the eyes of the public at least, as an anti-Communist party which regards any contact with the PCI as sinful and heretical. However, this has been truer of its words than its actions – the party has not gone in for the public burning of heretics! Indeed, a silent agreement between the two parties has slowly been built up which it has never been necessary to formalise.

Detailed research has shown that almost three-quarters of the legislation passed in the Italian Parliament between 1948 and 1971 has been supported by the Communists.[2] Laws thus passed are on the whole a means for feeding the two large parties' own *clienteles* – the great reservoir from which they draw their popular votes. They, in turn, become the measure to be used when it comes to deciding on the division of spheres of influence and the spoils of battle. This division leads to a kind of occupation of an institution, and sometimes it may happen that the institution, instead of being occupied by a single political party, is divided into lots to be shared out among a number of parties. One has to understand the machinery and the spirit of the system of proportional representation, in order to grasp this process of occupation of RAI by the DC, and also what followed from this – the sharing out of responsibility within RAI, in ways which were approved and sanctioned by the 1975 reform law.

The control which the DC managed to exercise over RAI from 1948 to 1963 by virtue of its position as the dominant party, was really and truly an 'occupation', in which the political parties were kept apart and prevented from joint activity. Under the system of 'occupation' the benefits derived from the control of an institution go to a single party, while under the system of 'divided responsi-bilities' these same benefits are parcelled out among those parties which have a share in its administration. This latter system, therefore, is normally applied in all those institutions whose directors are chosen by either local or national government, rather than by popular election. Quite naturally, RAI is one of these institutions. Its occupation or the possession of a share in the control of such a powerful and persuasive form of mass com-munication is an objective which no party can afford to reject. As we shall see, the battle to end the almost exclusive control of RAI by the DC, and to open the way for shared control, was long and bitter. The battle still goes on, and every new development is bound to have an effect on RAI, since no political party can choose to ignore the most powerful form of mass communication available.

The Control and Occupation of RAI–TV

In 1910, nine years after the signals which Marconi had transmitted from Poldhu in Cornwall were picked up in St John's, Newfound-land, the Italian state set about organising by means of legislation 'the setting up and running of radio-telegraphic and radio-telephonic installations and in general of all those means by which . . . energy is employed to obtain results at a distance without the use of wires'.[3]

The 1910 law, with a candour easily appreciated by those who like to see facts stated as they really are, declared directly and openly that any radio-telegraphic or radiophonic activity was reserved for the 'government' – the executive, that is – and not for the 'state' – an institution known for its impartiality and for its freedom from human error. Thirteen years later, in 1923, a year after Mussolini's 'March on Rome', at a time when neither legality

nor the state were held in very high esteem, a new law corrected
the mistake in wording and substituted 'State' for 'Government'.[4]
However, the laws of 1910 and 1923 made it clear that the state
(that is, the Italian government) had no intention of running those
activities which used 'energy . . . without the use of wires' itself. It
reserved the right to exercise control over them and to entrust
them to third parties through the use of concessions.

From 1919 until the present day, despite the presence of very
different political regimes, this system of concession has not been
abandoned. Indeed Law 103, which recently reformed RAI,
makes specific reference to the system in precisely the same terms
used in the very first laws in which the state reserved the right to
distribute these services.[5] The instrument of concession is no
better and no worse than any other. Much depends on the way it is
used. In turn the way it is used depends on the extent of the
powers of intervention and control which the government can
exercise over the holder.

In 1927, out of the ashes of a company which had in 1924
obtained an exclusive six-year concession to run the Italian
wireless service, there arose the EIAR (Ente Italiano per le
Audizioni Radiofoniche).[6] The law which set up the EIAR
organised and rationalised the sector. Its purposes were un-
equivocal: a closer link between the state and the holder of the
concession, which should take account of appropriate political
considerations. 'One can say that it was from that moment that the
state began to take an interest in the practical running of the
service, following a pattern which has remained substantially
unaltered up till the present day: it institutes a project for
extending radio broadcasting to remote areas to reflect the policies
of the fascist government.' There followed on from the 1927 law
an agreement between the Minister of Posts and the EIAR, in
which 'state control, envisaged as control by the executive, was
considerably increased'.[7] In 1933, SIP (a Piedmontese industrial
group whose main activity consisted in the production of hydro-
electric power in the Alps), became the majority shareholder in
the EIAR. At the same time a minority of the shares in SIP were
bought by IRI, a public holding company which saved many Italian
companies which collapsed during the world economic crisis of the
1930s. Thus the circle was closed. To the control exercised from above
by the government was added a control from below of the manage-

ment and the day-to-day running of the EIAR. Thus, especially through the influence of SIP and its directors, there grew up in the EIAR a managerial staff which reflected the professional values and the bourgeois habits of the Piedmontese business class.[8] Filled with a love of caution and discretion together with a preference for sound administration without much entrepreneurial imagination, such people were prepared to follow quite rigorously what the government ordained. Since a certain imagination in business presupposes a sometimes wild and undisciplined desire for freedom of action, in its absence there is a natural tendency to comply with the requests of the political authorities. Such characteristics were widespread in Italian industrial circles at the time, and these same groups did not hesitate, once things had settled down after the tumult of the Second World War, to transfer their allegiance to the new power in Italian politics, the Christian Democratic Party.

This is not to say that the DC can in any way be compared to the Fascist Party, indeed it is to the credit of the DC not to have been tempted in that direction, and to have remained true, on the whole, to its origins as a free popular party. Nevertheless, in choosing to 'restore the old state'[9] and in succeeding in that task, the DC accepted a large part of the old ruling class with its ingrained habits and methods.

Thus, from the end of the Second World War until the end of the 1950s, the RAI was administered by men who had been trained there before the war – in the old EIAR. The production of both news and entertainment programmes was in their hands. The DC had taken care to appoint men from its own ranks to fill the most important positions, including the Chairmanship and membership of the Board. All the same, it is always the cook who controls what is served up on the table; all he has to do is to learn the tastes of the master.

Throughout the twelve years from 1948 to 1960, the internal organisation of the RAI remained extremely simple. There was a central programme administration (under a Director and two Assistant Directors) and a separate central administration for radio news. The arrival of television in 1954 prompted the division of the central programme administration into two; one for radio and one for television. In turn the central administration for radio news became 'the central administration of journalistic services' with control over two subordinate administrations, one for radio and one for television news. The new jobs which television brought with it were shared out among the same directors. During this period, the organisational structure of RAI expanded principally and most significantly only in the administrative and technical fields. This was due to the rapid growth in the number of subscribers as well as to the need to reach an ever larger proportion of the population despite the difficulties imposed by the mountainous nature of the country.

Therefore there existed all the right conditions within RAI for the DC to develop and complete the process of 'occupation' during the course of the 1960s. The laws which the newly-born Italian Republic passed to deal with broadcasting seemed, indeed, to help the dominant party to gain control of RAI.

The first legal provision relating to broadcasting – Decree 428 of 3 April 1947, which remained in force until the 1975 reform – sought to safeguard the form and rules of democracy. However, in practice, the executive retained at its disposal ways and means of communicating its wishes to the management of the RAI and of keeping a check on all its initiatives. Paragraph 8 of this decree set up a 'Committee to establish the basic cultural, artistic and educational policies which should govern radio broadcasts, and to watch over their realisation'. Its job was to examine the 'preliminary programme plans' for the three succeeding months; once the committee had expressed its 'opinion', it was up to the Minister of Posts to give his approval. Committees of this sort which express 'opinions' of a consultative nature, about 'preliminary plans' and which lay down 'basic policies', tend never to have any real influence; their role is essentially ornamental and they remain outside the halls and corridors of power.

Paragraph 11 of the same decree established a Parliamentary Commission with the supervisory task of 'ensuring the political independence of broadcasting and the objectivity of its news coverage'. These provisions were also to apply to television when it came into being, since under the system of exclusive concession, both radio and television came under the aegis of the same governing body. The Commission was 'made up of thirty members appointed equally by the presidents of the two Houses of Parliament from among the representatives of all the parliamentary groups' (Para. 12), and it was to 'pass on its decisions to the Prime Minister's office which in turn' was to 'instruct the chairman of the company holding the concession as to how to put those decisions into action' (Para. 13).

Quite legitimate doubts arise concerning the effectiveness of the Commission's decisions. The definition of its role is set out in vague terms, and it is by no means clear what the term 'supervision' actually means in practice. In every instance, the decisions of the Parliamentary Commission reached RAI through the Prime Minister's office. This latter, therefore, has two functions, the first being to act as a filter through which all the Commission's acts were obliged to pass, the second to act as a kind of buffer zone to eliminate the possibility of any conflict between the Parliamentary Commission and RAI.

Furthermore, Decree 428 had, as we have observed, divided the task of supervision between two bodies and given them each a separate field of action. From a practical point of view it is doubtful whether the distinction between 'cultural, artistic and educational' programmes on the one hand, and news and current affairs programmes on the other, is strictly speaking valid. The overall message of radio or television has an intrinsic unity which cannot easily be broken up. Cultural and educational programmes, for instance, can contain a large amount of political information. A means of communication, whether it is on a large scale or not, needs to be considered as a whole, and not in parts. However, there was never any question of entrusting a single body (which was neither the Prime Minister's office nor RAI itself) with the sole right of judgement and control over broadcasting. Instead, the object was to minimise such power and make it as far as possible ineffective. Thus the government, by dividing the 'supervision', remained itself unsupervised and was left free to watch over RAI.

The executive could have asked for nothing more than this: a helpful law and a compliant and passive management to help it control radio and television as it liked. So it was until the beginning of the 1960s. For some years the Director General of the RAI had been Rodolfo Arata, a mild man who had been editor of the official Christian Democrat newspaper, *Il Popolo*. In 1961, his place was taken by the pugnacious and aggressive Ettore Bernabei, who had also been, until then, editor of *Il Popolo*, and was well known as a close and faithful associate of Signor Fanfani. Bernabei remained at the head of RAI until 1974 and proved to be a most able and undaunted advocate of what he and his protectors considered to be the supreme interests of the DC. He was able to extend the 'occupation' of RAI further than anyone expected, helped partly by a 1960 decision of the Constitutional Court which effectively stifled all attempts to breach the wall which protected RAI from outside competition.

Some years previously, the Rome daily newspaper *Il Tempo* had formed 'Il Tempo–TV', a company whose aim was to set up a television service to operate in Lazio, Campania and Tuscany, financed by advertising revenue. Similarly, certain private citizens had formed another company, called 'Televisione libera' in Milan. RAI was opposed to the proposed activities of these companies, and took them to court. This was the beginning of a long and complicated case which came finally before the Constitutional Court: it had, as it is its peculiar task, to decide on the interpretation and extension of the concrete liberties available to the citizens and sanctioned by the Constitution itself.[10]

The Constitutional Court declared the monopoly held by RAI to be legitimate, and the reasoning on which it based its decision is worth mentioning in detail. The judges of the Constitutional Court based their decision on the observation that 'there is a limited number of channels at present available' following the allocation of wavelengths to Italy by the appropriate international conventions. Such being the situation,

> television transmitted by radio-electric waves is undoubtedly an activity which is destined, in a free economy, to be in a state of at least limited competition, the range of the limitation depending on whether services are operated on a national or local scale. Since RAI finds itself among those undertakings which Article 43 of the Constitution considers to refer to positions of monopoly, for that same reason alone, it belongs to that range of activities . . . which the same article allows to be removed from the conditions of the market.

To avoid any misunderstanding, the Court went on to support its argument by specifying:

(a) that television broadcasting should be considered to be 'of especial public interest', in the words of Article 43, 'the very importance . . . of . . . the interests which . . . it tends to satisfy' whether these be of 'single members of society . . . or of society . . . as a whole'; and that

(b) to prevent television services falling 'into the hands of one individual or of a small number of individuals' answers the criterion of 'public interest' mentioned in Article 43, given the limited number of channels; the decision that the service could therefore be exclusively entrusted to the state was not arbitrary since the state 'is in the best position to run it objectively, impartially, and most extensively and continuously over the whole of the country'.[11]

Finally the Court went on to consider whether or not such a decision found itself in conflict with Article 21 of the Constitution. This is the Article which safeguards the right of expression of individual opinions in all media. Once again the Court fell back on the argument of the limited number of channels and came to the conclusion that since it was not possible 'for everyone who wants to . . . to run a television service . . . the state monopoly is, as an institution, in the best possible position objectively and impartially to overcome the difficulties imposed by the natural limitations of the medium . . .' After all this, the judges concluded that 'the state as holder of the monopoly has the duty to ensure . . . freedom of access to television . . . within the limits which apply to any such freedom . . . to anyone who wishes to use it to spread his ideas . . .'. No such argument has ever been enshrined in law, and the right of access which the Constitutional Court mentioned in its recommendations was only put into practice with the 1975 reform. As can be seen from the extracts quoted earlier, the Constitutional Court (decision 59, 1960) took the limitation in the number of channels available as its main argument to justify the constitutionality of RAI's monopoly.

Even without evidence, it is safe to assume that the judges of the Constitutional Court consulted the appropriate public body responsible for the administration of telecommunications, the Ministry of Posts, which is also responsible for the technical governance of RAI. This branch of the executive certainly had no interest in breaching the walls protecting RAI's monopoly, and presumably presented the Court with the conventional view that the spectrum could support only a limited number of channels.

The Court certainly treated this as axiomatic and did not seek to enquire into alternative systems of frequency administration. In fact, throughout the text of its decision there is no reference at all to the situation in other countries – the United States, for instance – where the UHF band has been used to multiply the channels available. On the other hand, the judges of the Constitutional Court would probably have considered the existence in the US of three large, privately-owned national television services as evidence of a necessary state of limited competition. In confirming the monopoly status of RAI the judges of the Constitutional Court also reflected a feeling and a view prevalent not only in Italy, but all over Europe, that state monopoly is preferable to private oligopoly. It is a conception of social organisation which may be open to criticism, but which cannot be considered invalid.

Meanwhile, at RAI Ettore Bernabei, the new Director General, had taken up his post in 1961 and was able to carry out his plans unchallenged. Being a faithful follower of Signor Fanfani, he enjoyed the protection of the DC, and what is more, the unambiguous verdict of the Constitutional Court forestalled any competition. During the course of the 1960s, RAI was free to expand and enlarge. The exclusive concession signed with the Ministry of Posts was not due to expire until 1972, which seemed far in the future.

A second television channel was opened on 4 November 1961, and there followed a steady increase in the proportion of the population reached by one or other of the two channels. By 1968, the first channel could be seen by 98 per cent of the population, the second by 90 per cent. A considerable amount of investment was required to achieve this result. The mountains and valleys which make the Italian landscape so varied and beautiful were a major stumbling block when it came to transmitting television pictures to the entire population, and considerable effort was needed by RAI in order to overcome the problem. RAI wanted to achieve these objectives (provided for in the instrument of concession signed with the Ministry of Posts) well in advance of the time limits set by the public authorities. It was a demonstration of good will as well as of technical capability; to reach the entire Italian population before the required date served to emphasise RAI's role as a public service and to justify in social and political terms the monopoly with which it had been entrusted. It would, however, be misleading to judge the Bernabei regime at RAI on this success alone.

Bernabei assumed the role of father figure in RAI, and every decision had to be personally approved by him. In 1963, shortly after he had taken up his position, a government was formed which for the first time included members of the Italian Socialist Party (founded in 1892) as ministers.[12] The Socialists demanded posts for their men within RAI, and from 1964 one of their number became Deputy Chairman of the Board; later, in 1968, another Socialist was appointed 'Amministratore Delegato' of the company, a post senior to that held by Bernabei. Even so, Bernabei managed to keep a firm hold on the reins, in such a way that, according to the circumstances, any Socialist proposal was either shelved or rejected, or accepted in such a way that the interests of the DC were not seriously damaged. The differences in strength between the two parties was a determining factor in favour of the DC, and Bernabei made very skilful use of it. Only by reference to this is it possible to explain how the DC 'occupation' of RAI was able to develop so smoothly before and after 1961 without encountering serious opposition.

In a short space of time, the organisational structure of RAI changed so much as to become unrecognisable, and quite unlike what it had been in the 1950s. New posts were added to those already in existence, rather like a new multiplication of the loaves and the fishes. New names would suddenly appear. The number of executive offices grew from around ten to something like fifty, each with its own director and assistant director. While the number of services and offices increased, the breaking up of responsibilities was not always justified by a corresponding expansion of the company or by an increase in the hours of transmission. The demands of efficiency are not always so crystal clear to the outside observer. Very often one can only surmise that a complicated distribution of responsibilities and tasks within an organisation conceals the desire to consolidate the control from the top. Thus RAI became like a large chessboard on which the Director General could play out his game unchallenged.

One must add to the directors, managers and journalists directly employed by RAI and to those involved in cultural, current affairs and entertainment programmes, all the freelance contributors, either employed for individual, specific programmes, or permanently under contract as advisers. Their precise number has never been ascertained, and the official figures have to be approached with caution. One would not be far wrong in stating that there are several hundred of them, mainly journalists, writers, university professors and intellectuals. These additional squares on the board allowed a more refined and elaborate game to be played. Furthermore, by means of these contracts of collaboration, people (and opinions) who could have caused trouble by maintaining a spirit of opposition, became tied to RAI – and to the political or internal principles on which it was run. Such opposition might have taken the form of criticism of the control exercised over political information and over themes and situations which it was considered best to avoid, specially in entertainment programmes.

The other pillar, apart from the employees, which sustained and made manifest the DC 'occupation' of RAI, was the control exercised over programme content, and particularly political news. Even before the advent of Bernabei, RAI had a kind of code of internal censorship. For instance, there was a ban on certain words innocent in themselves, but which in the Italian language could also quite legitimately have sexual connotations. Similarly, in entertainment programmes, situations which violated the basic principles of Catholic morality were avoided. The principles to be upheld included: the unity of the family and disapproval of divorce; procreation blessed by religious not civil marriage, and disapproval of extra-marital sexual relations, and especially of artificial methods of contraception; acceptance of the *status quo* and the need for the individual to resign himself to it since it had been sanctified by tradition. Otherwise, any sign of social impatience or rebellion had to be reconciled with the doctrines of the Church, with its teaching and with its views on the problems of justice and society. In short, it was not so much a case of censorship as of trying to keep out of dangerous waters. Rather than exalting the principles which it wished to defend and protect, RAI wanted to prevent anything which might seem opposed to them from emerging and developing in television. This included even small, banal but also grotesque examples of prudery, especially in popular entertainment programmes which naturally included the appearance of artists and entertainers endowed with charm, beauty and talent.

Similarly, in the political and cultural domain, an employee (or freelance contributor) of RAI would know which politicians were to be given preferential treatment on the screen as well as those who should be shown sparingly or not at all. The same went for political situations too; none were forbidden, and they could all be described, but only in a certain way, smoothly, never explicitly mentioning things as they really were, with the result that any description of opinion was lost in a grey, indistinct haze. The expression of provocative opinions as well as satire (even in entertainment programmes) was strictly outlawed. Events and developments in political life both inside and outside Italy constituted a special world, set apart, which it was forbidden to laugh about and which it seemed better not to think about.

The seeds of such practices existed before Bernabei, but under his guidance they become more refined and sophisticated, so that in the end they became the most striking characteristics of Italian television. They reached their apotheosis in the 'Telegiornale' (the news bulletin) and in 'Tribuna Politica' (a programme in which politicians representing the parties in Parliament talk to the people and are sometimes interviewed by journalists).

The rules applied to 'Telegiornale' were very simple. Above all there was to be a minimal use of live shots, instead of which still photographs were to be used to illustrate the words spoken by the news reader, who, 'though using the rhythm and expressions of the spoken language, was in fact reading from a written text, or at least conforming to a particular style of writing'. The content was simply handed to the news reader, and indeed the whole manner of presentation was set from above.[13]

'Tribuna Politica' went on the air in the late 1950s and at the start was something of an event. The programmes seemed to inaugurate a fruitful dialogue between politicians and citizens. However politicians failed to adjust themselves to the requirements of the new medium. The average Italian political leader, when speaking or when answering a journalist's question at a 'Tribuna Politica', speaks as if he were delivering a prepared speech, in which political jargon is mixed with the words of the bureaucratic and curial language. He always prefers to use long complicated sentences rather than to speak to the point. It is a way of convincing the listener that only the politician has the authority and the power to get things done, but which at the same time leaves what he appears to be committing himself to both vague and imprecise. In a country like Italy where ideology takes precedence over crude political facts, it is not usual to question a politician about his actions and his practical decisions. Instead it is the ideology and the myth which he stands for which are challenged. Thereafter, in the 'Tribuna Politica', journalists who share a politician's political views avoid asking embarrassing factual questions, while if they disagree with his ideological leanings, they will attack him on a theoretical level, avoiding the facts. Thus the discussion becomes colourless and the result is a programme which provokes boredom. In the case of 'Tribuna Politica' the blame cannot be put on 'occupation' alone. These characteristics apply to Italian politicians, regardless of their party, almost without exception. They do not like to be challenged and, in practice, they go unchallenged. Very rarely do interviewers expose to public scrutiny the actions of politicians in a live televised discussion and this coincides exactly with the goals of the 'occupation' policy, whose whole point is to avoid criticism, or to leave criticism undeveloped as is the case in 'Telegiornale'. Anyone who wanted to follow only through 'Telegiornale' reports the traumatic changes which have taken place in Italian society since the 1950s would have been struck by two conflicting impressions: on the one hand, celebration of the achievements of the government which benefited those in power; and simultaneously the determination of the political majority to find solutions to serious impending problems, of which he, the viewer, had been until then hardly aware.

It is worth recalling that towards the end of the 1960s, after much protest and criticism, RAI put a journalist who was not a Christian Democrat in charge of the 'Telegiornale'. Fewer pictures of DC leaders appeared on the screen and the programmes became rather more lively. It looked like the beginning of a real reform, but it proved to be only a beginning. A conflict of personalities soon arose and divorce was not slow in coming; the journalist, who had unwisely underestimated the rules governing the Italian political system, and especially those of the 'occupation', was dismissed.

By the late 1960s the machinery of 'occupation' was firmly in motion, and it was impossible to stop it. The larger it grew, the more difficult it was to contain. It reached the point where it seemed to propel itself; even those who had set it in motion were losing control of it. What is more it could no longer be hidden discreetly from the eyes of its critics. The Christian Democrat 'occupation' became a widely known fact. The other parties were jealous of the power which it exercised over RAI. Through television, many millions of Italians were exposed almost exclusively to the influence of the dominant party; in the medium term the effect could have turned out to be harmful and counterproductive, but the DC seems to have been entirely unaware of such a possibility. It was considered better to take the risk of over-exposure on television rather than limit the extent of its own control over the medium. Any such decision would have been interpreted by its competitors and political opponents as capitulation. Nevertheless, the DC managed to retain control of the most important and sensitive posts within RAI. It skilfully resisted the attacks of the other political parties as well as remaining blind to resentment expressed by groups within the public.

The Christian Democrat administration proved much less skilful in dealing with the internal disobedience, rebellion and conflict which were arising within RAI. These all had one thing in common: ideological and political opposition to the DC and to the directors of RAI (as representatives of the DC). This dissent arose particularly among programme makers, especially in the cultural and current affairs fields. The result was most clearly seen in the content of programmes which implied values or realities very obviously opposed to the political and electoral interests of the DC.

Every project carries within it the seeds of its own defeat and the DC plan to control RAI was no exception. In order to reinforce the DC position, Bernabei had sought to gratify a large number of powerful people and groups, taking on hundreds of writers, intellectuals and political hangers-on who worked more for their parties than for RAI, plus hundreds of outside collaborators, on the recommendation of influential figures in politics and the Church who belonged to the Christian Democrats and the other political parties. He hoped, by performing favours for everyone, to strengthen the position of the DC (as well as his own) and to minimise the hostile criticism levelled at RAI.

This policy did not in the event help the DC, because Bernabei only succeeded in filling RAI with political enemies. Even RAI's Christian Democrats were divided into groups according to their various internal factions; meanwhile, the representatives of the minor parties were all trying to maintain their respective shares of influence. The largest and most active contingent consisted of members of the Marxist left, and of the PCI in particular, the party traditionally most attractive to intellectuals. The chess board which the DC should have been able to control through Bernabei grew too large, becoming a scattering of miscellaneous political affiliations, all attempting to influence decisions and all loyal to their various parties rather than to television or to RAI.

In the end it was the company that suffered. Its whole hierarchy became politicised. Many employees were already politically committed before joining, while others became so in order to compete for jobs. Every problem and every undertaking was treated in terms of political categories. Petty struggles for the control of offices or programmes were ennobled by the skilful flying of ideological banners. Everyone hid behind the shield of ideology and politics. Personal independence, freedom of opinion and respect for the public – values which ought to have taken precedence – had little chance of gaining currency. Efficiency and professionalism suffered too. In order to be accepted, all plans and projects needed a political or ideological justification.

Thus the administration of RAI became the scene for continuous political skirmishing among directors, producers and journalists who often called on their external patrons to help them. This situation could only result in programmes which harmed the political and electoral interests of the DC, turning the effect of 'occupation' against it, or else in programmes which were cauldrons into which each political party or group was trying to fling its own ingredients.[14]

Reform, Monopoly and Sharing

The twenty-year-old agreeement by which the Ministry of Posts had assured RAI–TV the exclusive right to broadcast, was due to expire on 15 December 1972.[15] It was clear that any renewal of the agreement would not pass unchallenged. Indeed many different cultural and ideological groups had been preparing proposals for the reform of RAI–TV since the 1960s. Certain political parties had also put bills before Parliament,[16] but they had not even been discussed; the time was not yet ripe. The opposition parties (the PCI in particular) had not yet committed themselves seriously.

However, the right opportunity was indeed visible in the impending expiry of the agreement.

Parliament was dissolved in the spring of 1972, a year before its term would normally have ended. Following the elections, the DC formed a centre government which leaned slightly to the right, with the PLI (returning to the coalition after an absence of more than ten years), the PRI and the PSDI. Both the government and the political parties found themselves unprepared by the time of the crucial date on which the agreement ran out, and the government was forced to announce before Parliament that it was extending the agreement between the Ministry of Posts and RAI for a further year, until 31 December 1973.[17] On 13 December 1972, there was a stormy debate in the Chamber of Deputies. At that stage, Parliament, even if rather unwillingly, had to accept the government proposals. Still, the government was obliged to promise, through the Prime Minister Giulio Andreotti, that it would take certain practical steps.

Andreotti announced the setting up of a special commission whose job it would be 'to examine the various possible solutions [for the reform of the RAI] . . . and to prepare a report [on which] the adoption of the necessary measures could be based'. The commission was to deliver its report on 15 February 1973, and Andreotti promised to put a bill for the reform of the RAI before Parliament a month after that.[18] The commission duly completed its report,[19] but the promised bill never materialised. Andreotti's coalition was threatened by a crisis, and a few months later, in June 1973, the government resigned. As the parties had planned, a centre–left coalition replaced the centre–right government. The PLI returned to opposition while the PSI entered into the coalition with the PRI, PSDI and the DC under the Prime Ministership of Signor Rumor. The new government took office in July 1973, but it too was unprepared.

While the government, deeply concerned with the crises facing it, remained silent on the question of reforming RAI, parties such as the PCI and the PSI, as well as the regional administrations of the Abruzzi, Campania and Lombardy, prepared plans of their own. Such plans were intended not only to express publicly the ideas of the parties concerned, but also to challenge the plans which the DC would try to impose, as the strongest party in the coalition, in the ensuing negotiations. At that stage there was no public discussion or debate in Parliament. For the second time, at the end of 1973, the RAI agreement had to be extended, this time until 30 April 1974, but the government now found it necessary to grant a third extension which was due to expire on 30 November 1974.[20]

Following the plans of the PCI, the PSI and the regional administrations, the government finally expressed its own opinions, and on 21 May 1974 it put before Parliament Bill 2961, entitled: 'New regulations regarding the public radio and television services'.[21] In August a number of Deputies belonging to the left wing of the DC put forward their own plans which were much closer to those proposed by the regional administrations and the various parties mentioned than to those of the government.[22]

Very soon, however, the problem of constitutionality over-shadowed all these proposals even before any discussion or negotiation could begin. The Constitutional Court, in its Decisions 225 and 226, both dated 9 July 1974, imposed limitations on the exclusive monopoly held by the RAI–TV.[23] On 30 November 1974, the day when the agreement was due to expire, the government issued a decree which, apart from meeting the require-ments of the Constitutional Court, restated the contents of Bill 2961.[24] However, when this was put before Parliament for approval,[25] the bill was successfully obstructed by the MSI, the extreme right-wing party which had not been included in the ranks of those due to benefit from the reform. Time threatened to run out, and the government was forced to issue another decree, identical to the first, on 22 January 1975.[26] Yet even this second decree could have been stifled in the same way as its predecessor. Thus a danger-ous race against time formed the last phase of these dramatic events.

More than two years after the crucial date of 15 December 1972, the coalition parties (DC, PDI, PSDI, and PRI), encouraged by the decisions of the Constitutional Court, finally reached an agreement, which took the shape of Bill 3448 put before parliament on 8 February 1975.[27] Two months later this became Law 103 which effectively set up the new, reformed RAI–TV. On 7 August 1975, the Ministry of Posts and RAI–TV signed a new agreement to last for six years.[28] The reform of RAI–TV had been completed.

The attitudes of the various political parties towards the reform of RAI–TV, Decisions 225 and 226 of the Constitutional Court, and finally the content of Law 103 need to be closely examined.

As far back as 1970, the DC had set up a committee to define the party's attitude towards the reform of RAI–TV. The DC was perfectly well aware not only of the attack which the other parties were preparing to launch against it, but also of the strong possibility that the golden age of its dominance was drawing to a close. Proof of such an awareness can be found in a memorandum written in 1971 by a senior member of the committee. This document says at one point:

> A state monopoly is not, and cannot be a way of ensuring political conformity, let alone a support for various sources of political power . . . It is undeniable that the members of the board [of the RAI] are appointed, whether directly or indirectly, by the government through the majority shareholder, IRI, and that all the most important posts such as those of chairman, vice-chairman, chief executive and general manager are bound to the government by ties of personal trust. It is easy to see what effect . . . such a situation can have on programme planning, on the choice of staff, and on the appointment of managers and administrators . . .

The DC thus recognised the whole extent of its 'occupation', and realised that it could not continue as before.

The memorandum evaluated the objectives which the other parties were setting themselves, as follows: 'It is quite natural that in a situation of this sort the opposition parties should seek to . . . (1) take away from the government the power which it has over RAI at the present moment and (2) transfer it to Parliament . . . The intention is to transfer to Parliament not only the task of legislating on questions of broadcasting, but also that of making appointments and running the system.' The author of the memorandum was not overjoyed at such a prospect: '. . . such phenomena are merely the expression of a desire to transform parliamentary government, which is government by the majority, into government by the assembly, thus involving the minority parties too . . . It is only too easy to understand why this should please certain political groups anxious to shift the governmental axis.' Our author is clearly thinking of the PCI, even though he makes no specific reference to it. While, however, he recognises that 'the government's control of broadcasting cannot be upheld any longer', he insists that any move to give such a power to Parliament should be resisted.

The memorandum proposes, as a solution to this *impasse*, a radical reform of the old Committee to establish *the basic cultural, artistic and educational policies* which came under the authority of the Ministry of Posts (see under Para. 11, Article 8 of Decree 428). The new 'committee should be made up mainly of true representatives of the most important social, civil and religious organizations and institutions', since 'these too form part of Italian society'.[29]

The fundamental difference between the government's proposals (reflecting, of course, the DC's aims and worries) and all the other plans for reform, lay in the extent of the power to be given to Parliament. Through it, and a reorganisation, the opposition parties hoped to change the rather intermittent and precarious influence they had exercised within RAI into a legal right. There were naturally other, equally important differences, but they were all logical consequences of the first.

As the DC saw it, an increase in the powers accorded to Parliament would make it much more difficult to justify its 'occupation' of RAI–TV by means of legislation. Without legislative protection or justification, the DC would be forced to reckon with the other parties and would have to try to take from them in practice what it could not obtain by means of legislation. It therefore resolved to oppose any move to increase the powers of Parliament in this field.

Thus, it is not by chance that the government's Bill 2961 reiterated in 1974 the ideas expressed in the 1971 memorandum. Indeed, we find in the bill a proposal for a radical reform of the Committee to establish *basic cultural, artistic and educational policies* under the authority of the Ministry of Posts. It was to be rechristened the National Broadcasting Committee, to be no longer dependent on the Ministry of Posts; it was made up in a way that secured to the government a comfortable majority. The committee would be able to intervene in management and programming, while a Parliamentary Commission would be given much more general power to establish policy and control over RAI–TV. This Committee, on the other hand, does not feature in the opposition plans. Furthermore, in these plans, RAI ceases to be a company whose shares are owned by IRI (as the government desired) but becomes a public institution, so that it can more easily be controlled by Parliament.

In the government's proposals the appointment of the General Manager has to be approved by the Council of Ministers, and though his duties are more restricted than before, he remains a dominant figure. He also retains autonomy and freedom of initiative, while in the other plans the role of the General Manager is purely executive without any autonomy of action. In the latter proposals the real power within the company is exercised by the members of the board, in practice establishing a sort of collegiate administration of RAI–TV.

The regional administrations had naturally assigned themselves an important role in their own proposals. For instance, they wanted to supervise at least one third of transmission time, for both local and national programmes. Furthermore, they considered that the monopoly of the broadcasting services should belong to 'the state and the regions', thus assuming for themselves a position equal to that of the state. They also proposed to run any future cable television service with their own studios and transmitters. The PSI's proposals stated explicitly that cable television should be operated by means of concessions to the regional administrations. The government proposals, however, did not assign any particular role to the regional administrations.

The government document visualised a broadcasting company which, apart from some small modifications, was basically hierarchical and heavily centralised. The opposition's proposals were quite different on this point. The PCI's plans, and to some extent those of the regional administrations too, included the setting up of production units among the workers and collaborators of RAI–TV, which would operate as collectives taking initiatives in the conception, production and transmission of programmes.[30]

On two matters, the DC found itself in agreement with the other parties and with the regional administrations. The first concerned the establishment of special rules to govern the right of access to television, so that, as the government proposals put it, 'all parties and political movements with parliamentary representation, national trade unions, regional administrations and religious creeds could express their views in *ad hoc* programmes'. In other proposals, the right of access was more extensive. The terms employed were much less restrictive, as, for instance, in the proposals put forward by the PSI which gave the right of access to political, cultural and trade union movements and organisations, and also, to use its own words, to 'whomsoever applies'. It would therefore follow that in principle everyone had the right to apply for television time.

The second point that everyone agreed upon was that the RAI–TV was to continue to enjoy exclusive rights over broadcasting. Since any reform was to be the result of negotiations between the parties, it was quite obvious that none of them were particularly anxious to squander any of the influence they might retain or gain by spoiling the perfect completeness of the monopoly.

While the politicians, during the course of 1972 and 1973, were busy setting out their points of view, private radio stations operating within a local radius began to multiply in Italian cities both large and small, as well as a number of television stations which used cables to transmit their programmes directly to the homes of their subscribers. Even though these operations were not on a large scale, they were threatening the principle behind RAI's monopoly. If their existence had been tolerated it would have meant that the political establishment was not opposed to limitations being imposed on the monopoly. Thus, many of these stations were closed down by officials from the Ministry of Posts, while their promoters were taken to court.

It is difficult to convey to a foreign reader the enthusiasm which greeted these first experiments in cable television in Italy. The most emphatic and superlative language was used to describe them. The weekly magazines were full of articles which succeeded in giving one over-riding impression: that very soon Italy would be covered in cables, with hundreds upon hundreds of stations broadcasting their own programmes and points of view quite freely. The desire to demolish RAI's monopoly, like a latter-day Bastille, was mingled with the most hare-brained technological forecasts suggested by the new and compact gadgets produced by the electronics industry. This outbreak of collective enthusiasm for cable television took place in a period in which the secularisation process within Italian society was approaching its peak. The student protest movement and working-class protest expressed through the trade unions had acquired a full-blown status in the political scene and had shaken the traditional and hierarchical Italian social order, with its consolidated relations between the authority and the citizen. A year later the Church and the Catholics were to lose a national referendum calling for the cancelling of divorce legislation approved by Parliament on which the Christian Democratic Party was to find itself isolated. Authority had been effectively challenged, and was on the defensive. In this context, cable television appeared as a means for breaking a monopoly, which had become synonymous with traditional authority. However, cable television did not go beyond the stage of experiment scattered around many Italian towns. No one had taken any account of reality or of technology. The enthusiasm vanished as fast as it had arisen, and with it the cable television stations, thus confirming that behind this outbreak there were no big, well-organised interest groups.

Simultaneously, another more serious and actual threat was posed to RAI's monopoly, involving a drop in its advertising revenue. Some private companies set up installations which picked up signals from foreign television services (Switzerland, Monte Carlo and Yugoslavia) and re-transmitted them to an ever-growing number of Italian viewers. Advertising for Italian products flowed in to these stations thanks to their competitive rates. In this case too, the government intervened by closing the transmitters and commenced judicial proceedings.

In the meantime, the government's Bill 2961 was waiting to be discussed in Parliament and the opposition parties had prepared their own proposals. The armies were drawn up waiting for the start of battle, but the bill never in fact came before Parliament because of an unforeseen event – the publication of the Constitutional Court's Decisions Nos 225 and 226, which were soon widely known, and which caused the government a considerable degree of discomfort.[31]

The two decisions permitted certain exceptions to the absolute and complete public monopoly of broadcasting services; they permitted the installation of transmitters for foreign television stations and of cable television services, provided these remained on a local basis. In practice, these decisions made the way clear for two parallel systems, one local and one national.[32] While cable television services lost ground and disappeared, the number of foreign television transmitters increased. But private radio stations multiplied, thanks to the juridical and legislative lacuna. Before this decision, the installation of transmitters for foreign television programmes had been punishable under the law, but the Court now declared this situation to be unconstitutional because it considered that one could not force a citizen 'to obtain his information only from the national broadcasting services . . . by denying him the possibility of consulting other important sources of information, and choosing those sources according to his own criteria'.[33]

In permitting the national transmitters of foreign television services, the Court opened a door to a multiplicity of opinions and views. The new situation could endanger the RAI monopoly of national and public broadcasting services. The Court was quick to explain why in its view the monopoly could still be considered as constitutional, stating seven requirements which the national monopoly ought to fulfil in order to ensure the same multiplicity of opinions. Decision 225 declared that

> 'The denial [to undertakings owned by private citizens] of the medium of broadcasting is only legitimate if two fundamental aims [are fulfilled]: [first], programmes which [offer] the public a range of services characterized by objectivity and fullness of news coverage, by being open to all cultural developments, and by an impartial reporting of the ideas being expressed in society; [secondly] the favouring, application and guaranteeing of the right of access [to the RAI–TV] as far as technical limitations will allow.

The Court observed that if these two objectives were not maintained, 'the broadcasting medium runs the risk of becoming a powerful instrument in the hands of one faction and of certainly not being to the advantage of the whole community'. It could not have been more explicit in its criticism of the government and the party indentified with it.

In the view of the Court, in order for these objectives to be achieved, the following legal provisions should be adopted: (1) the administration of the concessionary company (that is, RAI–TV) should not be entirely or mainly a reflection of the government in power; (2) measures to guarantee the impartiality of news programmes; (3) the granting to Parliament, as the institutional representative of the community, of sufficient powers to carry out its directives and exercise effective control of the service; (4) the greatest possible objectivity on the part of journalists, giving them the opportunity of fulfilling their professional duties; (5) a restriction on advertising; (6) measures to govern the right of access; (7) measures concerning the right of reply. These conditions constituted quite clearly a number of yardsticks for determining the legitimacy of the monopoly and have proved to be guidelines for subsequent legislation. Indeed, Law 103 of 1975 was approved on the basis of a bill (3448) which 'made specific reference to these conditions laid down by the Constitutional Court'.[34]

The Court had made a significant contribution to the political debate over the reform of RAI–TV, and by its decisions it had, for better or for worse, dealt a lethal blow to the line adopted by the DC up to that point. Since the Court had decreed that Parliament should be given 'sufficient powers', the National Broadcasting Committee which the government had proposed to set up in order to maintain at least some control over RAI–TV, was clearly doomed. The existence of this committee could not be justified after these decisions, and the proposal was withdrawn. The way was now open for the parties to agree on the text of Law 103.

Law 103 takes account of all the directives which the Constitutional Court had set out in its Decision 225. Gone is the National Broadcasting Committee proposed by the government, and its powers are transferred to the Parliamentary Commission in addition to those already conferred upon it.

'The fundamental feature [of Law 103] is the destruction of the traditional relationship between the government and broadcasting . . . a situation is created whereby the national community is considered as having the right of control over the broadcasting which is otherwise designed to serve it.'[35] This was the opinion which the Christian Democrat Minister of Posts expressed before the Parliamentary Commission on 30 April 1976. The 'National Community' is represented by Parliament, which delegates the task of 'general policy-making and supervision of the broadcasting service' to a commission made up of 'forty members drawn from among the representatives of the Parties' parliamentary delegations' (Art. 1, Law 103). These fine words do not hide the reality: Law 103 has been basically the result of an agreement openly reached by the parties and only afterwards submitted to the Parliament. A dangerous precedent has been set. It amounts to a derogation from the authority of Parliament, and means that the forty parliamentarians will act more as party yes-men and less as officers of the legislative power.

The Parliamentary Commission has to deal, first and foremost, with the Board of RAI–TV. This is made up of sixteen members, which at the present moment can be divided up as follows, according to their political affiliations; DC, six members; PCI, four PSI, three; PRI, PLI and PSDI, one each. The Secretary, though not a Member of the Board, is a Communist.

The running of the company is in the hands of these two bodies, the ultimate loyalty of whose members is to their parties. The senior management of the company, though not elected but appointed by the parties, is in a similar situation, from the General Manager down to the directors of the various services. The extent of their subservence to their parties depends largely on the character, tastes and opinions of each individual. Even so, any possible personal freedom is inevitably limited by the fact that each director and senior manager owes his nomination, job and career to a party. He cannot afford to disregard or ignore its interests or demands. If he should ever choose to act according to his own opinions or convictions against the will of the party, he will sooner or later be faced with the choice of either submitting or resigning. Indeed such a situation has already arisen.

The Parliamentary Commission has to lay down the principles for the organisation of the company, while the Board has the task of putting them into practice and applying their decisions. The Board has to look after staff matters, especially the appointment of senior and middle management (including the transfer of officers from one job to another), and to work out the assignment of jobs, while the General Manager has to carry out its directives. The highest executive role is in the hands of the General Manager, but his task is formulated in such a way that he can only act as a co-ordinator of the various departments of the company and this allows him little chance of acting on his own initiative.

In order to deal with so many decision-making and operational tasks, the two bodies meet very frequently. The Parliamentary Commission and the subcommittee which examines and approves the applications from associations and institutions wishing to use some television and radio time, met thirty-seven times during the course of 1976 and twenty-five times in the first quarter of 1977. The Board of RAI–TV has met seventy-six times in the eighteen months from 23 May 1975 to 31 December 1976, and twenty-five times in the first four months of 1977, while its subcommittees have met in all for some 106 working days from 23 May 1975 to 31 December 1976 and for 30 days in the first four months of

1977.[36] It is only when a board is really a form of collective leadership that it meets so regularly and so frequently, and in this situation what was once a powerful General Manager becomes its executive secretary.

Furthermore, Law 103 transformed the two television channels into two separate and autonomous networks and gave the three radio programmes an equally autonomous status. It ordained that each of these networks should have its own organisational and administrative staff. It also gave particular freedom to the editors of the news programmes for each of the networks, giving to them the status of editors of ordinary daily newspapers.

Article 13 of Law 103 which set out what we have just described, also prescribed the organisation and the role of senior management for these and for all the other programmes and technical departments.

The new, reformed RAI–TV is actually a faithful reproduction of Law 103. Nothing in the law is left to chance or to the discretion of the proposed governing bodies of the company, apart from two things. Obviously, the law does not say who should fill the posts which it describes, especially those who should be on the Board, and it does not explain how the individual radio and television networks should increase 'the participation of citizens' or how they could help 'the social and cultural development of the country'. A law cannot be expected to go into too much detail. However even if this had been possible, the law would have refrained from doing so. Nominations, as well as the future of the broadcasting networks, were the task of the parties. The decisions on these questions would be taken after hard and exhaustive negotiations, which have been described as follows:

> . . . the form, the mechanism and the initial stages of the agreement between the parties which prepared the way with such difficulty for the reform, betray very clearly the concerns of all the parties. For the losers it was a question of agreeing while giving away as little as possible of the influence they had hitherto maintained; those who were new to the system were anxious above all to gain an influential foothold in the governing bodies.[37]

According to the author of the above quotation, the Constitutional Court had borne in mind when delivering Decision 225, a reform of RAI–TV characterised by '. . . an ideal model of participation . . . drawn from the experience of other European countries where social structure and opinions have a very different history and traditions from our own'.[38] If this is the case, and there is no reason to doubt this assessment, the Court certainly indicated one line of development, but at the same time showed scant regard for the deafness of the Italian political system to such an ideal.

The nature of the Italian party political system being what it is, the reform opened the way for two main developments. The first of these is described with considerable lucidity and perspicacity by the author of the article we have just been quoting. It concerns 'the special significance' and 'the particular role assumed in our system' by Parliament. Since Law 103 gave Parliament certain funda-mental powers as well as 'certain tasks which bear upon the very running of the company' a situation has arisen which 'is quite outside the normal Parliamentary system'. The second result is a logical consequence of this, and can be defined as the sharing of responsibility, or the division of the spoils of battle. The bargaining took place during a period when the PCI, despite the great advance it had made in June 1975, was not yet supporting the government under the six-party agreement signed after the National Elections of 1976. It therefore took no official part in the negotiations. Between 1975 and the end of 1976, the 'direct presence of the Communist Party' in RAI–TV was almost a symbol of its real strength in the country.[39] Thus it was to the PSI out of all the parties opposed to RAI's hegemony, that the lion's share fell. It was given the Chairmanship of the Board of RAI–TV, as well as control of the second television channel and the third radio programme. The DC gained control of the first television channel and the second radio programme. The demands of the PSDI were satisfied when they were given the first radio pro-gramme. All the parties agreed to run RAI–TV together as a joint venture. In this division of responsibilities, the DC managed to secure for itself the largest and tastiest slices of the cake. Proof enough of this fact is that it managed to gain control of the first television channel which has by far the largest audience.

The DC emerged quite respectably from the negotiations, while the other parties gained a great deal, not so much because of their individual bargaining power but by using the combined muscle of all the political left wing. The DC was unable to escape the collegiate atmosphere which pervaded and characterised the Board which now set eagerly about its work. In the course of a few months it produced several documents dealing with the organisation and functioning of the company.

In the first of these documents, on the 'Restructuring of the Company', the Board confirms right from the start that 'the main function of the company in the context of the reform is to conceive and produce programmes'.[40] What other function, one may ask, can a broadcasting company have? The document goes on: 'This task is in the hands of various units concerned with conception and production, of the programme department and of the directors of the channels.' Thus we see the resurrection of an idea contained in the proposals of the PCI and some of the regional administrations. The conception and production units are defined as the basic units of programme production; one of these is 'built up of a group of people, who may even come from outside the company . . . who must get together to conceive and produce a programme or a series and is characterised by a very high degree of freedom in matters of organisation; it can break up or be reconstituted with the same or different people according to the content of a programme or during the different phases of conception and production.' A programme department is on a 'higher level than these units'. The departments are given 'an amount of broadcasting time which can be reckoned as the total of the time allotted to the units which belong to each department'. These departments look after a variety of programmes broadcast regularly at particular times on certain days. Finally, each network is made up of a number of programme departments. All these different components of the company can propose the making of particular programmes, which must then be approved by the Board, and the Board alone can give permission for its decisions to be modified.

The other documents are concerned with journalistic services, the two channels, the role of management, and the decentralisation of the broadcasting services.[41] The last of these can be seen as the first step towards the subsequent decision of the Board to create a third television channel to start transmission in 1979, which will be principally in the hands of the regions. It will transmit programmes locally, but will also produce regional programmes for transmission throughout the country.

Clearly the reform had transformed 'occupation' into the sharing of responsibilities. Someone, when commenting on this situation, had used the phrase 'pluralist regime',[42] by which he wished to indicate the way in which the multiplicity of opinions in the reformed television service reflected a style and content which went arm in arm with the parties' interests.

Several protests had arisen in the press in the past when the appointment of certain RAI officials looked as if they had been imposed by parties (the DC or the PSI) seeking to extend their influence. The resentment against the DC's occupation obviously led the majority of the Italian press to castigate the main opposition party which showed no hesitation at all in adopting those same practices. A new stormy controversy arose in the summer of 1977 when the PCI flatly asked to be represented within RAI–TV in a manner more in proportion with its electoral strength. Thirty-four senior managers were appointed, fifteen from the DC, eight from the PCI, five from the PSI, three from the PSDI and three from the PRI. The DC was to appoint the Director of the proposed third channel. The PCI was given the Chairmanship of SIPRA, the powerful company which gathers advertising for the RAI–TV, as well as a number of assistant managerships in various departments within RAI or in companies linked to it.[43]

Press comment was highly critical. An article which appeared in the *Corriere della Sera* under the title 'The Communists also get a share', contained the following words: 'It may well be that the new managers of the RAI appointed by the PCI are experts in their field . . . but it remains the case that they hold party membership cards and that . . . without [those cards] they would never have crossed the threshold of Viale Mazzini'.[44] *L'Unità*, the Communist Party daily newspaper, objected that a great change had taken place, since all the parties had now been included and one could at last talk of the 'introduction of pluralistic criteria' in RAI. It was the end of the period when individual departments of the RAI were exclusively assigned to some parties or political groups. This, according to the article, was quite the opposite of a sharing of responsibilities.[45] This is a very curious piece of reasoning: a sin was no longer a sin because the Communists had joined the ranks of the sinners. The controversy continued vigorously in the course of the following days. One paper talked of 'invading parties', another asked in alarm: 'Is this the beginning of the great partition?'[46] *L'Unità* had to reply, and did so in an article entitled 'Concerning some not unfounded criticism'.[47] In practice, it promised that in future the PCI would not commit any more sins of this kind. Two days later, the General Manager of RAI–TV, Pier Antonino Berté, gave an interview in which he said that though there had been no 'wild sharing out' of appointments, the choice in this matter had not been entirely free. This was equal to an admission that the parties had expressed their views, and that they had been listened to.[48]

One gets the feeling when reading this controversy that the PCI was being accused because it had been considered incapable of the same sins as the DC. A large proportion of intellectuals and journalists thought of the PCI not only as the 'Opposition' (with a capital 'O'), but as the exact opposite of so many national faults. They liked to see in the PCI a kind of Jacobin resistance to the habits which the Italian political leadership had introduced to the nation during previous decades. When the time of reckoning came with the appointments to RAI–TV, such a hope proved abstract and unfounded, and it became obvious that despite the many fine words that it poured out so readily, the PCI was very much a part of the Italian political system and had no intention of turning its principles upside down or changing the way in which it worked. It was indeed through the system and its principles that it had been able to infiltrate Italian society (just like the DC) and prepare the way for its electoral successes. Many intellectuals and journalists had a vague attitude towards the PCI, amounting more to what they wished to see in the PCI than in what it really was and is. When the PCI finally entered into the portals of power, the spell was broken. Peter Nichols gives perhaps the best explanation of this attitude when he writes that 'like the students, some left-wing writers and intellectuals recoil in horror from the contagion of power'.[49] There was no doubt that the PCI wished to contract this very disease.

Like a novelist, we must ask the reader to step back in time, in this case from summer 1977 to summer 1976, when on 28 July the Constitutional Court in Decision 202 declared unconstitutional those parts of Law 103 which forbade 'the setting up and running of installations for broadcasting radio and television programmes without wires within a local radius'.[50] Just as it had authorised local private television stations using cables (which subsequently vanished), so the Court now authorised those without cables, plus local private radio stations.

Did the Constitutional Court in Decision 202 wish to challenge the 'pluralistic regime', thus loosening a screw in the mechanism which the parties had every interest in keeping tight? There is no answer to this question; the reader is free to answer it as he thinks best. The fact is that since 1976 no law has been passed to correct the unconstitutionality of those parts of Law 103 which deal with local private television transmitters.

Early in 1978 the text of a bill was published[51] which is designed to regulate private radio and television stations on a basis which the mass media experts appointed by the political parties appear to have agreed on. When the bill is finalised it will be submitted to Parliament. Its main legal provisions are:

(1) A tight control of licences (lasting no more than six years) to be approved by a nineteen member body called the National Broadcast Commission, eight of whose members are elected by the Parliamentary Commission set up by Law 103, a further eight elected by this same body on the basis of lists prepared by the regions and the remaining three appointed by the Prime Minister. This means that the same political balance embodied in the Parliamentary Commission will be reproduced in this new National Commission.

(2) A national frequency plan including a map indicating the limits of each transmission area to be adopted by the National Broadcast Commission, by which a private television station can obtain a licence if it accepts and observes certain requirements; namely transmissions cannot exceed a radius of 15 kilometers and must serve a population of no more than 100,000; in exceptional cases a station may be allowed to serve a population of up to 500,000; each station must go on the air for no less than three hours per day, and twenty-four hours per week; the percentage of original programmes (that is, autonomously conceived and carried out by the station) cannot be less than the 50 per cent of the total of a week's transmission hours; advertising time must be no less than the 5 per cent and no more than the 12 per cent of the transmission hours.

(3) No one can get more than two radio or television licences within a region, and no more than five in the whole national territory, and there must be no contiguity.

(4) Mergers and or other forms of liaison are strictly forbidden; the transmission of the same programme in the same hours or on the same day by different stations is forbidden; however, more stations may broadcast the same event live, but they cannot pool their technical equipment.

It is doubtful, to say the least, whether a television station could easily meet all these requirements *and* run a profitable business. Be that as it may, the fact is that these proposed rules are strikingly similar to other current pieces of legislation tailored to fit the needs of the parties (such as, for instance, the new law for press subsidies presented before the Parliament). In practice, the new text envisages a private television system heavily dependent on the will of the political establishment. It apparently aims at reproducing in the private radio and television area the same sharing of influence now bearing upon the life of RAI–TV.

Obviously the relationship between television and politics in Italy still has some distance to go before it stabilises, but it would be more than mere speculation to suggest that as long as Italy maintains its present party system, radio and television are likely to reflect the opinions and wishes of the parties. The present organisation suits them well and the successors of the present party system will hesitate before abolishing a mechanism that has stood them in such good stead.

4 Federal Republic of Germany

From Democratic Showcase to Party Domination

Alfred Grosser

Television has influence, and television is subject to influence. It is influenced by the society on which, in turn, it exerts its influence. It is also influenced by the past of the society to which it belongs; it is influenced by the ebb and flow of ideological currents. This applies to the Federal Republic of Germany (FRG) just as it does to other countries, and much of what we shall have to say about television in the FRG does not in essence differ from the state of affairs described in the other chapters of this volume. This is true, for instance, of the wave of systematic questioning which marked the 1960s. But like every case, the case of the FRG is a special one; in fact it is more of a special case than other countries since its origins have an individual history, since it has a very special problem of identity, and because it has a very special relationship to democracy.

The FRG is a very strong state whose origins go back to 1948–9, to an act of double rejection: a rejection of the Nazi past and a rejection of the Communist present. This double 'No' – 'No' to Hitler and 'No' to Ulbricht – produced at one and the same time a sense of certainty and a feeling of insecurity. People knew full well (only too well) the meaning of democracy: the opposite of what all Germans experienced between the years 1933 and 1945 and the opposite of what seventeen million Germans have been experiencing in the GDR since 1946. At the same time, there is a great deal of uncertainty about exactly what the FRG represents in the world. The FRG is not Germany: 1945 witnessed a rupture in history as well as a rupture in geographical terms which divided Germany into at least two parts.

Other countries experienced a process of detachment from their history due to the technological transformation of society and to an exaggeratedly sociological attitude to society. In the FRG, over and above this, a different – and more thorough – process of uprooting occurred, a process to which President Scheel rightly often draws attention.[1] It is almost as if people would rather not have had a past at all, merely because one part of that past – only twelve years, but what a twelve years! – is accounted for by the Nazi era. At the same time the founders of the new German state faced the clear task of 'overcoming' this past, that is, the task of making known the facts about and the origins of that past in terms of precise knowledge and sober but committed reflection.

Moreover, foreign countries insist that the criminal past should not be forgotten or passed over in silence. This insistence carries with it certain negative consequences. The other countries' self-righteousness, which causes them to forget their own crimes, tends to reinforce the tendency in the FRG to say 'let the past bury the past' or to embellish what has happened. And those who are anxious to enlighten their fellow citizens, the educators, are constantly being shaken in their assumptions by the mutually contradictory strictures being voiced abroad: when nothing much is said about Hitler, this is taken to betoken an evil desire to obliterate the past by a conspiracy of silence; when Hitler is mentioned this is taken to prove that he is back in fashion, in other words that the Germans are about to be led astray by Nazism once again.

Television, which had from the outset assumed (with great, and somewhat naïve, assiduity) the role of educator and instructor, is constantly being subjected to foreign criticism and has for nearly thirty years now been trying to guard against it. But how? Whenever a 'neo-Nazi' incident occurs (when a grave is daubed with paint or something occurs in a military academy, etc.) the difficult decision has to be taken whether to say little about it – thus proving how incorrigible the Germans are ('where are the protests?'), or to give the matter extensive publicity, thus attaching a significance and importance to such incidents which they do not deserve. The foreigner is thus shown how significant and extensive 'neo-Nazism' is in the FRG. Since the end of 1969, that is since the neo-Nazi NPD party failed to poll 5 per cent of the vote – which meant that it obtained no seats in the Bundestag and which in turn resulted in its rapid decline – the television networks have had to face one problem less. That problem was: ought one to give screen time to the NPD people to show how stupid they are, or should one give them scant exposure in order not to strengthen them and to prevent their importance from being over-rated abroad? At all events, an unimportant incident such as the flight to Germany in the summer of 1977 of the SS leader Kappler, who had been held in prison in Italy, underlined once again the customary dilemma.

Even disregarding foreign reaction, the question of the amount and kind of exposure of the Nazi past is a very delicate one. Television films about this past are frequently shown and the work of enlightenment which goes into this effort is generally good.[2] However, it is only a few films which create a stir, and such films nearly always become the subject of violent debate. This is true, for instance, of Joachim Fest's *Hitler – A Career*, which was attacked in the FRG as being insufficiently critical. This in turn caused important foreign newspapers to brand the film, without having seen it, as a glorification of Nazism,[3] which was by no means the case.

The question how the past is to be depicted, or even to be hinted at, is the more difficult as nobody can foretell how the public will react. The best example of this is the series 'Ein Herz und eine Seele' (A Heart and a Soul), the main character of which, called Alfred Tetzlaff, had been cast by the editor as a repulsive individual. However, his constant, fanatical, obstinate, dogmatic and genuinely reactionary critique of politics and society met with too positive a public reaction. The lively debate about the series had been forgotten by the time Tetzlaff last appeared on the television screen, in November 1976. Occasionally the past is really treated with shocking indifference, for instance when Leni Riefenstahl, the producer of the films about the 1936 Olympic Games, talked about her past or when the actress Christina Soederbaum spoke about the anti-Semitic films on which she worked under the direction of her husband Veit Harlan.[4]

The character of the FRG has also since its very inception been determined by its anti-Communism. When Berlin was threatened in 1948 and saved thanks to the air bridge, a political and psychological reality came into being which has endured to this day. The threat was real, as was the healthy determination to withstand it. At the same time it was not disagreeable to become, thanks to the menace, an ally of a great power, the USA, while as it were shedding the past in the common defence of freedom, with anti-Communism becoming the measure of one's dedication to democracy. It now also became more important to protect Western Germany and the West in general from the menace than to proclaim one's dedication to national unity.

In the meantime all the fundamental questions regarding the German problem remained unanswered: the feeling was that the Oder–Neisse line was not a final frontier and that the other German state was not a state. Television has played a particularly important part in this context, by making the public in the FRG aware of the realities of the situation – in advance of every political party and almost every politician – by means of accurate information and what, at the time, was very courageous comment. Programmes about the finality of the absorption of the refugees from the East, about the Oder–Neisse line, and about the GDR (then commonly called the Soviet Zone of Occupation or Central Germany) contributed to the gradual transformation of the FRG's eastern policy, a transformation which culminated in the years 1970–72.

In the last few years television has been carrying out a double task, and a difficult one. On the one hand it is playing an important role in the GDR, which is the only country in Eastern Europe whose population regularly watches the television transmissions of a Western country in its own language. This brings with it both responsibilities and criticism: the problem is to decide whether one is to put out programmes strongly critical of FRG society, knowing that such programmes are liable to be used in Socialist Germany as evidence of the sins of capitalism. The answer to this question is, of course, that such programmes are proof of the freedom which prevails in the West and make this freedom seem desirable. On the other hand, the information available in the Federal Republic about the other Germany is unbelievably poor (even the FRG's best newspapers publish virtually no information at all about the politics, economy and society of the GDR), with the result that television has a particularly important part to play in this connection, a part to which programmes such as the series 'Kennzeichen D' ('Registration mark D') seek to do justice.

Television also tries to shed light on the human and political aspects of the existence, side by side, of the two German states. This is not always an easy task; it is, moreover, generally neglected by the press. In August 1977 the ZDF (Second German Television) network broadcast a documentary film 'Deutsch–deutsche Perspektiven' (German–German Perspectives) which in its final part – the theme of which is the love story of a West German chemist and an East German hairdresser who is helped by her lover to escape to the FRG – describes the destructive effects of the difference between the two societies on each of the two lovers, differences which finally bring the story to an unhappy ending. The film does not set out to portray this as a typical fate but merely to draw attention to the objective forces to which the fate of individuals is subject. The fate of Wolf Biermann, the poet and singer who was expelled from the GDR but who has nevertheless remained a Marxist, is even more characteristic of the political and ideological situation. There was much controversy about the amount of attention FRG television paid to him after his arrival in the West. Some asked was it right to give him so much exposure? Others asked, on the contrary, whether more of his song programmes should not have been shown on television. Was Biermann's case evidence of Western freedom as against Eastern intolerance, or was he a particularly credible critic of Western capitalism?

A well-known song of the nineteenth century asks: 'What is the German's fatherland?' For thirty years now, this question has again been very topical. There can be no doubt that the Federal Republic is not a fatherland in the same sense as France, Sweden or Holland. Hence the tremendous importance of concepts such as 'free and democratic institutions' and a 'state based on the law': the ideological content of the Constitution is in a sense a surrogate for the absence of patriotic allegiance to a community. The British and the French ought not to feel that so much talk in the Federal Republic about democracy is unnecessary since it fortunately enjoys a completely normal liberal–pluralistic political system. True, it does have such a system and one which, moreover, functions better than, for instance, the systems in Italy, France and Belgium. The fact is that the democratic concept is particularly valuaole in the Federal Republic. Its 'free and democratic institut' ns' and the existence of a 'state based on the law' are meant to provide it with solid foundations, which it would otherwise have to seek in the fear of Communism. Hence television is bound to talk more about democracy, and its democratic character is subject to more careful scrutiny, than the television networks of other countries.

Democracy means pluralism, precisely because the rejected past and the rejected institutions of the neighbour country are in turn based on the rejection of pluralism. It is the political parties which are the embodiment of pluralism. This is even more the case as the parties go back to 1946, that is, they antedate the FRG by three years and had presented themselves to the citizens in regional elections before the birth of the Federal Republic. Anyone who wishes to understand the power the political parties wield over television – a subject which we shall deal with later – must first grasp the favoured position which they enjoy in the structure and day-to-day life of the FRG. Nowhere else has the role of the political parties been defined in such generous terms. It would be worthwhile in this context, to quote textually Article 1 of the 1967 law about the political parties:

The parties are a constitutionally essential part of the free democratic order. They fulfil, with their free and continuous participation in the shaping of the people's political will, a public task which is imposed on them and guaranteed by the Constitution.

The parties share in shaping the political will of the people in all spheres of public life, in particular by:

promoting the citizen's active participation in political life;

training citizens capable of assuming positions of public responsibility;

participating in federal, Land and local elections by putting forward candidates;

influencing political developments in Parliament and the government;

introducing their political aims into the shaping of the state's political will; and providing a constant, living link between the people and the organs of the state.

If, as was the case in the Weimar Republic, splinter parties and the multi-party system had created disorder in the country's political life, the legitimacy of the parties would have been shaken even in their own eyes. However, the public's sober attitude, as well as the functioning of the electoral law's 5 per cent clause, have simplified and justified the party system. Since 1961 there have been only three parties in the Bundestag (if we regard Franz-Josef Strauss' CSU in Bavaria and the CDU in the other provinces as one), and these parties together obtained in the 1961, 1965, 1969, 1972 and 1976 elections an aggregate of 94.3 per cent, 96.4 per cent, 94.6 per cent, 99.1 per cent and again 99.1 per cent of the votes cast, with the two big parties – the CDU/CSU and the SPD – averaging together 91.2 per cent of the vote. Since the FRG does not have the British electoral system (which is capable of giving the Liberals 2 per cent of the seats when they have polled 20 per cent of the vote), the FDP, with its 7.9 per cent share of the vote and 39 seats out of a total of 496 (CDU/CSU 243, SPD 214) plays a decisive role. The same applies to the Land diets and governments: everything depends on the three parties, and frequently it is the smallest of the three which decides which of the two big ones shall govern.

The FRG is a federal state, the more so as the Laender existed prior to the federation and as such endorsed the Constitution. Although the reality, and also the text of the Constitution, is much less federal than that of the USA, Article 30 nevertheless remains an essential element of the country's legal and political structure: 'It is up to the Laender to exert the state's powers and execute its tasks unless otherwise provided for in or permitted by this Constitution.' It was above all on this article that the Federal Constitutional Court based itself in declaring, on 28 February 1961, the establishment by the Federal government of a German television company, as being contrary to the Constitution. In its judgement, it said, among other things:

The provision of broadcasts is, in accordance with German legal history, a public responsibility. Should the state assume this responsibility in any shape or form whatsoever, this would become a 'state' responsibility, the implementation of which, according to Article 30, is, however, up to the Laender . . . Nor may it be concluded that this is a matter for the Federation merely because a given task (e.g. the transmission of a television programme) is not being undertaken by each Land (or its television corporation) separately but by the Laender (or respectively by their television corporations) jointly or according to individual arrangements . . . It makes a decisive difference to the federal state whether the Laender agree among themselves or whether the federation shall be empowered to make decisions legislatively or administratively in an individual case contrary to the will of the Laender or of individual Laender.

At that time various Laender were already co-operating in this way. After the war various broadcasting institutions came into being whose statutes were frequently influenced by the occupying Powers. They were all public institutions whose statutes were entrenched in state treaties and broadcasting laws.

The problem of television became topical in 1950. The world's first regular television service was started in Berlin in March 1935. The development of television was subsequently interrupted by the war. In August 1948, the administrative council of the Northwest German Broadcasting Company (Nordwestdeutscher Rundfunk) took the decision, in agreement with the British military government, to resume the development of a television system. The first experimental programmes started in Hamburg in November 1950. The other Land broadcasting corporations put television transmitters into operation from 1953 onward. The joint television programme 'Deutsches Fernsehen' (German Television) began on 1 November 1954.

This joint programme was based on an agreement which in June 1950 gave birth to the ARD, or Working Community of Public Broadcasting Corporations of the Federal Republic of Germany (Arbeitsgemeinschaft der oeffentlich-rechtlichen Rundfunkanstalten der Bundesrepublik Deutschland). The ARD's statutes, modified in 1962, must be considered together with other important texts, above all the 1964 Administrative Agreement on Co-operation in Television (the television agreements); the basic principles governing co-operation in the ARD joint television programme 'Deutsches Fernsehen', agreed in 1971; and the 1975 administrative agreement on the central licence office.[5] Of the present members of the ARD, two are institutions established under federal law: they are 'Deutsche Welle' – a shortwave transmitter whose task it is 'to provide listeners abroad with a comprehensive picture of political, cultural and economic life in Germany and to explain to them the German view on important topics' – and the 'Deutschlandfunk', whose task it is to give listeners in both parts of Germany a comprehensive picture of German events. Both of these institutions are concerned with sound broadcasting only and not with television and are based on Cologne.

The corporations which concern themselves with television are all Land broadcasting institutions, with the largest of them, the North German Broadcasting Company (Norddeutscher Rundfunk), being provided by three Laender (Hamburg, Niedersachsen, Schleswig–Holstein). Baden–Wuerttemberg, on the other hand, has two such corporations. Under the television agreement, co-operation is organised along the following lines:

(1) The broadcasting corporations provide a joint television programme consisting of the programme contributions of the corporations.

(2) The joint television programme consists of the following parts:

(i)   The evening programme, from 8.00 p.m. onwards;

(ii) The afternoon and evening programme, from Monday to Friday;

(iii) The weekend programme, consisting of: (a) the Saturday afternoon and evening programme; (b) the Sunday morning programme; (c) the Sunday afternoon and evening programme.

(3) The broadcasting corporations undertake to provide the joint television programme according to the following percentages:

	Per cent
Bavarian Broadcasting Corporation	17
Hesse Broadcasting Corporation	8
North German Broadcasting Corporation	20
Radio Bremen	3
Saar Broadcasting Corporation	3

	Per cent
Transmitter Free Berlin	8
South German Broadcasting Corporation	8
South-west German Broadcasting Corporation	8
West German Broadcasting Corporation	25

The percentages of the programme contributions to be produced in Munich, Frankfurt, Hamburg, Bremen, Saarbruecken,
Berlin, Stuttgart, Baden–Baden and Cologne correspond to the
population figures and hence to licence revenue. The various
transmitters are thus left above all with the 6.00 p.m. to 8.00 p.m.
time slot for regional programmes. To this should be added the
'Third Programmes', which are put out regionally and which in
general either have a regional content or else consist of culturally
and politically demanding features. The 12 May 1971 administrative agreement on the co-operation of the Third Television
Programmes facilitates the co-ordination and exchange of these
programmes.

The programmes are known as 'Third' because the figure two
was reserved for another institution, which originated from the
television judgement of 1961. The fact is that on 6 June 1961 the
Laender concluded a state treaty providing for the establishment
of a public corporation, the 'Zweites Deutsches Fernsehen' or
Second German Televison Programme. The corporation's seat is
in Mainz. While the ARD is a sort of co-operative of Land broadcasting corporations, the ZDF is a central establishment owned by
the Laender. In its tasks and organisation the ZDF resembles the
Laender corporations. Paragraphs 2 and 3 define the basic tasks of
the ZDF, and these are also reflected in other statutes.

Paragraph 2   Character of the Transmissions
   (1) The transmissions of the corporation are to provide television viewers throughout Germany with an objective view of world
events and in particular with a comprehensive view of German
reality.

   (2) These transmissions are to serve, above all, the cause of
Germany's reunification in peace and freedom, and international
understanding. They must conform to the country's free democratic institutions and promote the free formation of opinion.

Paragraph 3   News information

(1) News information shall be comprehensive, true and factual. The origin and content of reports intended for publication shall be carefully scrutinised.

(2) News and comment shall be separate; comment shall be identified as an individual's view.

As is the case with the other corporations, the structure at the head of the ZDF is three-fold: a wider committee (in the case of the ZDF the Television Committee); a more restricted body with wider powers, the Administrative Council, and the Intendant. The Television Council has sixty-six members, the seats being distributed according to a key laid down in the agreement. This key corresponds to the principles which govern institutions in the south of the FRG, the ruling principle being that the institution shall be based on 'the socially relevant forces'. In the case of the West and North German Broadcasting Corporations, on the other hand, the councils are elected by the appropriate diets, each party receiving the proportion of seats it has in the diets.[6]

The ZDF Television Council is composed as follows:

(1) one representative each of the Laender which are a party to the agreement, the representative being nominated by the Land government concerned

(2) three representatives of the Federation, nominated by the federal government

(3) twelve representatives of the political parties, the seats being distributed according to the various parties' strength in the Bundestag and the appointees being nominated by their party executive committees

(4) two representatives of the Evangelical Church

(5) two representatives of the Catholic Church

(6) one representative nominated by the Central Council of Jews

(7) three representatives of the trade unions

(8) two representatives of the FRG Federation of German Employers' Associations

(9) one representative of the Central Committee of German Agriculture

(10) one representative of the Central Federation of German Craftsmen

(11) two representatives of the FRG Federation of German newspaper publishers

(12) two representatives of the German Journalists' Union

(13) four representatives of the Free Social Welfare Associations

(14) four representatives of the Local Government Association

(15) one representative of the German Sports Association

(16) one representative of the Refugees' Association

(17) ten representatives of the educational world, as well as of science and art, and one representative each of the free professions, of organisations concerned with family life, women's interests and youth.

Quite apart from the fact, to be analysed further on, that many representatives of 'unpolitical' bodies actually have party political allegiances, one is prompted to ask whether such a council is 'representative' in regard to its age structure and the division of its members into such groups as employees and employers. Thus, the DGB (the German TUC) with 7.5 million members has just one seat, in common with the Union of German Employees, with 1.4 million members and the Civil Servants' Federation with 0.7 million members. Together, they form a tiny group of employees' representatives, while the employers and the free professions are represented under several headings.

The Television Council issues directives for the programmes and advises the Intendant in regard to programme planning. The nine-member Administrative Council decides the terms of the Intendant's contract of employment, supervises the activity of the Intendant and decides on the budget submitted by the Intendant. The membership of this body (the members being appointed for five years) is composed as follows:

(1) three representatives of the Laender, who are selected by the respective Prime Ministers; the latter shall endeavour to make their nominations, as far as possible unanimously

(2) five further members, who are elected by the Television Council by a majority vote. These members shall belong neither to a government nor to a legislative body (thus, contrariwise, the three Laender representatives may be ministers or even Prime Ministers); members of the Television Council are eligible for election

(3) one representative of the Federation, who is appointed by the Federal Government

The Intendant is elected by secret ballot for five years by the Television Council. A minimum of three-fifths of the members' votes is required for such an election. Re-election is permissible. The Intendant may be dismissed by the Administrative Council with the agreement of the Television Council. He is responsible for the entire programme output. He requires the agreement or approval of the Administrative Council, among other things, for the appointment of the Director of Programmes, the Chief Editor, the Director of Administration and for the conclusion of contracts of employment with the most senior members of staff.

The directives for the fashioning and judging of programmes go very far in two respects: in twenty-five paragraphs they demand, on the one hand, truthfulness and objectivity and, on the other, a commitment to the support of a number of other basic social and political values, promotion of which does not necessarily accord with the call for truthfulness.

In recent years, financial problems have been increasingly in the forefront of attention. The ZDF receives 30 per cent of the total licence revenue and also has an income from advertising. As of 1 October 1977, there were in the Federal Republic including West Berlin 20,500,000 radio and 18,800,000 television sets for which a licence fee was payable. The word 'payable' is important in this context, for the economically or socially underprivileged do not have to pay these fees. The details of the application of this provision depend on the regulations in force in individual Laender. In respect of television, this applies to no fewer than 1,300,000 licence fees which are not levied and which thus represent, as it were, a social contribution made by the broadcasting institutions.[7] The financial difficulties are mainly due to inflation (and the now slow growth in the number of television sets). The fact is that viewers have paid the same licence fee, i.e. DM 10.50 a month, since 1974; only on 1 January 1979 will this figure rise to DM 13 a month.

The money goes to the broadcasting corporation of the Land where the owner of the set resides. Since the Laender have very unequal population figures and contribute widely differing proportions to the programmes which go out, the financial share-out among the Laender tends to be a matter for constant dispute. In 1977, the share-out was as shown in Table 1.[8]

TABLE 1

	Contributes	Receives
	(in millions of DM)	
Bavarian Broadcasting Corporation	16.24	
Hesse Broadcasting Corporation	5.60	
North German Broadcasting Corporation	24.28	
Radio Bremen	0.71	16.45
Saar Broadcasting Corporation	0.90	20.16
Transmitter Free Berlin	2.37	28.34
South German Broadcasting Corporation	4.80	
South-west German Broadcasting Corporation	6.25	
West German Broadcasting Corporation	54.50	
	115.65	64.95
ARD receives from Deutsche Welle, from Deutschlandfunk and from RIAS Berlin for the execution of joint tasks	0.90	
It spends on items of joint expenditure		18.00
It finances Deutschlandfunk to the tune of		33.60
	116.55	116.55

It is all the more difficult to achieve a balanced budget as nearly all the broadcasting corporations are constantly in the red.[9] The North German Broadcasting Corporation has the biggest deficit, and this accounts for a considerable part of the crisis with which we shall deal later. There are many considerations involved, among other things the salaries and number of staff members, i.e. whether or not programmes are to be made with many or only a few original contributions.

A new element which has contributed to finance and programme problems emerged in 1977. Up to that time many of the journalists and other contributors were 'freelance', that is, they had no claim to established employment. They did much of the creative work, if only because many of them belonged to the younger generation. On 22 June 1977 the Federal Labour Court recognised claims to established employment based on working relationships which had arisen by dint of actual practice. Thereupon a number of freelance contributors sued for permanent employment. This has induced the corporations to employ fewer freelance contributors and to use those they do employ only at irregular intervals. The West German Broadcasting Company (WDR) has now submitted a constitutional case to the Federal Constitutional Court against the Federal Labour Court on the grounds, among other things, that the latter court had infringed the constitutional task of the broadcasting corporations and the freedom of broadcasting since the compulsory permanent employment of freelance contributors, with all the consequences that this entails, restricts the freedom of programming and the possibility of creating adequate programmes.[10] The corporations certainly share the burden of responsibility for the present state of affairs, owing to their refusal to grant normal pay conditions to many regular freelance contributors. Although many of the 83,000 freelance contributors have other main outside jobs which preclude their being taken on to the establishment, the court judgement nevertheless gives rise to a real danger that the corporations will grow old and ossify.

Despite some difficulties and friction, the system functioned well for a long time, providing a guarantee of political quality and independence much more effectively than was the case in France and Italy. In many respects the guarantee was as good, if not better, than that which existed in Britain. The federal structure has had (and still has) one enormous advantage: any political prejudice or influence on the part of one corporation could be compensated in the ARD by the opposite tendency on the part of another. In any case, everyone has been compelled to keep within bounds: 'If you make your share of the programme more red, I shall make mine more black . . .' All have joined in keeping a wary eye on the common newscast 'Tagesschau' which, according to the 1971 principles for ARD co-operation, 'must not contain any expression of editorial opinion'. 'Reports by correspondents may, however, contain expressions of opinion. Commentaries put out as part of the "Tagesschau" must be clearly separated from the news.'

For many reasons, however, one cannot take a very positive view of developments over the last few years. Tendencies making for bias have always been in evidence.[11] This trend evoked a reaction when, as hitherto, it tended to favour the left; when it favoured the conservative camp, on the other hand, the bias was, if anything, reinforced. This is connected with the general development of the intellectual climate in the Federal Republic, but needs to be analysed on a number of levels.

First, there was a possible menace to co-operation within the ARD from the Bavarian Broadcasting Company (BR). The latter, becoming increasingly one-sided, was threatening to go its own way. In November 1977 an incident occurred which was not in itself tragic but was nevertheless sensational in the light of the general relations between the Bavarian company and the ARD. The Bavarian corporation's Intendant had vainly sought to have cuts made, totalling 100 seconds altogether, in a film contributed by the West German company (WDR). The WDR Intendant refused to agree for reasons of principle (he had not himself seen the film at the time): if he did agree, would this not amount to conceding the right to every corporation to exercise a censorship of sorts over the network contributions of the others? The Bavarian Intendant thereupon dropped the film, in other words he cut out the ARD transmission altogether and replaced it with other material. His point was that he could not show the scenes in question (they were in fact the face of a girl who had become the sex object of the inmates of a welfare institution as well as the picture of female genitals in a pornographic film which was being shown in the house of a deputy) without violating the viewers' moral feelings. Since the Bavarian Broadcasting Act forbids the transmission of programmes which violate moral or religious sentiment and since the ARD State Agreement says under Article 6 that 'every broadcasting institution is entitled to forego the transmission of parts of the common programme and to replace such parts with contributions of its own', the Intendant was no doubt entitled to act as he did. However, this was just one more incident involving the Bavarian corporation and the ARD, the Bavarians having repeatedly refused to carry joint transmissions, especially of satirical New Year's Eve programmes.

The ARD's general structure does not seem in danger, however. The same cannot be said of the internal structure of the North German Broadcasting Company (NDR) which is threatening to break up, in 1978, as a three-Land institution since the powerful figure of the Christian–Democrat Prime Minister of

Schleswig–Holstein, the former Federal Minister Gerhard Stolten-
berg, has given notice of his intention to renounce the state agreement. The crisis has been brought about as much by financial and
administrative problems as by political differences over the control
of programme content. In April 1977, after the Administrative
Council consisting of four CDU and four SPD members and sitting
under the chairmanship of the Minister of Culture of Lower
Saxony, had harshly criticised a series of programmes about
works' councils, the Intendant of NDR, Martin Neuffer, himself a
Social Democrat, brought a court action against the Administrative Council on the grounds that it had violated the neutrality rules
of the state agreement. In June, after the Christian–Democrat
members of the Administrative Council had deliberately deprived
it of a quorum by absenting themselves, the Broadcasting Council
adopted a resolution calling on them to resign. The resolution was
passed since there is an SDP/FDP majority on the Broadcasting
Council.

The bare facts of the affair point to a development which is not
peculiar to NDR – the importance of party allegiances among
members of the companies' administrative bodies, and to the
massive presence of important politicians as members of these
bodies – a state of affairs which has altered the entire nature of
state supervision. This applies to the broadcasing institutions in
the southern part of the country nearly as much as to the others,
for the representatives of theoretically apolitical organisations are
increasingly behaving as members of political parties. In fact, they
frequently hold important party positions and occasionally even
elective office. On the Broadcasting Council of the Bavarian
company (BR) the percentage of politically committed elements
rose from 33.3 per cent in 1959 to 54.4 per cent in 1972.[12]

The Administrative Council of the ZDF, as constituted in
1976–8, has as its Chairman the President of the CDU and shadow
Chancellor, Helmut Kohl. The Deputy Chairman is the Mayor
and President of Bremen and concurrently Deputy Chairman of
the SPD, Hans Koschnick. The representative of the Federal
Government on the Administrative Council is none other than the
Vice Chancellor, Foreign Minister and Chairman of the FDP,
Hans-Dietrich Genscher. As you can see, the parties are not
exactly blind to the importance of television! The situation is not
very different in the Land corporations. Hans Kuehn, an SPD

Prime Minister, and Kuppler, the leader of the CDU opposition, both sit on the Administrative Council of the West German corporation.

The elections of Intendants are more and more tending to become party battles. (Alternatively, where a party enjoys a clear majority, a candidate is simply appointed who belongs to the 'right' party.) Creative qualities, television professionalism or administrative skill are not as important as party allegiance. It would hardly be possible nowadays to conceive the election of a fine independent Intendant such as Klaus von Bismarck, who directed the West German corporation (WDR) from 1961 to 1976. In 1977 Prof Karl Holzamer had to go into retirement, a man who had for fifteen years since its inception been at the head of the ZDF. True, he was a committed Catholic and a member of the CDU, but prior to his appointment he had for many years been an expert on broadcasting and, in addition, a professor of psychology and education. The struggle for his succession ended in March 1977 after long and not always very dignified disputes with a compromise solution which admittedly resulted in the appointment as Intendant of a brilliant individual. After twelve hours, seven ballots and the defeat of three candidates, the diplomat Karl-Guenther von Hase was elected. He had up to then been FRG Ambassador in London and from 1962 to 1967 State Secretary and head of the Federal Government's Press and Information Office – a fact which at one and the same time qualified and disqualified him so far as responsibility for television information policy was concerned.

When an Intendant is elected anywhere, his party allegiance is common knowledge. In June 1977 the former chairman of the SPD group in the Berlin Chamber, Wolfgang Haus, was elected Intendant of the Berlin station (SFB). In July the successor to Franz Mai, the Intendant of the Saar Broadcasting Company (SR) was appointed with effect from 1 January 1978. Mai had been Intendant for twenty years (his attitude becoming increasingly authoritarian and conservative in recent years). The post went to Hubert Rohde, professor of education and, first and foremost, Vice Chairman of the CDU group in the diet.

This development should be seen in an international context: such differences and political disputes are still far more democratic than the political appointments, made without any discussion and

by secret decision, which are customary, for example, in connection with the appointment of French television network controllers. Nevertheless, the fact remains that this is a negative
development, as Klaus von Bismarck pointed out in an address
which he gave in December 1977. He said:[13]

> I have come to realise that where professional politicians are
> concerned the party political balance of power is in the final
> analysis decisive. To assume anything else would be to put an
> idealistic gloss on the situation. What does this mean? It
> means, for instance, that politician A, a member of the
> Administrative or Broadcasting Council, is swayed in making
> his decisions as a member of these bodies by his wish to project
> his personality in the eyes of his party colleagues . . . It means
> that politician B may say to an Intendant: 'I shall work for your
> re-election.' But a meeting of his party caucus is enough to
> change his mind, i.e. a man is chosen who has the right party
> membership card. It means, for example, that the politicians
> of party A, given a certain political situation, will be swayed in
> arriving at their decisions as members of broadcasting bodies
> primarily by considerations of a party political nature, i.e. they
> weigh up what course of action will most surely assist them in
> forming a coalition.
>
> What is the reason behind this increasing tendency towards
> 'party-politicisation'? The pressure of the parties, in practice
> above all of the party groups in the Land diets, on the members
> of broadcasting bodies has grown in intensity . . . As a result,
> the freedom of the majority of these members, who depend on
> party support, to take decisions which are in the best interests
> of broadcasting is strictly limited . . .
>
> In my opinion, it was quite legitimate for the Prime Ministers
> to insist on various conditions being fulfilled, in connection with
> the 1973 increase in the licence fee, with a view, for instance,
> to ensuring greater clarity as regards the financial situation. It
> is, however, a very different matter when Prime Ministers insist
> on deciding the details of the Third Programme . . . Leaving
> aside whether they have the legal power to do so it is simply a
> question of their not having sufficient expertise.
>
> It runs counter to the principles of a liberal society that the
> parties, in their capacity as the bodies responsible for articula-

ting society's political will, should behave as if in their sum total they accounted for the whole of society. This is why resistance is called for against party political domination of public broadcasting, even though we must be on guard against excessive sensitiveness *vis-à-vis* the political parties. If broadcasting were to become nothing more than the mouthpiece of the political parties, this would put paid to the making of lively programmes, of programmes capable of serving as the vehicles of new ideas.

[This is not to say, of course, that other segments of society are less] selfishly blind, less obsessed with satisfying their own interests . . . There is little evidence of the presence of a rational counter-impulse, one operating, for instance, with a view to asserting the community interest. No, the dominant attitude is determined by tradition, with all its prejudices. This is just as true of older, conservative members of the bourgeoisie as of young socialist trade unionists.

The editor of the South-west German Company (SWF) has similar things to say:

I regard the belief that representatives of the socially relevant forces will treat the common interest as more important than the interest of their own group as a superstition – and I know of only a few exceptions to this rule. I regard as a nightmare the idea that the Farmers' Union should appoint the editor of the agricultural programme or that the trade unions should appoint the person responsible for programmes dealing with social problems.[14]

There is, of course, a danger that in the broadcasting companies staffing policy may come to be regarded as 'a way of making appointments in accordance with the political parties' relative strength'.[15] People who – somewhat exaggeratedly – believe that this situation is already with us here and now, see things shaping as follows:

The editor who has sole responsibility for output is given a deputy who belongs to the other party, whichever it may be . . . But a true balance does not come about as a result of this.

Internally, within each editorial office, balance assumes the
form of tactical shifts, with a counter-course being steered
occasionally . . . (The journalist who readily adjusts himself
to this state of affairs enjoys advantages, but there is a price
to pay.) He pays by having to judge his own work, and that of
his colleagues, not in terms of professional competence but in
purely ideological terms. He pays in terms of having to plan
his programmes no longer in the light of the public interest but
according to parliamentary business and party political events
and conferences. He pays in terms of betraying his editorial
duties in the face of outside pressures . . .[16]

The question whether journalists are in fact simply pawns in the
hands of the political parties was considered very frankly and
soberly at the Mainz conference on television criticism by the
Editor of the ZDF, Reinhard Appel, who can look back on a
career of seventeen years in journalism with the liberal and 'non-
party' papers *Stuttgarter Zeitung* and *Süddeutsche Zeitung*, and
then as Intendant, from 1973 to 1976, of the Deutschlandfunk.

The political parties' power of attraction is not to be denied, and
the temptation is very considerable so far as many journalists
are concerned to give way and go along with the party even
against his or her own convictions . . . The parties have created
a state of affairs which makes it more difficult for journalists
in public broadcasting to escape their influence . . . [However],
the governing bodies in the sphere of broadcasting are responsible for making staff appointments for the most senior positions
only and much depends on how the powers-that-be in the
various broadcasting institutions use the rights and privileges
they enjoy under the law . . . However, I would not go so
far as to say that there is a clear-cut difference between
journalists who owe allegiance to a political party and those who
do not, for I know journalists who do belong to a party but
whose independence is nevertheless greater than that of journalists who owe allegiance to no party . . . Authority by dint
of competence is one way of fighting the temptation to become
a party pawn. Take the case of a duty editor who was criticised
at the end of a shift by his colleagues because he had treated
the views of the Young Socialist League's executive as interesting and, therefore, as worth including in the news while he had

ignored the reaction of the Socialist Party proper. Is such an attitude not proof that the journalist in question was – wittingly or unwittingly – a pawn in the hands of the socialists' adversaries, who have an interest in depicting the radical views of the youth organisations as those of the party as a whole.[17]

Naturally, the discussion in Germany about the relationship between the political parties and television resembles in some of its aspects the controversies which rage in other countries. A constantly repeated reproach made by the parties and important associations reflecting sectional interests is the excessive presence on the television screens of politically or socially unimportant minorities. The journalists' answer is that it is their duty to provide an outlet for precisely such minorities, which have no other mouthpiece. Such is the democratic way. Yes, but suppose that through the power of television the small are made great, be it in terms of numbers or in terms of influence? Who has authorised journalists to exercise such a power?

This controversy reflects the influence of television as a living reality which is not to be underestimated, especially since, as in France, there is a tendency in the Federal Republic to deplore the present state of affairs and to praise bygone days – the achievements of which went unnoticed at the time. And yet, the fact is that there are achievements to boast of in the Federal Republic of which France can only dream. This applies particularly to the exposure given to minorities, which – it is quite true – are being favoured by some editorial offices or at least by individual editors. There is quality to be found, too, in such programmes as the Sunday 'International Morning Break' by Werner Höfer. Thus, foreign participants in the programme have been able to speak frankly about the Oder–Neisse line, and this at a time when the subject was still taboo as far as the political parties were concerned. What they had to say was relayed live, something that has always been unthinkable in France in connection with such themes as Algerian independence. It has been, and to a considerable extent remains, possible to voice criticism freely in the current affairs programmes, though this tends to apply rather more to (carefully chosen) outside contributors than to staff journalists.

Although the daily news programmes ('Heute' – Today – on ZDF and 'Tagesschau' – Newsday – on ARD) have long been monotonous in style and content, it nevertheless remains true that German television retains a breadth of accurate information about foreign countries which it would be hard to find elsewhere. For the French observer the comparison with France is particularly depressing as French television's reporting of events in the Federal Republic is notably poor, while German television's reporting of France is extremely good.[18] The splendid reports and films of the ZDF studio in Paris, and especially ARD (for example two films, in 1977 and 1978, by Ernst Weisenfeld – one about the division of France into two camps and the other about the crisis of the left) furnish much more accurate information about the fundamental facts of French politics than does French television itself. In general, the ZDF series 'Auslandsjournal' (Foreign Journal) and the ARD series 'Weltspiegel' (World Mirror) are of high quality. It is also generally true that the problems of the developing countries are depicted less inadequately by ZDF and ARD than by most foreign television companies.[19]

This is not to deny that German television's reporting of foreign news and politics is open to criticism. But the point is that criticism is encouraged, especially criticism contained in reviews of media output. Thus the series 'Betrifft Fernsehen' (Concerning Television) by Helmut Greulich (ZDF) in July 1977 carried the critical film entitled 'Das ist der Gipfelt. Fernseharbeit bei einer internationalen Konferenz' (This is the Peak. Television Work at an International Conference). 'Betrifft Fernsehen' (About Television) and 'Glashaus' (ARD) have accomplished pioneering work of international importance in the sphere of media criticism, that is, in trying to educate the television viewer in his attitudes towards and expectations of the media. Many programmes put out in both series are worthy of a mention in this connection.[20] Will they be able to continue doing this work? 'Glashaus' is facing growing difficulties in dealing with really burning topics while 'Betrifft Fernsehen' is to lose its peak viewing time as from September 1978. It will be shown as late as 10.00 p.m., which would entail a radical change in its audience and hence in the nature of its impact.

These restrictions are but one symptom among many of the indisputably deteriorating situation in most of the FRG's television institutions. In a fairly sharply worded 'Declaration about freedom in broadcasting', the Central Committee of German Catholics (by no means a revolutionary organisation) noted in

June 1977: 'In spite of directives entrenched in law, developments have been in evidence for some time which give cause for concern. The citizen's right to free access to information and the duty of broadcasting to practise and safeguard freedom of information have been increasingly circumvented and ignored.'[21]

Examples and warning signs could be cited *ad infinitum*. Let us take the case of the youth programme 'Direkt' (ZDF). It has repeatedly provided good examples of the unpatronising approach to television: it has helped youth groups to express themselves through the medium of television; it has not just treated the young as objects. After six years of ups and downs, the programme appears to have been finally 'tamed' at the end of 1977.[22] It became clear in September 1977 that Günther Wahlraff's report about the 'Bild-Zeitung' would only be shown by foreign companies. The report, let it be admitted, was made by somewhat dubious means, for Wahlraff had joined the Springer paper's editorial staff under a false name. By the beginning of 1977 the internal disputes and attempts at browbeating colleagues which have occurred in the Bavarian company had become public knowledge.[23] While Gerhard Löwenthal's 'right-wing' political 'ZDF-Magazine' was left untouched, the (always stormy) history of the ARD magazine '*Panorama*' reached a low point in October 1977, the programme having been watered down, possibly beyond redemption. The most important alteration, however, is probably that which has taken place in WDR. When Werner Höfer retired in the summer of 1977, it became clear that he had held a protective hand, as a well-informed and conscientious Television Controller, over his editorial staff, who had long been under attack because of their alleged 'left-wing' sympathies. The new Controller, and especially the new Editor, the journalist Theo Loch, who as a CDU man can scarcely be called 'left wing', have seemingly started to put on the brakes fairly systematically. However, let it also be said that many of the attacks on their new approach are not in fact well directed.[24] In July 1977 things reached such a pass that trade unionists, politicians of the left and intellectuals organised a 'citizens' initiative' under the motto 'Save freedom of broadcasting in the WDR', a move which greatly resembled the Bavarian initiative for freedom of broadcasting. At the same time the corporations seemed to give way more readily to pressures by outside bodies. An example of this occurred in

Saabruecken, where the Intendant of SR appears to have sided, in June 1977, against his own editorial staff and with the German Football Association, the latter having criticised a religious broadcast in the course of which the Association had been accused of failing to make a protest, during the preparations for the finals of the World Cup, against torture in Argentina.[25]

The television corporations have become an object of controversy in the press (with fierce denunciations of their 'trendy left-wing sympathies' especially in the Springer papers). *Spiegel* and *Stern* frequently criticise the corporations' alleged domination by the left in exaggerated terms; the excellent *Allgemeine Deutsche Sonntagszeitung* takes them to task in soberly critical liberal language, while *Zeit* denounces all and sundry with words of biting condemnation. The situation is such that the need for calm reflection about the role of television in FGR politics tends to lose out.

As in other countries, television's role is of course questioned during election campaigns and afterwards. Questions are asked about the way it has reported a given campaign and how it has influenced people. As elsewhere, the problem exists in the Federal Republic of 'political marketing' that is of the 'selling' of politicians as if they were mass consumer goods. And as elsewhere, those concerned are particularly anxious during election campaigns to preserve a careful 'balance', that is, they tend to be even more cautious than usual. This caution can go so far that programmes are taken off the schedule if they are liable to be interpreted as indirectly bringing an influence to bear on voters. The election year of 1976, however, produced very open television, with a particularly interesting experiment by Reinhard Appel, in the series 'Citizens Ask – Politicians Answer' (ZDF). Important politicians were confronted face to face with members of the public in workshops and factories. The current affairs programmes gave a great deal of exposure to the electoral contest, with each series paradoxically (but is this really a paradox?) giving much more time to its potential adversaries than to the political leaders with whom it sympathised. 'Panorama' mentioned Franz-Josef Strauss seventy times, while the 'ZDF-Magazine' mentioned Helmut Schmidt eighty times and Willy Brandt sixty-six times. On the other hand, it did not mention the CDU leader Helmut Kohl at all.[26]

After the narrow victory of the SPD/FDP coalition a discussion took place on the part television had played in bringing about this result. Professor Elisabeth Noelle–Neumann, who is in charge of the Allensbach Institute for Public Opinion Research, indicated at a meeting of the German Television Corporation's Media Commission that the majority of radio and television journalists had believed in a victory for the coalition and had expressed that belief by using the media in a way that had in fact strengthened the coalition.[27]

At times when there is no election pending – and such times are rare in the Federal Republic, where there is always some election campaign in progress, be it only for a Land diet of importance to federal politics – it is the relationship between politicians and television journalists that is the problem. Who influences whom? Who tames whom? It depends on the politicians concerned, and some of the outstanding ones among them are treated with respect. Taken all in all, however, the interpretation favoured by Joachim Obst in his film 'Ihr Auftritt, Herr Minister' (Your Turn, Minister) – part of the 'Betrifft Fernsehen' series – seems to be right. Obst suggests that there are politicians who give way to television journalists in the hope of getting plenty of exposure in return.

The 'depoliticisation' of television programmes had given rise to widely voiced complaints. It is said that entertainment programmes are getting a constantly rising share of air time, and in this context the political effect of entertainment programmes is mentioned, their role of 'making people passive through entertainment'.[28] This function of television had been clearly defined by the Federal Constitutional Court in its 1961 television judgement. Anxious to ensure the application of Article 5 of the Constitution, according to which 'Everyone has the right freely to utter and spread his views by the spoken word, in writing and by means of pictures and to seek information from all universally accessible sources without let or hindrance', the Court had stressed: 'Freedom of the press and freedom of information in broadcasting and film are guaranteed . . .'

This co-operation [of radio and television] in moulding public opinion is by no means limited to news broadcasts, political commentaries, or programmes about political problems of the present, past or future. Public opinion is formed equally when

plays are broadcast, musical programmes, cabaret . . . Every
programme broadcast is bound to have a definite tendency by
virtue of selection and presentation, and especially as a result of
the fact that it is up to the programme-maker to decide what
shall not be put out, what is supposedly of no interest to the
listener.

Such problems also exist elsewhere. And yet, complaints about
television having lost its cutting edge are particularly strong in the
Federal Republic. Are they justified? That there has been a
change, there can be no doubt. This change reflects the peculiar
situation in the Federal Republic. For one thing, there are the difficulties connected, for instance, with terrorism and the violence
which threatens to erupt as a result of the debate about nuclear
energy. The reporting of the incidents in Wyhl, Brokdorf and
Kalkar led to a vigorous discussion.[29] The self-discipline which
television imposed on itself in September 1977 while the police
were searching for the kidnapped Hans Martin Schleyer also gave
rise to many questions.[30]

Over and above this, the Federal Republic has undergone a
development in the 1970s which is unique in Western Europe. At
the beginning of the 1950s a certain hardening of attitudes
occurred everywhere as a result of the cold war. During times of
relaxation of tension, the FRG is, however, the only country
which is inwardly worried and therefore outwardly intolerant. The
public employment prohibitions imposed by the authorities are
merely a sign of a hardly justified insecurity which breeds intolerance.[31] This insecurity is reflected within the television corporations by a new conformism, a fear of questioning. There can be no
doubt that in the 1960s people indulged to excess in criticism of
everything and anything. Now the pendulum has swung too far the
other way.

It has not swung so far, however, as to destroy the positive
qualities of FRG television. It may be that I am generalising my
own personal experience to excess. I am often asked for help, as it
were, by German television journalists and producers. I am asked
to put in a word of criticism here or to plead for tolerance there.
But my experience is precisely that I am able to tender this help
frequently and without obstacles being put in my way; I can do so

moreover, in a manner and on a scale which would be unthinkable in France. But then the television workers of the Federal Republic would hardly draw encouragement from a comparison with France!

5 Sweden

Freedom's Boundaries

Åke Ortmark

A Threatened Idyll

Sweden is small, homogeneous, prosperous, isolated and free
from conflict. Its success in avoiding wars and crises almost
constitutes a challenge to others. This idyllic background has
largely determined the development of television and the
conditions in which it functions.

Sweden's stability in the party political sense has likewise been
striking. The Social Democratic Party dominated government
practically without interruption during the period 1932–76; few
democratic governments anywhere in the world have enjoyed so
long a stay in office. Political stability can affect the freedom of
television in two opposing ways. On the one hand the absence of
divisive national crises ought to create a calm working atmosphere
and considerable room for journalistic freedom. On the other,
links can easily develop with the dominant party. In Sweden such
links have appeared to a remarkably small extent.

Now, the picture of Sweden has partly changed. In the 1960s
came the wave of the left, with its drastic social repercussions; in
the 1970s came long-term economic problems and terrorist
activity. Added to these are the social tensions generated by the
immigration of foreign workers. The proportion of immigrants in
the total population has risen surprisingly quickly to about 10 per
cent. The homogeneous Swedish pattern is beginning to break up.
The social and political consequences of this dramatic transformation cannot yet be measured, but it is possible already to
speak of the disintegration of the unified culture of the past.

At the election of 1976 the non-socialist parties (the Centre – formerly the Agrarian Party – the Conservatives and the Liberals) finally managed to defeat the Social Democrats, and a 'bourgeois' government was formed. The election result was not surprising. The Social Democrats have been declining in strength for a number of years, partly in consequence of structural changes in the composition of the population. The introduction in 1970 of a new electoral system allowing rapid transfers of power made it only a matter of time before a change of regime took place. Sweden will experience more frequent changes of regime in the future, and probably new governmental constellations as well.

Television reflects changes in society. Up to the end of the 1960s at least, Sweden ought to have been able to realise the dream of free television, that is, a television enjoying approximately the same journalistic freedom as the press in relation to the state and pressure groups. The external conditions were favourable: absence of problems, social and economic progress, respect for democratic ideals of which freedom of expression is one of the most important. On such terms, journalists of the air ought to be able to enjoy the classic freedoms. In such a model, journalists seek out the truth and publish it without sideways glances, without reference to party interests or sectional ideologies. The attitudes, passion for truth and integrity of journalists, then, correspond basically to those of scientists, even though the differences in the selection and demarcation of subject-matter, in working methods and level of ambition, are usually very wide.

Journalists who try to work consistently with this model can play an important role as watchdogs of authority in various sections of the community. What is required of politicians is that they shall accept – even create and finance – a system under which they themselves will be exposed to close and critical scrutiny in an open arena, and which will mercilessly show up their own shortcomings in the discharge of office and perhaps even their purely human weaknesses, which are of course not without political significance.

This demands much of politicians, and perhaps the demand can be met only under special conditions; it is questionable whether such conditions in Sweden or any other country have ever been met. There is a constant danger that politicians may so exploit their power as to confine television within a straitjacket of dependence, incompatible with the model itself; government and opposition can exercise parallel influence towards this end. The politicians can justify this by referring to the unique character of television, its great range, its special technical nature and its presumed power to influence. These factors turn television into an activity which has to be regulated and controlled, and at this point scruples about the libertarian ideal are sometimes overlooked. Certain leading Swedish politicians have spoken many fine words about the freedom of television, however – especially the Social Democrat who has probably had more to do with the development of television in Sweden during the 1960s and 1970s than any other politician – Olof Palme. In the mid-1960s he was Minister of Communications, and in that capacity he vigorously defended, in a Riksdag debate of 1966, the principles which he considered ought to guide the broadcasting media in Sweden. He struck up a song of praise to free and critical television – in a society where the wave of the left had still not gathered strength, where student revolt was still unthinkable, where long unofficial strikes in key industries were unknown.

Palme said that 'we must safeguard, uncompromisingly and with a steadfastness bordering on passion, the right of television to make open criticism of society, of the authorities, and of private interests. On this point we must not yield for an instant, no matter how the bassoons may blow or the trumpets bray.'[1] Palme went on to say that the best possible guarantees against abuse and for freedom of expression are to be secured through a corporation operating in the service of the public, that is, a corporation that is not owned by private interests nor financed by advertising. A corporation founded on the philosophy of public service, in Palme's view, has greater freedom in its choice of programmes and produces better, bolder and more varied programmes than its commercial equivalents. Palme reverted several times during the debate to this desire for television to produce *bold* programmes. It was natural for Palme to speak thus in the mid-1960s. The idyll did not seem to be threatened; the ideal of freedom of expression could be apostrophised in high-flown declarations in one of the world's most successful democracies. The future seemed bright. Palme, like other observers, was blissfully unaware of the political and economic shocks that Sweden was to sustain within a few years.

Philosophy, Organisation and Economy

Radio Sweden (Sveriges Radio or SR) is founded on the public service philosophy. Regular sound radio broadcasts have been made since 1925 and regular television broadcasts since 1957. The second television channel was inaugurated in 1969. The Swedish system is unique from the international standpoint since a measure of competition or 'stimulating rivalry' has been introduced between two equal and national television channels, both of them units within the same corporation. When the system was being worked out in 1966 the alternative of creating separate corporations for TV 1 and TV 2 was naturally discussed. The argument for such an arrangement can be grounded partly in classical mass media theory. It can be argued that diversity and free expression are encouraged if several organisations, entirely independent of each other, are working in open competition. However, the parliamentary situation of the mid-1960s made it easy for the Social Democrats to force through SR's monopoly of radio and television broadcasting. There were two main arguments for this arrangement: it would save money and offer better opportunities for sensible co-ordination of the two channels while simultaneously generating a 'stimulating rivalry' between them. However, the object was to avoid 'commercial' competition, which is characterised by the broadcasting of similar programmes by the various channels at the same time. Planning was to aim at a 'reasonable measure of contrast and therefore freedom of choice for the viewers'.[2]

Foreign observers sometimes say that Sweden adopts centralised monolithic solutions, and there is probably some truth in this assertion. But TV 1 and TV 2 did become independent units to an astonishing extent both in relation to each other and in relation to the top management of SR. Competition between the channels has become very real as far as news programmes and programmes on social problems are concerned – even though it is possible, of course, that the advantages of competition would have been reaped in even larger measure under another system.

However, the central point here is that the decision over the two channels was taken in a climate of opinion that can be described as favourable to the development of a relatively free and unfettered television service. Palme's words in the Riksdag debate were not mere lip-service. In leading political circles in the mid-1960s there was a clearly articulated will to safeguard the journalistic freedom of television – to the largest possible extent. It is on this question of *extent,* the degree of freedom, that the discussion becomes interesting and complicated, especially when comparisons are made between different situations and epochs and note can be taken of the varying degrees of pressure to which the corporation has been exposed.

The government grants SR the economic resources for its operations, establishes the laws and agreements applicable thereto, including the requirement that the right to broadcast shall be exercised factually and impartially, and determines the times of transmission, that is, the quantity of programmes. For the rest, the self-evident general principle, in accordance with the public service ideology, is that there shall be no interference in programme matters. What programmes shall be transmitted and who shall take part in them are matters decided within SR. So runs the general rule. The exceptions we shall come to shortly. It is with them that this chapter is largely concerned, that is, with the complications that arise when the public service ideology and the classical model of freedom are confronted with emerging social and political tensions and with attempts to change the prevailing power structures.

Television and radio are financed by licences – (costing Kr 400 per annum in 1978, including a charge of Kr 120 for possession of colour television).[3] It is inherent in the nature of the system that the allotment of funds must not be coupled with any kind of directive governing the use of the funds apart from the provisions of the Radio Act and the agreement between SR and the government.

In form SR is a limited company, but it most resembles a non-profit-making public corporation. The state does not own any shares in SR. There are three shareholders: the 'popular movements' (folkrörelserna), 60 per cent; the press, 20 per cent; and the business community, 20 per cent.

The 'popular movements', whose proportion of SR's share capital was increased in 1968 from 40 to 60 per cent, have played a fundamental role in the evolution of Swedish society since the end of the nineteenth century. The category includes trade unions and religious organisations, consumer and temperance associations, and other groups as well. These extra-parliamentary organisations have achieved an influence in Sweden to which there is no equivalent in most other countries. More than 90 per cent of workers in Sweden are organised in the Confederation of Trade Unions (Landsorganisation), the trade union wing of the labour movement. The corresponding figure in Britain is about 50 per cent and in the United States 20 per cent. The Swedish Confederation of Trade Unions is one of the strongest and most centralised trade union organisations in the world. Sweden is commonly called a thoroughly organised society, and with much justification.

Certain features of Swedish society – including the operating conditions and development of television – are incomprehensible unless account is taken of the influence of the popular movements in all the different parts of its social machinery. For instance, these organs have functioned as nurseries for talented individuals from the working classes. Many have been able to use the popular movements as a springboard from which to vault into influential positions in government or the Riksdag. Many of the latter's members have their background in the popular movements, no fewer than 20 per cent (65 out of 349), for example, being organised temperance reformers compared with only a few per cent in the population as the whole.

The popular movements and organised interests have always had a very strong if not dominant position on the Board of Governors *(styrelse)* of SR. The highest decision-making body has thus incorporated within itself all the important power groups of Swedish society: representatives of the big parties, corporations and organisations.

It is easy to perceive that a programme policy capable of always satisfying – or refraining from irritating – all these representatives of diverse and often conflicting interests would be of a notably bland and official character. Only in the period after the Second World War was SR able to begin liberating itself from what may be called the official grip. For example, not until twenty years after it had started could sound radio claim to be actively journalistic as far as domestic politics and controversial affairs were concerned. During the Second World War the corporation was still prohibited in principle from having anything to do with news. It was the news agency Tidningarnas Telegrambyrå (TT) that had the sole right to broadcast news over the air. Under such circumstances the radio's own 'news programme' entitled 'Echo of the Day' (Dagens Eko), took on a remarkable character. When Nazi Germany invaded the neighbouring countries of Norway and Denmark on 9 April 1940, 'Echo of the Day' consisted of two items: one official spokesman explaining how hoarding of sugar was to be prevented and another describing a study of the cost-of-living index. From the standpoint of news journalism and social criticism radio was asleep, a product of the passive tradition of popular education and improvement evolved within the popular movements.

Not until 1947 was the corporation granted the formal right to gather and edit news itself. Developments since then can be described as a protracted process of liberation, with uneventful periods punctuated at irregular intervals by explosive steps forward. The advances made have been achieved at times in tough confrontations with government, parties and the Board of Governors.

In principle, it is exceptional for the Board of Governors to concern itself with individual programmes that have been or are to be transmitted. Routine oversight of the details of programme policy is the responsibility of the Radio Council (Radionämnden), whose task is to determine whether programmes already transmitted are in accordance with the rules prescribed in the Radio Act (Radiolagen) and in the agreement between SR and the government. The Council consists of seven members appointed by the government. It examines programmes following representations from the public or on its own initiative. The Radio Council's composition, like that of the Board of Governors, reflects the power structure of Swedish society, although the Council's limited numerical strength precludes detailed adaptation to all the convolutions of society at large.

The passing of power to the non-socialist parties in 1976 has in the short run had relatively little identifiable impact on television. Basic principles and rules have not been changed. Most non-socialist politicians have always cherished the same sort of fundamental respect for the public service ideal as the majority of Social Democrats, and the sympathy found formerly in non-socialist circles for financing broadcasting by advertising has lost a great deal of ground, partly because of the economic difficulties of the press. Thus, no drastic alteration of the system or of the corporation's operating conditions has come on to the agenda. It is true that criticisms of SR have been more vigorous on the part of non-socialist politicians – chiefly Conservatives – but these have been concerned mainly with alleged deviations from existing rules and regulations which the critics have thus been endeavouring to safeguard.

However, a change of regime in one of the world's stablest – not to say dullest – democracies is a very important event. It mirrors a long-term shift of opinion within the community which will gradually have repercussions on SR, both directly and indirectly, through a variety of subtle mechanisms, half hidden from view, of which recruitment is one. But it is a process that will take a long time and may be interrupted if the Social Democrats get back into power again. After its victory at the polls the new government appointed a non-socialist Chairman to the Board of Governors of SR, but this was a measure almost completely without short-term effects, partly because the weight of SR's own apparatus gave it a sufficient degree of independence *vis-à-vis* the Board of Governors and the power groups within it.

However, there are some vital changes of principle that can be linked to the change of regime. First, the Riksdag decided in the spring of 1978 to offer idealistic, religious, trade union and political groups, organisations and folk high schools (*folkhög-skolor*) the opportunity of making their own local radio broadcasts alongside SR. This represents an infringement of SR's monopoly. It involves a number of local transmitters with very limited power (1 watt, range 2.5 – 10 km). The operation will be experimental to begin with, covering between fifteen and twenty localities over three years. If the experiment proves successful, a substantial expansion may take place. The object of the experiment, according to the cabinet minister responsible, is to enable organisations of the type specified to reach their own members and the public at large with information about their activities. It is difficult to judge what significance this so-called short-range radio (*närradio*) will assume. The important principle of monopoly, however, has been renounced. The government's bill also provides for one or two experiments to be made with short-range television.[4]

Secondly, the same bill provides for a reorganisation of SR with effect from 1 July 1979. Under a common parent company there are to be four subsidiary companies of equal status, for television, national radio, local radio (not to be confused with short-range radio) and educational radio. The subsidiary companies are to be independent of one another and will all have their own budgets and be responsible for their own programmes. The television company will continue the competition between TV 1 and TV 2. The principal task of the umbrella or parent company will be the allocation of transmission times and resources, and it will not influence programmes in any other way.

This organisational change has drawn fierce criticism from the management of SR and from the Social Democratic opposition, among others. It has been alleged that the splintering of SR will produce a number of weaker and, from the standpoint of pressure groups, more manageable organisations. And indeed this, in the eyes of certain critics, is the government's real intention: they want to create the conditions for firmer direction of the broadcasting media. The government's champions retort that the freedom and independence of the programme companies are exactly what they are trying to safeguard. If the programme companies had been entirely independent and not combined within a parent company, the state would have been forced to make decisions on a larger number of matters concerning radio and television than now. One example is the question of the allocation of cash between the companies, a task in future to be handled by the parent company.

It is impossible as yet to assess the effects the organisational change will have on television freedom. But it should be noted that despite everything, the change is relatively minor, that television freedom is probably determined more by factors other than relatively small-scale organisational changes, and that the change now being initiated may be expected to affect journalistic freedom both for good and for ill. One critical point, however, concerns the number of Board Members, which is increased drastically by virtue of each programme company's having its own board. The parent company will have fifteen members on its board and the programme companies fourteen members each. This completely new system of boards obviously means that their work will be shifted, as it were, much nearer to programme production than has previously been the case. This naturally does open *possibilities* for a greater degree of direction of policy.

It must also be said that the 1978 bill diverges in certain crucial respects from the bill which the Social Democrat government introduced twelve years before.[5] The equivalent sections of the non-socialist government's bill are much longer, and this is probably not fortuitous. It is very probably the manifestation of an increased propensity to direct policy. This emerges with particular clarity in the parts of the bill concerned with the details of programme production. There are a number of pointers here to which there were no equivalents in the writings of the 1960s. There are admonitions, framed in very anxious terms, against violence, alcohol and swearing in programmes. For example, dark suspicions are harboured in Swedish political circles concerning the alcohol habits portrayed in such a series as the English 'The Brothers'. There is disquiet over 'the attitudes to the use of alcohol' characterising certain parts of the programme output.[6]

The minister responsible also makes an attack in the bill upon the use of bad language on radio and television: 'Swearing should be avoided except in contexts where it is justified by artistic values or the requirements of authenticity.'[7] An earlier, unpublished version of the bill revealed an even more restrictive attitude to the use of bad language on radio and television.

Impartially and Factually

The authorities exercise their control over broadcasting in Sweden in a variety of ways. Important general instruments of control are the Radio Act and the agreement between the state and SR on the conduct of the latter's operations. The rules have, with minor revisions, remained the same for decades. The same basic approach has dominated throughout.

According to the Act, the right to broadcast shall be exercised impartially and factually. This is the fundamental duty of a public service organisation. Furthermore, the Act contains a prohibition against censorship. Neither government authorities nor any other public organs may scrutinise programmes in advance. SR is also charged with giving, 'in suitable form', information about current events and an insight into the more important cultural and social issues, and with stimulating debate thereon. Likewise it is laid down that programmes are to be diversified in character and content and to offer sound recreation and entertainment with due consideration for different tastes.

A key question is how the requirements of impartiality and

factuality are to be interpreted. What restrictions do such requirements place upon programmes? This controversial question has played an important role in the mass media debate in many countries. The requirements offer ample scope for the exercise of both political differences of opinion and philosophical subtleties. It does not take long to slip into the debate over the possibility or impossibility of objectivity that has accompanied the emergence of the new journalism since the mid-1960s, a style of journalism which, in contrast to the classical ideology, does not seek to distinguish in the same way between news and commentary, because it is regarded either as impossible in principle or as foolish, since a medium with wide coverage ought to be deliberately exploited in the political struggle.

An important deviation from the impartiality requirement occurs already in the basic rules, inasmuch as SR is not to be neutral in the contest between democracy and dictatorship. 'The company shall assert the fundamental ideas of a democratic constitution in its programme policy.'[8] The formula alludes to the values customarily regarded as those of formal political democracy: freedom of expression, freedom of assembly, free and secret voting, etc. This passage was written in the mid-1960s, before the debate on the meaning of democracy was complicated by increased interest in economic equality.

In a stable liberal democracy in which freedom of expression is regarded as a great merit, the boundaries of journalistic freedom will be very wide, at any rate as long as one abstains from violent criticism of the system or the irresponsible persecution of individuals. The agreement between the government and SR states that the rules on impartiality and factuality are to be applied bearing in mind that an ample measure of freedom of expression and information is to prevail in radio and television. This can be interpreted as a call to those responsible for programmes to present controversial material even if this should be provocative to large minorities. And during the 1960s and 1970s, SR has increasingly made room for extremely controversial programme features, often without any attempt at an all-round view in the short run.

A very important rule says that the programme policy 'as a whole' is to be marked by a judicious balance between different views and interests. This mode of expression is an indication of the freedom of producers and reporters. Thus, it is not always required that balance shall be achieved within each individual programme. The requirement is to be met in the long term, in which the whole programme policy of each channel will be judged.

The formula has often been invoked by programme-makers under criticism for partiality. They have declared that any short-comings or bias in a programme will be balanced by other programmes in the near future, or even perhaps that balancing has already been effected through items in the past. The rule had been used, for example, in defence of the radicalisation that certain areas have undergone. It has been considered possible to argue that radical bias in social programmes is not even enough to balance the conservative propaganda or spirit manifested in many entertainment programmes. At this point the discussion becomes unmanageable. It is often difficult enough to determine whether a balance has been achieved within the framework of a single programme. When the assessment is to span thousands of programme hours of radio and television, many will find the task daunting.

In practical programme production, the concepts of impartiality and factuality were for a long time interpreted in sturdy, not to say stolid, terms which in themselves adhered closely to the relevant written rules. To be impartial was to let all the parties affected have a say. This applied especially of course to the party falling under direct criticism. In order to 'balance different views in a fair manner' – to use a common formula – then obviously the simplest procedure was to let the parties concerned all speak in the same programme. A similar practical interpretation of the factuality requirement means that factual information given in the pro-gramme by SR's staff shall be true as far as verifiable facts are concerned, and is assumed to be so unless its incorrectness can be quickly and certainly demonstrated.

In everyday life the conceptual analysis often does not need to be any more sophisticated than that. It is simply a matter of basic attitudes: does the journalist share the scientist's ambition to describe and explain reality and to disseminate knowledge of his observations and conclusions? Or does he want to change society by favouring a certain class or party, or to promote a particular solution of a social problem? The broadcasting journalist who shares the fundamental ambition of the scientist will not feel unduly hemmed in by the requirements of impartiality and factuality.

This traditional attitude to the problem of impartiality was called increasingly into question from the end of the 1960s. This happened not only at the level of philosophical analysis in which the essential nature of objectivity was dissected and exposed, but also in political pamphlets. This discussion has increased freedom – and self-indulgence – in programme production at SR, as the complications and relativity of the concept could be illustrated very effectively. For example, it has been pointed out that the concepts of partiality and impartiality are relevant primarily to categories of problems where relationships between the parties and clear differences of opinion have been established. The programme producer who wants to introduce new topics finds the concepts more difficult to handle.

Abolition of the veto right represented a very important advance. As late as the middle 1950s the requirement that on controversial issues all parties concerned should be represented simultaneously was still being strictly enforced. The consequence of course was that any party who for some reason did not wish to participate had an effective power of veto. He could prevent the programme from being made. This practice was a seriously inhibiting factor not only on programmes debating social questions but also on the news. In this area a new ruling was made in 1956. The Social Democrats issued a government statement jointly with the then coalition party Bondeförbundet (the Agrarian party, now the Centre party). The Social Democrat party leader declined to take part in the radio news programme commenting upon the government statement, and the chairman of the Agrarian Party was not available. The statement was read out during the programme and then commented upon by the leaders of the Liberal and Conservative parties.

It was such an important deviation from established practice that it was regarded as something of a sensation. The newly-appointed and independent-minded Head of Radio (the title encompasses overall control of television and radio), Olof Rydbeck, came under heavy pressure. A chorus of indignation welled up from platforms and printing presses all over Sweden. The radio was threatened in various ways, and there were suggestions of financial reprisals by the government.[9] The latter is – and under the prevailing system must be – the government's ultimate weapon. A successful democracy can tolerate a great measure of freedom, but drastic deviations from what is regarded as established convention can quickly provoke financial consequences, at all events if those in power feel the new departure to be a threat to their own position. The Swedish broadcasting media can never forget that the budget process in which they are involved is one where the politicians have the last word. The public pays the licence fees, but the government and Riksdag vote the funds.

In this important instance, however, victory went to the radio and the cause of journalistic freedom. Time had worked in favour of liberation from the traditional veto. Since then the Radio Council has many times established SR's right to make programmes even if one of the parties affected refuses to participate. It is one of the corporation's most momentous advances.

Pressure from the Popular Movements

Thus, SR lives under the latent threat emanating from the holder of ultimate economic power. It is in the nature of a well-organised, idyllic democracy that such threats materialise very seldom. By and large, relations between SR and the politicians are good. This is not because television is so timidly well-balanced as to avoid offering politicians any provocation, but because the problems during this idyllic period are relatively small, and because politicians often like to demonstrate support for journalistic integrity. Some leading politicians do have a serious interest in the quality of current affairs journalism; and among others, obeisances in the direction of journalistic integrity have a certain snob value, since it is intimately bound up with democratic orthodoxy.

The main impression is thus that to a large extent politicians are reluctant to exert pressure or manifest disgruntlement over day-to-day programming. General experience, indeed, suggests that pressure, often of a disagreeable sort, is more commonly brought to bear by the popular movements, the labour market organisations, private business, religious groups, the police and defence interests. It is much easier to find examples of pressure from among these groups than from political parties. Pressure is to be understood here as attempts to interfere in decision-making with the intention of guiding programme policy, for example, by trying to induce SR to make or not to make a particular programme, to make changes in a programme, and so forth.

It seems as if representatives of the popular movements, organisations and corporations do not have the same respect for journalistic integrity, the same training in submitting to public scrutiny or the same desire to fly the flag of respect for the rules of the democratic game. Nevertheless the world of reality is full of contradictions. Instances have occurred where the popular movements have opposed proposals that would have restricted journalistic freedom, as for example when they resisted the idea that SR should be compelled to transmit programmes arranged and financed by the authorities. This proposal, which is a grave challenge to the classical model of freedom, had been mooted by a government commission but was buried thanks to vigorous criticism by the popular movements. Despite such important reservations and amplifications, however, the main impression remains unshaken: representatives of the popular movements are usually more troublesome sources of pressure than are politicians as far as day-to-day programme matters are concerned.

The attitude of the popular movements to SR can best be described as one of disappointment. Representatives of these organisations are deeply conscious that they represent some of the most central and characteristic of Sweden's social structures, and they were given a degree of precedence in the allocation of places both on the Board of Governors of SR and as shareholders. But the relationship with SR has been tense for long periods and characterised from time to time by acute conflicts bordering on breakdown. In a sense it can be construed as testimony to the freedom of SR *vis-à-vis* powerful interests. An organisation capable of living and thriving in the teeth of so large a measure of disapproval on the part of the popular movements can be no feeble one.

Representatives of these organisations have often complained of a sense of alienation in regard to SR. Many of them have their roots in the working class, while SR on the other hand has long been dominated by people of middle-class and often academic background. A conversation with a trade unionist on one occasion brought the following retort illustrating his alienation: 'I grew up in a working-class home in the thirties. They had a children's programme on the radio in those days called "From the Nursery" (Från barnkammaren). I never understood what the title meant. Did they have special rooms for children? Didn't they know that in the thirties Swedish people lived in one room and a kitchen, regardless of the size of the family?'

When broadcast journalism became active from the mid-1950s, this hardly made the representatives of the popular movements any happier. It was the Anglo-Saxon liberal press ideology that was paramount, with its predilection for unusual happenings, for deviation, for news, for events. This meant that the activities of the popular movements were not heeded in the way that their representatives had hoped. Programmes seemed to be preoccupied with critical scrutiny of unusual problems but seldom dealt with straight accounts of the day-to-day work of the organisations, which were apparently much less appealing.

Later on, when the wave of the left thundered its way forward during the late 1960s, the disappointment of the popular movements turned to deep pessimism, occasionally spilling over into resentment and aggression. The wave of the left in Sweden was not accompanied by any appreciable recruitment into television of staff from the broad masses. To a large extent, individuals of middle-class background and academic education were still recruited, but there was now the interesting difference that in many cases the newcomers had crossed over to the left wing of the Social Democrats or to positions even further left. These employees felt themselves to be possessed of a special knowledge of the true interests of the people, whose real representatives they considered themselves to be. Following from this, the representatives of the popular movement were regarded as 'bigwigs', part of the despicable anti-popular establishment that had to be fought. This idea, and programmes inspired by it, led to an acute conflict between SR and the popular movements, chiefly the trade union component.

Viewed in longer-term perspective, however, and leaving aside the events of the late 1960s and early 1970s, it is the less obtrusive disappointment over programming that has coloured the attitudes of the popular movements. The representatives of these organisations have sighed bitterly over what they feel to be the failure of programme executives to understand their importance. The decision to start a second television channel naturally aroused great expectations. Television air time was to be doubled, and this would surely mean more time for the message of the popular movements. And this was a prospect the politicians had held out when the expansion of television was being discussed. The politicians had not wavered in fact. No politician in Sweden remains one for long if he fails to affirm regularly the importance and value of the popular movements. However, practically nothing came of the promises. The first reason was that TV 2 started transmitting in 1969, which was not exactly a gala year for these traditional popular movements. The wave of the left had gathered momentum and it had become a journalistic aim to scrutinise in a spirit of scepticism the very representatives of the popular movements who were expecting congratulations on their altruism. Secondly, the Riksdag had decided that both channels were to be national in scope. They were to compete with but not to supplement each other in the sense of each offering different material. And so the inauguration of a second channel meant there would be more of the bold and inquisitorial type of programme. The amount of time available for straight accounts of the daily toil of the popular movements did not increase, however. The broadcasting media of the late 1960s had little enthusiasm for that sort of approach.

The aggrieved reactions of the trade unions were the most important, but other organisations, including religious ones, have aired their displeasure. Sweden is a relatively secularised country and has been so for a long time, but religious programmes have always been allowed an important role. Thus the religious groups, like the farmers, have enjoyed a specially favoured position. The disappointment in religious circles was that much the greater when it turned out that TV 2, unlike TV 1, did not intend to transmit any religious programmes, at any rate not programmes of religious services in the traditional sense. Instead, the new channel went in for a series of programmes on life-stances, in which different ideas were allowed to contend with one another in the context of multilateral debate. TV 2 became impartial, as it were, on the subject of religion. This breach of a central broadcasting tradition provoked sharp criticism among the Board of Governors of the corporation. One representative of Free Church interests argued that TV 2 was not fulfilling its agreement with the state, while the head of the channel took the opposite view. Up to now the Controllers of TV 2, with the support of the Head of Radio and the majority of board members, have managed to hold out against the demand for religious programmes.

SR and Election Campaigns

In principle, SR decides the number, scope and form of programmes even when power is at stake in election campaigns. In practice, however, there are detailed negotiations between SR and the parties over election broadcasts. The negotiations become difficult occasionally when SR's programming considerations run up against the tactical judgements of the politicians. The outcome of the negotiations, quite naturally, is determined by the degree of unity between the parties. If they form a united front, SR has to give way.

The parties have a strong position in relation to SR during election campaigns for two reasons. First, of course, it is always the parties that have the final economic and political hold over SR. This circumstance constitutes the basis of the parties' power. Nothing, of course, can shake the leaders of the five Riksdag parties[10] in this respect – when they are resolute and united. Resolution is not usually lacking during these negotiations. It is unusual, too, for party leaders at election periods to be tormented by an over-tender concern for journalistc integrity. Secondly, attractive public figures are always in a very strong position *vis-à-vis* a mass media corporation engaged in negotiations about the format of programmes. During election campaigns the party representatives are not just good programme value, they are indispensable.

During the election campaign of 1976, which was followed by the non-socialists' assumption of office, the power of the parties was brought home with unusual clarity. TV 2 wanted to change the format of a series of long planned interviews with party leaders by SR journalists – an innovation of the 1966 election brought in with some misgivings and after lengthy negotiations with divided parties, and regarded at the time as a notable journalistic achievement in election broadcasting. Ten years later TV 2 wanted to revise the format of the programme: the party leaders were to be confronted in the studio not only by SR journalists but also by so-called ordinary voters, 'the grass roots', that is, non-professional questioners who would be allowed to bring up their own problems. Filmed reportage illustrating these problems would also be used.

The proposal encountered fierce resistance from all parties except the Liberals. SR found itself involved in an argument of unusual asperity. It would be difficult, it was said, for party leaders to argue against filmed material dealing with cases whose details it was impossible for them to have at their fingertips. It would also be difficult to choose 'grass-roots' representatives impartially. In sum, it would be impossible to ensure that the interview situations would be the same for all party leaders, whereas such equality had been quite well guaranteed, it was considered, when SR journalists alone did the questioning.

Four of the five parties adopted an inflexible attitude on the issue. The Head of Radio requested a meeting with the party leaders during the closing phase of the negotiations in order to discuss the setting up of these dialogues, but the party leaders refused to attend. It was not a matter that needed discussion. The Conservative Party employed an extreme argument, to the effect that it was the political parties in the first place that should decide the format of programmes at election times and that programme considerations must be ignored.

Two important points must be added: first, of course, the Conservative Party's argument is incompatible both with the Radio Act and the agreement between SR and the state. It is unlikely, moreover, that in a less tense atmosphere any party would pursue the line that SR can ignore programme considerations in election broadcasts. The argument was brought up in the closing phase of these protracted and exasperated negotiations, and it hardly represents a considered position. This ought to be said even if the episode at the same time offers a clear illustration of how tough and almost provocative the pressure from leading politicians can be when they feel really vital interests to be threatened. In such situations the public service ideology can be undermined.

Secondly, the outcome of these negotiations can give a completely false impression of the success of politicians by comparison with SR. Viewed over the longer term it is undoubtedly the broadcasting media that have triumphed in negotiations: or, to put it in another way, freedom of the broadcasting media has been helped by the ways in which society changed during the 1950s and 1960s. A whole series of advances has been achieved. News coverage, for example, has become intensified during election campaigns, both in the ordinary news programmes and in special feature programmes. This has taken place side by side with election broadcasts proper. Journalistic judgement has almost always been the criterion in these news programmes. No attempt at punctiliously measured justice has been made or demanded. The so-called 'abstention rules' *(karensbestämmelser)* have now been relaxed so that in practice they no longer inhibit programme-making to any appreciable degree. Previously, SR was forced to refrain from programmes on political issues at election times apart from the special election broadcasts and ordinary news programmes. That this restrictive rule has disappeared in practice is to be counted a success from the journalistic standpoint.

Some politicians, by virtue of their positions and their person-alities, have had special opportunities to influence programmes both during election periods and at other times. The best example, typically enough, is the role which a Minister of Finance can play in relation to broadcasting media financed by licence fees. During the prolonged reign of the Social Democrats the consequences of this relationship were particularly pronounced. The Social Democrats have had several Finance Ministers, including Ernst Wigforss and Gunnar Sträng, of unusual political and personal eminence both in their party and in society at large. Wigforss had several periods as Minister of Finance, retiring finally in 1949. This extraordinarily successful politician, renowned also as a theoreti-cian and ideologist, accustomed both SR and the Swedish people to the idea that every year in January when the budget was to be presented he would comment on it in an address over the radio. This tradition, developing as it did during the lectures-and-popular-education epoch of sound radio, that is, long before active journal-istic broadcast coverage of the domestic political scene had been thought of, was continued by subsequent Finance Ministers, in-cluding Gunnar Sträng, who made a considerable success of it during the period he held the office from 1955 to 1976.

Sträng was a Finance Minister of unusual importance. He radiated all the confidence that a successful career in the popular movements confers upon those so favoured; he had taught himself the terminology of economics and politics; he had decades of experience in trade union, party, Riksdag and government work; he was a colleague for most of his time as a cabinet minister of a party leader (Tage Erlander) who did not keep as tight a grip on the reins as did his successor (Olof Palme); his command of language was such that even in the context of a brief conversation he was able to ring the changes elegantly between the genial and the magisterial.

It is interesting to study the relationship between this formidable politician and SR, since it illustrates in some measure the opportunities and limitations of broadcasting journalism. When review of the domestic political scene was activated, SR staff began not unnaturally to question the justification for the Finance Minister's annually repeated budget address, which in the fullness of time had become an institution in television as well. It was obvious that the budget would receive detailed attention in programmes, but it seemed fairer that an interview with the Finance Minister should take its place as one ingredient of the editorial staff's own presentations of the budget material. Simply to place programme time at the disposal of the Finance Minister, on the other hand, seemed difficult to reconcile with the requirement of freedom of the broadcasting media *vis-à-vis* politicians.

Sträng readily agreed to be interviewed about his budget proposals but stipulated that this was to take place alongside the traditional solo address and independently of it. He refused to give up the address, and his personal and political prestige enabled him to do this. SR was helpless when faced with such a minister. What should be observed particularly is that this could happen despite the fact that in Sweden the government has no 'reserve power', no formal right to demand transmission time in any situation whatever.

That Sträng had this effective power over an important programme stemmed partly from the fact that it is difficult to break an established tradition, especially when the tradition is thought desirable both by the central figure involved and by the public, partly from Sträng's unique status as a politician and public personality, and partly also from the fact that Sträng was – and is – an outstanding television performer. It is not always certain that programme quality is improved when Sträng is forced to share the television screen with one or two interviewers.

After the change of regime in 1976 the situation altered. The

Finance Ministry was divided into two, the economy and budget departments respectively. Thus, two Cabinet Ministers shared the responsibility, and neither of them had had the opportunity of building up a position like Sträng's. The budget proposals of 1977 and 1978 could be presented more journalistically. A tradition linked with a single personality has been broken.

When there is war or danger of war the demands made of SR are intensified as part of the total defence effort, which means that the government and the military leadership obtain real influence over programme production. But in normal situations the freedom of SR *vis-à-vis* the government is in principle well guaranteed and in practice highly respected – with the reservation made earlier and others to be made below. The Swedish system differs on paper at least from the rules applying for example to the BBC. In Britain the government has its formal reserve powers and other indirect power over BBC programmes because the BBC's Board of Governors is ultimately accountable to the government for the entire range of the Corporation's activities. However, the development of Swedish radio and television has been largely modelled on the BBC, so that in practice the similarities probably outweigh the differences.

In rare and exceptional cases it can be said that Swedish Cabinet Ministers have made use of a reserve power that exists *de facto*. The action of Finance Minister Sträng with regard to presentation of the budget is perhaps the best example. But there are more. In other – and infrequent – instances as well, Cabinet Ministers have appeared alone on television without any obvious journalistic justification. When the oil crisis shook the world in 1973, the then Prime Minister, Olof Palme, was allowed to deliver a television message to the nation, which probably would never have happened if the chancellery had not made an approach to SR's controllers.

Palme made another notable appearance on television when King Gustaf VI Adolf died the evening before the Riksdag Election of 1973. Palme was thus afforded an opportunity of an appealing appearance before the public after the election campaign proper was over. One or two factors in the situation are of interest: the King had been very popular, and his prolonged struggle with death had overshadowed part of the election contest. Now, a few hours before the opening of the polling stations, Palme had the chance of a vote-winning gesture. He was able to appear composed, free from the aggressive overtones of the election campaign, and grieving as if his party had never had the unpopular demand for a republic in its programme. This politically vital appearance, however, did take place as the result of a plan made long before. It had always been regarded as natural that the head of the government should appear on the broadcasting media to express sorrow at the passing away of the head of state when eventually it should occur. No one could have foreseen that the King would die the evening before the election – and no Social Democrat had dared to hope for it.

SR and the Minorities

Large power groups, long and securely established in the community – parties, popular movements and so forth – have an important influence in their various ways over the activities of a broadcasting medium. The system contains an inbuilt meanness towards philosophies and parties which have not been long established and are unable in the short run to secure some kind of broad popular support. It is true that in principle the democratic ideology does demand generosity towards people of unorthodox and even extreme opinions, and according to the rules in force SR is supposed to make special efforts to provide for the interests of minorities. The ungracious treatment meted out to minorities in the political arena is palpable, however.

Political broadcasting journalism centres around the large power groups. The crucial boundary line in Sweden is representation in the Riksdag. The five parties that have succeeded in crossing it (4 per cent of the voters) are also assured at election times of large and broadly equal programme coverage (that is, in the special election broadcasts). The five parties participate in the great election debates, and their leaders are questioned in long interviews on numerous separate occasions. Parties which have not reached the 4 per cent figure – including a party based on religion and some of the left-wing factions – can only reckon on getting a brief presentation programme apiece.

This treatment of minorities results partly from the indifference of the large parties to the interests of the smaller parties and a fear of losing votes to them, partly on the indifference of the broadcasting media to whatever does not seem to be journalistically and politically important, and partly from the factor of convenience for the media: the 4 per cent barrier constitutes a neat rule that prevents the election debates from becoming too clumsy because of the numbers of participants.

The treatment of the Communists is particularly interesting. The Communist Party has certainly secured a place in the first division by virtue of its representation in the Riksdag, but periodically it has been subjected to special treatment. At the end of the Second World War the party was quite large. Communists then formed about 10 per cent of the electorate, that is, about the same proportion as is constituted by the Liberal Party today. In recent years Communist figures have fallen to about 4–5 per cent.

Communist participation in political programmes was a controversial question for a long time, despite the Communists being represented in the Riksdag: this exemplifies the fact that even in a democracy it is difficult to tolerate criticism of the system. During the era of the cold war there were many who questioned whether the Communists should have the right to take part in programmes on the same terms as other parties. The atmosphere in Sweden during this period was anti-Communist to a high degree. The Prague *coup* of 1948 had an intense impact on Swedish opinion. Numerous cases of spying for the Russians had been discovered in Sweden and no one had any doubt, at the time at any rate, either as to the guilt of the individuals concerned or as to the serious consequences of their espionage. The Russians had also shot down Swedish aircraft over the Baltic. It was consequently in a very heated atmosphere that the question of Communist participation on the radio was discussed. The main argument against them, more or less clearly formulated, was that they represented a foreign power that threatened the security of the Swedish nation. The Social Democrat Party leadership opposed Communist participation in election broadcasts for a long time, as for instance in the party leaders' debate on the radio in 1952. On behalf of the radio, however, the objection was raised – by reference to the usual principle – that the party could not be excluded since it was represented in the Riksdag.

Another episode from this epoch is illuminating. A member of the permanent staff was excluded from programme duties on the grounds that he was a member of the Communist Party. He received a letter from the then Head of Radio from which it appeared that 'the management has decided that until further notice you will not be employed on announcing duties because of the political opinions which you have stated that you hold'. The cold war was thus reflected in the corridors of the radio. The important point is that the Head of Radio does not refer in his letter to any official misconduct of which the person in question was held to have been guilty as a result of his political leanings. To judge from the letter it was his political views in themselves that disqualified him – even for entirely neutral duties as an announcer. Such an incident would be unthinkable today. But even now great caution would probably be exercised in appointing a person known to be a Communist to any post where he would be handling politically controversial material.

The Shock of the 1960s

The revolutionary events at the end of the 1960s have been frequently referred to. But we must look in more detail at the series of shocks that befell the astonished members of the Swedish establishment in the late 1960s and early 1970s, the period when it turned out to be difficult to 'safeguard, with firmness bordering on passion, the right of television to make open criticism of society, of the authorities, and of private interests', to cite Olof Palme once more.

Palme's basic principle, as developed in the celebrated Riksdag speech of 1966, involved the consequence that tolerance of what we may call 'overstatement' (meaning cases of sensationalism, exaggeration, distortion and selectiveness) in programming must be very high.

Nothing is easier than to refrain from illuminating and exposing some unsatisfactory state of affairs. It is seldom necessary to have a factual basis for describing a powerful figure in laudatory terms. He will not enquire suspiciously after the evidence. Anyone attempting 'open criticism' on the other hand, must really tread warily. It does not always work. Sometimes the critical journalist makes mistakes, however serious and sound in judgement he may normally be. It is in such situations that public figures must demonstrate their tolerance as required by the classical model, their awareness that overcaution or 'understatement' is possibly the real danger, that is, all the sins of omission of journalists in the critical surveillance of public figures and powerful institutions. The tolerance of public figures is particularly tested, of course, when political and social tensions are snowballing and when journalists have the audacity to present their material in satirical form.

Broadly speaking, criticism of SR up to the end of the 1960s came chiefly from the popular movements, private business and the non-socialist parties. Social Democrat criticism, on the other hand, was not so articulate. In passing one may pose the question why the Social Democrats were less critical than the non-socialist parties. Was it because SR was compliant towards social democracy in a country long governed by Social Democrats? The answer is probably no. The situation is considerably more complicated than that. A more likely explanation is that the non-socialist parties, beaten by the Social Democrats in one election after another, vented part of their disappointment upon the dominant mass media organisation.

The resurgence of the left in the latter half of the 1960s, however, radically altered the conditions of debate and criticism in Sweden as in most other similar countries. It was soon to be revealed that Social Democrats reacted with extraordinary sensitivity as soon as the perspective of political criticism shifted to bring the traditional labour movement seriously into the firing line.

Certain subversive happenings on the Swedish domestic scene helped to create not only an entirely new framework of debate but also a vitally altered social atmosphere. In 1969 an unofficial strike broke out in the iron ore mines of northern Sweden. An unofficial strike in a showcase industry in a land noted for the extreme tranquillity of its labour relations compared with others was a sensational and terrifying experience for established interests, including the Social Democrat Party then in power, which had believed that its close links with the trade union movement and the sedulous welfare work of many decades had abolished the conditions that provoke unofficial strikes in less fortunate countries. The miners' strike came as a devastating shock.

For the very active groups on the left wing of the Social Democrats or even further to the left, the strike came as manna from heaven, partly because it was unofficial. It seemed to testify that there was an opposition to the Social Democrat establishment, which, in the eyes of the left-wing groups, had betrayed the ideals of socialism; it could be interpreted as proof that there was a revolutionary glow among the miners, the masses who, it had hitherto been believed, had been lost among petty bourgeois ideals.

A large section of the Swedish establishment, including the Social Democrat leadership and the trade union movement, regarded the journalistic coverage of events in the mining district with a scepticism that quickly grew to alarm and dismay. For in the first place there were journalists, even in SR, who seemed to have difficulty in controlling their enthusiasm for the strike. Secondly, and probably more importantly, even an impartial account of events in the north could seem disquieting from the establishment's standpoint, especially with the vast growth in the volume of coverage as an army of journalists invaded the area. The selection of material itself involves an important exercise of judgement and determination of attitude, and these have an effect on the shaping of opinion and the solution of society's problems. Thus, those in power could argue – with an intrinsic logic and comprehensibility – that SR bestowed an immoderate amount of attention upon the unofficial strike, which was a pure exception to the hallowed rule, while the unremitting day-to-day exertions of the organisations and popular movements scarcely had a metre of film devoted to them.

The miners' strike hit Sweden in an atmosphere that had already been radicalised for some years. The international wave of the left had rolled in over the peaceful boundaries of the nation several years before, spreading confusion, crises of identity and conflicts of loyalty right in among the middle classes; students had revolted against the established order in a dramatic occupation of the student union building in Stockholm in 1968; vehement criticism had been levelled at many aspects of representative democracy and thus at the whole social system. Now activist groups were trying to provoke unofficial strikes everywhere, and one extra-parliamentary action followed on the heels of another. The Swedish idyll was being threatened.

The miners' strike came about, too, as though initiated by a master director at a very critical point in the history of young

Swedish television. TV 2 began transmitting on 5 December 1969, and the strike broke out on 13 December. Thus it was surveyed and described by a highly activated television furnished with increased resources. TV 2 in particular devoted much attention to the miners' strike. It was a natural consequence of the historical trend. TV 2 had grown up during a period of radicalisation and was not rooted in the same way as TV 1 in the earlier, more official television. But TV 1 did not lag far behind during the miners' strike. Neither did any of the mass media. Interest was whipped up.

Representatives of established, official Sweden – politicians, trade union leaders, business leaders and senior officials – were seriously perturbed. Some years afterwards it emerged that the threat to the established order was a real one only to a degree: there are links between the political terrorism of the 1970s and the radical wave of the 1960s in the sense that a small minority of young radicals began to express its protest in violent action at the same moment as its political ideals were fading or losing focus.

But to begin with, no one could really tell where the forces that had been unleashed might end up. And even those who were careful not to exaggerate the consequences involved for the established order were quite sufficiently irritated, if not outraged, by growing criticisms on television, criticisms directed in large measure against the representatives of the labour movement. These people considered themselves to have battled selflessly day and night in the service of the people – now they found themselves portrayed as self-appointed busybodies without any real contact with the true needs and desires of the broad masses and as having betrayed their political ideals.

It is not surprising that the political atmosphere in Sweden during this period stimulated a number of programme-makers to undertake a critical scrutiny of the policies of the labour movement. There were long programme series and dramatic treatments of the subject. TV 1 put out no fewer than eight programmes in a series entitled, typically enough, 'From Socialism to Increased Equality'. The keynote of the series was indeed that the movement had betrayed its socialist ideals, which little by little had been replaced by naïve strivings for equality within the framework of the existing society. It is not difficult to see why this very long series cast both the Social Democrat Party and the trade union movement into uproar. The series viewed events from a left-wing socialist perspective, which certainly could have been defended successfully at the bar of mass opinion if it had been done within the framework of programmes in which, for the sake of impartiality, other possible views had also been put. But such was not the case. Television made one single, ambitious, thorough and expensive series about the labour movement, and it was cast in the form of a criticism of the compromise policies of the leading Social Democrats.

Then came what was to be considered television's kidney-punch against the labour movement, a satirical programme containing a sketch depicting a named labour leader of the 1930s, allowing himself, while inebriated, to be duped into a bad deal with the representatives of big business. The essential features of the situation are: first, that the sketch purported to deal with a very important actual event of modern Swedish history; secondly, that the thesis of betrayal of the working class by its own leaders was again hammered home; thirdly, and principally, that the man was represented as being the worse for drink. It may be difficult for foreigners to appreciate fully what a sensitive point this is in Sweden. The influence of the temperance movement on public opinion is so strong that the consumption of alcohol is not regarded as a really normal or acceptable phenomenon, and this despite the fact that Sweden, including its labour leaders, holds its own by any international standards in the consumption of alcohol.

Anyone who describes a Swedish public figure in a satire as being under the influence of drink during the exercise of his office – or even in his spare time – is therefore taking a grave risk. And in this instance, furthermore, the labour leader in question happened to be a member of a temperance organisation. There was a scandal indeed. The reaction was violent.

The General Secretary of the Social Democrat Party made a fierce attack upon SR in a television programme. Shortly afterwards the Board of Governors of SR met amid almost tumul-tuous scenes. The sketch about the labour leader was condemned in drastic terms while criticism of SR swelled up. It was as though a dam had suddenly burst. Representatives of different parties and interests all testified to their dissatisfaction.

Vexation with SR was now so general that the corporation could not count on the support of any influential group in the community. Practically all parties, institutions, organisations and corporations joined in the chorus of criticism, citing a long list of grievances. There had also long existed disapproval in government circles of the expansion of SR. It was felt that the corporation had become too big and too expensive in relation to the volume of programmes produced. It was natural in this situation that the government should have recourse to its ultimate weapon against SR, namely, financial contraction.

But all this was played out in a political atmosphere which, despite all disturbances however unexpected and dramatic, still retained its basic features of stability and calm. There was no question of any attempt to tear up agreements, of making radical short-term changes in the corporation's conditions of operation, or of drastically reducing the allocation of funds. But the financial cutback was a perceptible one. That disapproval of programme policy played an important part in it is not to be doubted; indeed, that interpretation was placed on it by the Deputy Head of Radio in a public speech.

The cutback left SR's total financial resources for the budget year 1973/4 and 1975/6 about 15 per cent below the level of 1972/3. The contraction of resources had serious consequences. Among other measures, SR had to reduce its personnel by about 5 per cent. To judge from the available figures, SR was among the most heavily hit of European radio corporations as a result of the measures of economic retrenchment during the early 1970s. Only the Finnish YLE fared worse. Organisations such as the BBC and RAI were much more fortunate.

In the spring of 1976 the Riksdag, surprisingly, decided to increase the grant to SR. The initiative came from the then non-socialist opposition and went through with Communist support despite the resistance of the Social Democrats. In the late 1970s SR is again living in a more favourable climate. The main reason is the slackening of the political tensions, but another is probably an increasing realisation that the public has reason to feel that the licence fees are low. Total licence revenue rose by 45 million Kronor at fixed prices between 1970 and 1976. At the same time the public could afford to increase its purchases of diverse kinds of domestic electronic equipment (radio and television receivers, record players and video recorders) by no less than 1500 million!

The cost to the public of its television and radio consumption fell sharply in Sweden during the first half of the 1970s. The reduction was in fact sensational. Table 2[11] shows the cost trend at 1976 prices for purchases of radio and television receivers and for licences.

TABLE 2

	1970	1976
Battery radios	350	235
Colour TV receivers	5500	3650
Colour TV licence fee	455	320
Total kr.	6305	4205

The Board of Governors and the Radio Council

The Board of Governors acted with great vigour at a meeting in 1971, as has been shown. It was a unique reaction in a unique situation. But there are many less spectacular examples of actions and interventions on the part of the Board of Governors through the decades, which does not mean that the Board has had the function of guiding or influencing programmes in detail. The opposite is rather the case, seen in long-term perspective. But the interventions of the Board are noted and disputed precisely because of their relative rarity.

Sometimes the Board of Governors – acting in accordance with normal procedure – has dealt with programme matters in broad terms, for example when important programme changes have been introduced or have been imminent.

It is necessary to distinguish between two sorts of action on the part of the Board of Governors. Sometimes the Board acts formally in its collective capacity, following a recorded decision supported by the whole Board or a majority thereof; in other instances action is taken informally behind the scenes by individual Board Members or by the Chairman. This latter type of influence or attempted influence is no less interesting when the Board is one in which every group of significance in the country is represented.

The abolition of the veto power in 1956 has already been dealt with (p. 154). That was when radio broadcast a news feature on a government statement despite the refusal of the Social Democrat Party leadership to comment. It was one of the most important advances in the history of SR. The Board Chairman, the influential Social Democrat Per Eckerberg, rang up the then Head of Radio, Olof Rydbeck, and said that his telephone was being 'besieged' by people expressing indignation that the leader of the opposition had been allowed to speak despite the fact that the other parties had refused or been unable to take part. According to Rydbeck, 'Eckerberg expressed serious misgivings lest what had occurred should endanger the increase that had been requested in licence fees'. Rydbeck thus received the impression that threats had been made about this to Eckerberg, who indeed also personally disapproved of the form which the news feature had taken. Eckerberg himself has affirmed that threats were made to him, and these threats must of course have come from those leading Social Democrats who considered themselves to have influence over licensing and budget policy.

This incident has been referred to a number of times in this chapter as it is of great fundamental interest. It shows, first, that leading politicians act via the Chairman of the Board of Governors when they feel that intervention is really called for, and secondly, that their action does not necessarily have any effect despite the brandishing of the powerful economic weapon. Rydbeck urged upon Eckerberg the view that the whole principle of freedom of radio *vis-à-vis* the state was at stake on this issue, and in the end it was Rydbeck's view that prevailed.

The Head of Radio was stronger than the government, to put it in bold terms. However, the abolition of the veto ought not to be regarded as following from the outcome of a duel between a champion of freedom and an obdurate government. As always it is the changes in society that in the end determine which side will triumph. Developments in various countries during these years favoured the growth of a freer, more independent journalism in broadcasting as well as outside it. He who acts in harmony with the climate of opinion or an incipient change in it is always in a strong starting position, of course, in the subtle interplay between diverse forces that determines the programme policy of the broadcasting media.

Since the end of the 1960s, the Board of Governors has started to concern itself increasingly with programme matters and to some extent even with individual programmes or programme series, despite the general rule that its influence is supposed chiefly to be confined to the long-term planning of programmes and to programme matters that raise important issues of principle.

But exceptions to the general rule do occur, and their frequency seems to have increased. Per Eckerberg, for example, has disclosed that during his tenure of the chairmanship the Board of Governors took an initiative 'directly in a programme matter' in connection with the debate over narcotics. It happened during the late 1960s, when disquiet over the rapid growth of narcotics abuse was an important element in the general deterioration in the social climate. Eckerberg writes: 'The Board of Governors has decided that SR shall actively campaign through its programmes against the narcotics epidemic and has thereby established the corporation's programme policy in this respect.'[12]

A decision made by the Board of Governors in the autumn of 1969 deserves mention as well. The Board decreed that there should be no direct broadcasts of the European sporting events in Athens. This was intended as a mark of disapproval of the then regime in Greece.

Formal Board decisions of this sort are very rare, however. Informal approaches or pressures from Board Members are more customary, either during discussions in the corridors before or after Board meetings, in the course of deliberations at Board meetings, or between them. It is in such situations that programme suggestions and programme criticisms are often made, for example, complaints that TV 2 does not broadcast religious programmes or that the co-operative movement has been dealt with misleadingly in programmes.

However, it is matters of an entirely different character that dominate meetings of the Board. According to one of the corporation's internal studies, 164 matters were dealt with at Board meetings during the budget years 1972/3 and 1973/4. Economic questions predominated with thirty-seven items, and in these cases formal decisions were reached. Twenty programme matters were considered without any decisions being taken. These twenty items were dealt with in the following ways: information in thirteen cases, discussion in three cases and shelved in four cases.[13]

A major question is whether the Board of Governors can be regarded as standing up for SR's journalistic demands and aims, for example, *vis-à-vis* the government, the Riksdag, the organisations and the public, or whether the Board's members consider it their principal task to represent the special interests of their own groups. In the history of the corporation over the years there have been examples pointing in both directions. First it should be observed that the Board of Governors neither could nor would have prevented the important advances that have occurred since the middle 1950s: the abolition of the veto power, the activation of news journalism, the overhaul of election broadcasts, and so forth. The Board of Governors has often given active support to the journalistic aspirations of the staff.

But of course the picture is splintered. Board Members, not unexpectedly, have acted on behalf of their special interests when these have been felt to be threatened or little regarded. Such riding of private hobby-horses was particularly common during the critical years around 1970. The following formula may serve to describe the general principles on which Board Members act: when there is a conflict between special interests on the one hand and journalistic aspirations and judgements on the other, a Board Member usually supports his own side. When no such conflict is involved, in all probability he supports the staff of the corporation, provided he is satisfied that the corporation's policy is in accordance with the law, the agreement and, in general, the conditions he considers ought to be fulfilled.

It is of course legitimate to pose the question why special interests should be represented at all on the Board of a mass media corporation which is supposed to be neutral as between different parties and to scan their activities critically. Anyone given the task of drawing up rules for such a corporation and starting from scratch might well be at pains to shun representatives of special interests altogether in favour of independent publicists, scientists and scholars, lawyers, etc. A Board of Governors so composed would probably be more competent, since it need never risk provoking the situation of conflict that arises when journalistic interests and collective egos are set against one another. Neither would it need to refrain from intervening to correct unsatisfactory situations, as it would be able to win the confidence of both employees and the general public in quite a different measure.

However, the principles of recruitment to the Board of Governors were laid down as long ago as the 1920s, when sound radio was starting. The people then in power wanted to make radio an instrument of popular education and uplift. The ideal of a new independent and critical arm of government did not exist. The intention was to anchor the new medium as broadly as possible in the existing power groups. The broadness would guarantee many-sidedness and comprehensiveness of vision. In this fashion a system was created which invites abuse and is in fundamental conflict with the idea of free journalism.

Finally, it should be noted that on various occasions – the last time in 1977 – the Board of Governors has vigorously opposed the constantly repeated suggestions for the introduction of so-called Programme Councils. Such Councils, composed of representatives of different parties and interests, do exist in other Nordic countries. Their function is not only to review and scrutinise the programmes transmitted but also to submit ideas for programmes. SR staff have naturally always opposed the idea of such organs, since in all probability they would limit journalistic freedom. The Board of Governors has supported the corporation staff on this very important point.

In Sweden it is the Radio Council that scrutinises programmes after transmission – either following reports from outside or on its own initiative – in order to determine whether any breach of law or agreement has taken place. Thus the Council is an indispensable adjunct to the Board of Governors. The system requires a council, since in principle the Board of Governors is supposed not to concern itself with individual programmes.

It is a fairly general belief that on the whole the Radio Council has safeguarded SR's journalistic freedom. The Council has usually supported SR in accomplishing such advances as the abolition of the veto power. Council members have displayed an appreciation of the needs of modern broadcast journalism, which has to advance in competition with the daily press. It would be a fatal blow to the competitiveness of broadcast journalism were it not permitted to evaluate news material in broadly the same manner as the daily press. The confidence of the general public in the broadcasting media would then diminish. On the whole the Council has exhibited an understanding of such general considerations equal to that of the Board.

However, one important reservation has to be made which has relevance to the actions both of the Board and of the Council over the years. SR has succeeded, often with the support of Board and Council, in developing an active news journalism including techniques of firm questioning. The corporation has made its presence felt in the field of the creative arts (the theatre, etc.) as well. However, political satire normally seems to meet with resistance. One may wonder for what reason a corporation which has shown a desire to experiment in so many fields has been unable to develop a satirical tradition. Some attempts have been made, but when the inevitable excesses have occurred, these efforts have languished again, at least temporarily.

It is possible that the strong power group representation on the Board of Governors and in the Radio Council inhibits efforts in the satirical genre. It is as if public figures, though they have learnt to put up with critical and intensive scrutiny and with being made to answer for their sins of commission and omission, have none the less a low threshold of tolerance when someone satirises their activities.

Their solemnity towards satire is illustrated in various statements by the Council. In dealing with such material it has not merely examined programmes in terms of the requirements of factuality and impartiality but has also paid maximum regard to an obscure requirement not previously discussed in this article: that programmes shall be cast in 'suitable form'. In 1977 the Council said on the subject of certain satirical programmes that they contained 'certain sections which contain insinuations and far-fetched allusions or are offensive . . . the satirical and parodical intentions have miscarried and what has emerged is simply abusive'. We are now manifestly in the realm of pure matters of taste – quite apart from the fundamental difficulty of satirising without insinuating.

In the autumn of 1978 SR underwent an important reorganisation, as already noted. In conjunction with this the number of Board members was increased considerably and the resources of the Council were strengthened. It remains to be seen how these changes will affect journalistic freedom.

Social-Democratic 'Affairs'

A series of scandalous incidents befell the Social Democrats prior to the election of 1976. The world-famous film director Ingmar Bergman decided to emigrate after a tax prosecution, in a protest which was exploited politically against the Social Democrats. A Social Democrat party official was caught at an airport attempting to smuggle money to party comrades in Finland. It was revealed that the Minister of Finance, Gunnar Sträng, had exploited the tax laws to his own profit in a house transaction. It was not a question of any sort of formal crime but rather of skilful adaptation to the laws in force, but even Sweden's biggest Social Democrat newspaper criticised Sträng's action. There were other 'affairs', about six or seven altogether.

An interesting measure can be obtained of the real freedom of a mass media corporation by studying how material of this special character is handled by its news editors. The situation is in many ways critical or even explosive. An election of great significance is approaching, throwing its shadow over all news evaluation and programme decisions. The prevailing opinion is that scandals, in fact, scarcely occur in Sweden. It is widely regarded as unbelievable that establishment figures can be guilty of trans-actions bordering on the criminal in Sweden to the extent that occurs in other countries. Official incorruptibility is widely considered (even in sociological literature) as a speciality of Sweden. Sweden is also such a small country that practically all of its establishment is on first-name terms. Journalists too are involved in this network of interlinked friendships.

The question is how far such a climate encourages the operation of self-censorship and the corruption of friendships. Alongside the laws, agreements, programme rules, procedural arrangements, and indeed alongside the personal pressures, there exists inside every journalist or editor-in-chief an inhibition of profound conse-quence. What are the normal taboos? and in election years? Every editorial judgement can give some advantage or disadvantage to one party or another. Impartiality is impossible in such a climate. The news editor who inflates Social-Democrat scandals to large dimensions favours the non-socialists, and he who plays them down favours the Social Democrats.

In form, the freedom of SR to make use of this type of material is just as great as that of any newspaper. There is nothing in the law or the agreement that would have prevented complete coverage of the 'affairs'. And the broad impression, indeed, is that the news editors gave a worthy journalistic presentation of them. A television service that was in the pocket of the dominant party would not have devoted so much attention to the smuggling scandal, for example, as actually happened. And there was much complaining among Social Democrats about the volume of the television coverage.

However, no one has ever imagined that Swedish television was controlled by the Social Democrat Party. The discussion does not centre on such melodramatic accusations. The problem is whether self-censorship nevertheless dampens the activity of a broadcasting corporation in situations where the morals and honour of establishment figures are called into question. There are some indications to suggest this may be so. In the first place, there is considerable respect at SR for what may be termed 'good taste', defined within the framework of traditional and official criteria, which have survived the more liberated less conservative mood of the 1960s. That the tradition has shown itself to be so strong may stem partly from the fact that quite prominent and independent-minded journalists in SR accept it. For instance, there has been some anxiety not to pay excessive attention to crime or scandals of a personal nature. Such values within a public service undertaking probably cause the news editors to place less emphasis on scandalous political revelations than would be necessary to comply with the law, the agreement and procedural practice. Self-censorship on some scale occurs.

Secondly, prominent personalities in a society such as Sweden can in certain situations exploit the hold they have over the public service corporation. The news editors did after all give full coverage to the revelation. That seems fair to say. But the Finance Minister's house transactions were not featured, despite the fact that they occupied a prominent place on the front pages of the daily papers. This is probably connected, at least in part, with a sense of respect for the position which Gunnar Sträng then held in Swedish life. We come back time after time to the power which, all else notwithstanding, rests in the hands of the minister holding the purse-strings. Top executives of SR cannot entirely avoid feeling this pressure, even if it is not (and need not be) mentioned often.

In a critical situation where great personal and political interests are at stake, it is possible to perceive the difference between a public service undertaking economically dependent upon the government and a free newspaper enjoying a sound economic position thanks to the support of readers and advertisers. The point is that interference with press freedom cannot take place within the framework of discussions about agreements or negotiations over the allotment of funds. There are no agreements to discuss and no funds to allot. Interference with newspaper freedom would demand a much more powerful weapon than that, and to acquire it would be impossible for any government within the constitution, or even the prevailing social system. Influence can be exerted on SR in quite different measure within the framework of the existing system.

A degree of caution is observable within SR when it comes to the treatment of certain persons and topics. It feels sometimes as though there is in the corporation a high level of awareness of where the taboo boundaries run. It does not mean that such persons or topics are never brought under the searchlight, but the consequence is often a carefulness of approach, such as an unusually high insistence on quality in the research carried out.

There are certain things which a reporter or producer at SR definitely does not do. For instance, he does not question a prominent individual about his consumption of spirits even if there is reason to suppose that these may be affecting Sweden's success in international negotiations or the nation's image abroad. And there are other matters which SR staff approach with caution: critical scrutiny of the popular movements, the monarchy, defence and the police, including the security police. The classical list of taboo areas has been increased by one in recent years, namely, the so-called common man, the man in the street. Many programme-makers have taken up the cause of ordinary people, and brought out their desires and demands in programmes. Debates have been arranged in which ordinary viewers were encouraged by the programme-presenters to attack important public figures who find themselves at a disadvantage in circumstances where their formal language and fear of committing themselves in matters of detail renders them unable to communicate effectively, especially under emotional pressure. It was not an aim of these programmes to turn a critical spotlight on the wishes and demands of 'ordinary people'.

Few have questioned the extent to which these are defensible – for example, when compared with demands from other 'ordinary people' not present. (The refusal of the political parties to take part in question-and-answer sessions with 'ordinary people' during the electoral campaign of 1976 should be remembered in this connection.)

The programme-producer is particularly dependent upon the structure of the debate which has evolved in society as a whole. There are widespread and definite ideas about which problems are worth discussing. A topic that does not fit into the pattern risks being passed over, and even if it is dealt with the response will be slight. The consequence is that the topic or problem disappears from debate. It was revealed in a television programme in 1977, for example, that a large number of powerful individuals – leading politicians and others – had free passes for themselves and their families on SAS, the Scandinavian airline, a perquisite worth tens of thousands of Kronor or more. This was discussed in the programme mainly as a problem of corruption. The question asked was whether there was a danger that leading politicians would treat the airline more favourably in situations where they were supposed to make judgements of SAS. The debate after the programme was prolonged and passionate, but what was considered was chiefly the tax problem. Ought the holders of free passes to pay tax on their perquisites or not? This approach to the problem fits in entirely with the prevailing structure of debate. Questions touching tax levels and tax evasion have an obvious and dominant position in Swedish debate, while corruption, hidden perquisites and pressures are scarcely discussed at all. A foreign observer once remarked that there is no corruption in Sweden because no one looks for it.

Does Television Control the Politicians?

When television came to Sweden the expectations of politicians were great, and so were their misgivings. It was imagined that television would bring a revolution of political life, including new principles of recruitment. It was widely assumed that the image on the television screen would be of vital importance, and that, moreover, it was not easy to make an impression on the public via this medium. The general opinion was that new qualities would be required of politicians. Special 'television personalities' would be needed. A prominent Swedish politician predicted, for instance, and not entirely in jest, that television would finish him as a politician because he was not handsome enough, while he foresaw a brilliant career for one of his rivals who was better favoured in looks.

Such sentiments were reinforced by the 'television election' in the United States in 1960, when Kennedy beat Nixon. It was presumed by most analysts that the four television confrontations played a large part in the election results, and Kennedy himself said that he probably would not have won without them. (The confrontations attracted an average public of 71 million viewers, about 20 per cent more than the popular entertainment programmes that would have been transmitted at the same time.)

Kennedy played a role as a trend-setter in Sweden too, and Swedish politicians hastened eagerly to the training schools, to hurriedly fitted-out studios, to learn the most effective tricks. Gestures were rehearsed, the pitch of voice was changed, the gaze was adjusted, the hair-do was re-done, the warts were removed, the teeth beautified or replaced. The atmosphere was at times a trifle hysterical, to the delight of, among others, television reporters who could now make money on the side as teachers of ambitious politicians, especially those of the younger and more malleable generation. A new era seemed to have dawned: charm was to signify more than the party programme, personality more than issues.

However, it quickly transpired that a large part of these reactions were based on an utterly erroneous conception of the importance and function of television. The politician who was apprehensive about his appearance achieved great success as a narrator of stories on television but most of all as a spokesman for his party in debates and interviews; international experience showed that professional television personalities who tried their luck as politicians had little success; the researches of political scientists and communication theoreticians showed that television did not really play the vital role popularly ascribed to it in its early years. The practical conclusion gradually drawn in political circles was that a person who is effective and forceful in speeches, conversation and discussion will probably succeed on television as well, although the latter tends to reinforce both positive and negative points. Politicians took a more sober view and began to study their party programmes again. It was not necessary to create special television personalities after all. Television could be reduced to a more modest role, even though its coverage and its significance in the everyday life of the people still made it the most important medium.

What television has primarily affected is the planning of political information and propaganda. This is most noticeable, of course, during election campaigns, which are organised and planned in detail largely by reference to the distribution of television programmes during the campaign period. The procedures and preferences of television with regard to the choice of interviewee has increased the pressure on leading personalities in the parties. Party headquarters must see to it that attractive representatives of the parties are available at short notice to comment on problems which have suddenly cropped up, new moves by rival parties, and so on.

This is practically the only effect of television that emerges indisputably from the interviews and study of the literature carried out for this chapter. Other effects are more difficult to assess. It is sometimes said, for example, that television favours the superficial and the over-simplified, reducing the political message to a set of slogans. It is by no means certain that television has had this effect. The searching and forceful questioning technique that has been developed is more likely, at its best, to bring out subtleties and details that would have been missing from a polemical speech or an exchange of repartee in the Riksdag where the parties talk over each others' heads.

What significance does television have in the selection of political leaders? Even if a more moderate assessment of television's role has emerged since the early 1960s, it might be thought that, despite everything, television can still be regarded as having a certain special influence in selection of leaders. It is difficult to isolate the effects of television even here, however. What we can say is that there is an increased interest in external details to do with appearance, mannerism, etc., and that although these personal characteristics seem to be discussed nowadays more than they were in the 1950s when it comes to internal party nominations they are still not a major issue. But 'How does he go down on TV?'

is a frequent question, despite the playing-down of the medium's power and influence.

This increased interest in external details, however, does not lead to the favouring of a particular political type. It may be of interest in this respect to compare the present opposition leader, Olof Palme, with the Prime Minister, Thorbjörn Fälldin. Repeated comparisons made in the press have pointed out that Palme comes across as quick-witted, well educated, intellectual, fluent, skilled in foreign languages as well as in Swedish, while Fälldin seems slow, fumbling, sometimes uncertain both of his facts and of his words. But the makers of such comparisons are frequently people who think of themselves as members of a quick-witted and educated elite. It is possible that people in general feel a greater affinity with Fälldin because of the very qualities that he displays. It has often been said that Fälldin inspires trust, while Palme, despite his advantages, does have difficulty here.

What effect did television have on the result of the 1976 election, the one that brought the non-socialist parties into office for the first time in many decades? Opinions about the reasons for the non-socialist victory at the polls are naturally divided. Some have pointed to the impact of such current topics as the debate over nuclear power on the outcome of the election. Others stress long-term changes in population structure and the climate of opinion. What one can say is that politicians often plump for the short-term explanations in their election analyses, while re-searchers tend to attach greater weight to the long-term changes in the composition of the electorate, that is, such factors as its distribution over different regions of the country, residential areas and occupations.

What needs to be explained about Sweden, however, is not the background to the non-socialist election victory but rather the reasons why it did not happen much earlier. The Social Democrats had been hard pressed for a long time but were saved by a variety of factors, sometimes of a unique character, such as abstentions by opponents in the Riksdag, and the electoral system in force until 1970. In that year the new unicameral Riksdag was introduced, giving Sweden a system facilitating more frequent transfers of power. To secure office, it is now sufficient to win a single election. Under the previous system, the government in power could hold on with the aid of a majority still retained in the First Chamber.

So there was nothing remarkable about the result of the 1976 election. Neither, of course, is there any ground for concluding that television played a decisive role in the outcome. However, the exaggerated emphasis which politicians probably place on short-term factors produces the direct consequence that they ascribe altogether too much importance to television programes. One sometimes even hears the view expressed that isolated appearances on radio or television can change or at any rate substantially influence a current of opinion. This is a throwback to the unrealistic theories of the early 1960s. A typical instance occurred during the election campaign in the autumn of 1976. In a notable radio programme, Thorbjörn Fälldin, the Centre Party leader, launched an attack upon the then Social Democrat government's energy policy, one aspect of which was a relatively large investment in nuclear power. Fälldin described in highly emotional terms the dangers to life and health which can be associated with this form of energy.

This was nothing more than a Centre party policy that had been established long before. The crucial and politically interesting aspect was that Fälldin brought the issue so forcefully to the forefront during the final phase of the electoral campaign, spelling out certain new details and consequences of his party's policy. The appearance had an important impact on the mass media debate. Nuclear power became the dominant issue. The impression was further reinforced when Fälldin was questioned shortly afterwards in a series of television interviews with party leaders and once more attacked Social Democratic energy policy.

Leading Social Democrats have claimed that Fälldin's nuclear energy ploy influenced not only the mass media but the voters too. The latter, frightened by Fälldin's doomsday visions, are alleged to have forsaken the Social Democrats in sufficiently large numbers to make the non-socialist victory possible. But it is far from certain that this analysis is correct. One may very well believe that nuclear energy had more influence on the election result than any other single issue, but it does not follow from this that the Social Democrats would have won if nuclear energy had not been made an election issue. The cardinal importance of the long-term structural factors cannot be ignored.

In the debate after the election, however, the Social Democrats levelled heavy criticism at SR. The critics alleged that the corporation's staff had paid far too much attention to nuclear energy, and this, along with all the mass media publicity given to the 'affairs', was one of the principal reasons why the important Social Democrat election message did not reach the voters. Thus, like so many other earlier losers of Swedish elections, the Social Democrats put much of the blame for their failure on the broadcasting media. This allocation of blame is no surprise. Television has an important function as a scapegoat.

In a Calmer Climate

It is inevitable that scapegoats are taken out and shaken every now and then. Even so, SR at the end of the 1970s, as we have seen, has entered upon a considerably more tranquil phase both economically and politically. What is the reason for this? Did the establishment attain its purpose through the rebukes and cutbacks of the early 1970s? Did these measures lead to a revision of programme policy that has ultimately been rewarded by the dishing out of more money?

It is almost impossible to give a definite answer to such questions. The decision-making processes are too difficult to interpret, because they are integrally geared to a wider social transformation and cannot be viewed in isolation. It is certainly true that a programme series such as 'From Socialism to Increased Equality' would be unlikely to be produced in the late 1970s, but this is bound up with the fact that since the wave of the left began to ebb away society has developed in such a manner that a different perspective would automatically be chosen. Programme production by the broadcasting media can largely be regarded as reflections of national and international changes in the political, economic, social and cultural climate. It means that various groups among the staff, as well as certain approaches to given topics and events, become prominent at one period but not in the next, as circumstances change. It is not useful to view the differences between periods as the result of 'interference' by vengeful power figures. These are not processes that are governed by the thumping of fists on conference tables.

It has to be said, furthermore, even though the difficulties of measurement are insuperable, that television programmes at the end of the 1970s do not seem any weaker than they were in the middle or late 1960s. Attacks on the labour movement from the left are of course much less frequent but this is bound up with shifts in the climate of opinion in society as a whole, with the changes which go with the swing back to the right.

Moreover, it is evident that television retains much of its unruliness, capriciousness and subjectivity. Toleration is accorded now to a subjectivity on the part of those who present programmes that would have been unthinkable before the 1960s swing to the left. There has been no tightening-up in this respect since the end of the 1960s. The spread of 'committed' journalism in the broadcasting media is a fact even if it cannot be said to predominate.

However, there are at the end of the 1970s scarcely any regularly recurring television programmes which politicians or other prominent figures need regard with disquiet. It does happen that their activities are subjected to a scrutiny that is searching, critical and well-informed, but that sort of programme is not put out every week. This is partly because resources are insufficient. Searchingly critical journalism requires research at a level which SR can afford only occasionally. The value placed by establishment figures upon well-informed investigative journalism is not so high as to help SR towards an abundance of resources. And the non-socialist government's bill proposed for 1978 does not have much to say about the value of a journalism of social criticism.

In Table 3 an attempt is made to summarise schematically some of the developments dealt with in this chapter. In this summary, the 1950s are called the 'Decade of Respect'. It was the time when active news journalism and interviewing technique had still not developed, and when SR staff acted as polite officials rather than as journalists demanding information. This was partly a consequence of recruitment, which in turn reflected a social climate. There were not many journalists in Sweden in those days who were knowledgeable about social questions. A start had been made on recruiting specialists in politics and economics or trade union affairs, but that was all. The questions put to politicians were often so formulated that the respondent could use the programme time as a propaganda vehicle if he so wished. Penetrating follow-up questions aimed at clarifying obscure points were seldom put. The hypothesis was that the distinguished interviewee was hiding nothing.

'Journalistic Liberation' really got under way during the 1960s. News journalism was activated and the interviewing techniques developed. SR's political journalists were able to appear on a more equal footing with politicians. Distinct progress was made. SR staff secured a more important role in election programmes. Their attitude became more critical and inquisitorial, their questions more direct and designed to elucidate situations and fix responsibilities.

The turbulent years were those of the transition from the 1960s to the 1970s. A deliberate subjectivity manifested itself clearly in programmes and led to some excesses which, in the inflamed atmosphere, attracted wrathful attention in the form of attacks by the Board of Governors and sundry power groups and economic reprisals by the government. Gradually matters settled down and a calmer era began. Financial grants were increased again. Subjective journalism is still alive, along with the more traditional form in which impartiality is the top priority. There is a clearly increased propensity to let ordinary people have their say.

When new heads of the television channels were appointed in 1978 the power of the leading politicians was also very clearly demonstrated; the selection of people for these important posts was not only a task for the Board of Governors of SR; in practice it became the concern of politicians active in party conflict – an unpleasant experience for those who believe that politicians should not be involved in such matters. It does not follow from this that the new appointees will simply obey party instructions; the system does not work that way at all, although the appointments still have political implications. A Liberal head of a channel will presumably in the long run favour different ideas and approaches from a Conservative or Socialist, even if he tries to act independently of party pressures.

The 1970s have been called here the 'Years of Stagnation'. The idea behind this designation is that no new ground has been won during the 1970s. The process of liberation that was begun in the 1950s and gathered great momentum in the 1960s has not developed any further during the 1970s. This is not necessarily to be construed as a bad thing. It may simply be that during the 1960s, the public service system reached its own limit. If so, the standstill of the 1970s does not constitute a problem, since the goal has been attained: journalistic freedom in television can go no further.

TABLE 3 *History of current affairs programmes, 1950–80*

	1950s	1960s	1970s
General characteristics	'The Decade of Respect'	'The Decade of Liberation'	'The Decade of Stagnation'
Important events	1957 Start of regular TV broadcasting	1966 Palme's bill and Riksdag speech; 1969 Start of TV 2 Miners' strike	1971 SR's Board acts. Budget cutback — Grant increased — 1978 New bill
Programme forms	More active news journalism — Searching questions —————————————————→	SR journalists conduct interviews in election broadcasts ——————————————→ 'Grass roots' given a say ——————————→	
Programme attitudes	Polite, official ——→ Searching, persistent —————→ Striving for impartiality —————————————————→		Deliberate subjectivity ————————————→
Recruitment	Middle class, academic ————————————————————————————————————→ Specialist reporters ——————————————————————————→	Left wing, academic ——————————————————→	
A typical interview question	'May we trouble you, Minister, for your comments on the situation?'	'How do you explain that . . .?'	'Don't you realise that . . .?'

But there are some reservations that must be added. First, the advances achieved cannot become significant until SR enjoys sufficient economic resources for its freedom to be expressed in forceful programmes. Such is hardly the case at present. There is no power group anywhere in Swedish society that has the creation of a rich, free, independent and audacious television as one of its primary goals.

In the second place, it is possible, even probable, that the general climate for the mass media in Sweden is deteriorating. Much of the mass media debate revolves around alleged excesses on radio, television and the press especially in the satirical form. Over-caution, on the other hand, is seldom or never complained about. It is difficult to escape the impression that politicians and other prominent figures feel happiest when the broadcasting media are slightly weak in resources and inactive. Critical scrutiny can so easily make mistakes, and whenever it does hit the target, that may be even more damaging to powerful interests. Thus, a broadcasting medium in a public service system is like a well-loved child that certainly has the benefit of a good upbringing and tender care, but which in critical situations feels the weight of his father's firm hand. Papa makes the rules, Papa sees that they are obeyed.

Such control is most easily exercised, of course, under a monopoly system that arises naturally from a tradition of centralised institutions.

6 Holland

The Shaky Pillars of Hilversum

Herman Wigbold

Dutch television contains all the ingredients of the perfect system. There is no government interference, which in any case is forbidden by law. The political parties exercise no control, apart from certain negligible indirect influences. There is a certain amount of controlled advertising but no private commercial television. The individual programme-maker has very wide freedom and television as a whole is not the object of crippling rules and regulations. Nor are the parties, business interests and government clamouring for a new system over which they would have more power (although all of these groups complain about specific programmes from time to time). Yet, quite emphatically, the Dutch have failed to produce the perfect television system.

The Dutch system is based on the principle of open organisation. Every group capable of enlisting enough members is legally entitled to broadcasting time. To qualify as a broadcasting organisation one has to meet certain standards: the organisation's principal purpose must be the transmission of radio and television programmes, it must broadcast a comprehensive radio and television schedule, comprising all categories of material including entertainment, information and culture; it has to satisfy the religious or cultural needs of the population, it has to be a non-profit-making organisation and it has to have a certain minimum number of members.

There are five large organisations: AVRO (neutral, conservative), TROS (neutral, leaning to the right), KRO (Catholic),

NCRV (Protestant), VARA (Socialist); two smaller ones: EO (fundamentalist), VPRO (non-conformist); and also one candidate organisation: VOO (neutral). All these broadcasting organisations have – by law – to co-operate in the NOS, which has a dual character. It provides all technical facilities such as studios, cutting rooms, outside broadcast equipment, etc. (and employs two-thirds of all personnel in television) but it also produces certain programmes itself: news, sports, Eurovision and certain other community programmes. It is the link between the various broadcasting organisations but is at the same time in competition with them. The system in fact contains further complexities, including special organisations for the churches, and for scientific material – but we will come to those later.

The influence of television on politics and of politics on television cannot be understood without looking into the peculiar way the Dutch have chosen to organise television. But in turn, their peculiar system cannot be understood without looking into the whole fabric of Dutch society.

The broadcasting system is a direct result of the rebellion of the Catholics and Protestants at the end of the nineteenth century against the dominating position of the conservative liberals. This struggle was fought out over the school system. Catholics and Protestants did not demand the right to found their own schools (they already had that at the beginning of the century) but they demanded equality, that is, that their schools be subsidised in exactly the same way as state schools provided they met the same requirements of class size, examinations standards, etc. This struggle was crowned with complete success at the beginning of this century.

This so-called school struggle shaped the whole of Dutch society resulting in what is called 'pillarisation'. Catholics and Protestants not only founded their own schools, political parties, trade unions, employers' organisations and hospitals but also their own welfare organisations, travel organisations, sporting organisations, etc. The religious affiliation of a citizen decided the community he lived in from cradle to grave. A Catholic, for example, learned arithmetic at a Catholic school, learned chess in a Catholic youth club, played football in a Catholic team, learned typing at a Catholic course, went on holiday with a Catholic group and sometimes even preferred to do his shopping with a Catholic shopkeeper. The same applied to the Protestants. Seeking shelter within the group was seen as a pre-condition of emancipation.

Although Catholics had been tolerated since the seventeenth century, entry to important social positions remained closed to many. The orthodox Protestants, too, were mainly humble people, struggling against the powerful in society. By keeping to themselves they hoped to achieve two aims: internally, to strengthen their self-respect, externally to find their place in the sun.

The Socialists, also subject to repression, adapted themselves only hesitatingly to the system. Although they remained ardent defenders of the state schools, they found themselves forced to start their own youth organisations, cultural and housing associations, sometimes also old people's homes. They created their own world. The conservative liberals, however, did not create a parallel system since they were already in power.

The main communication medium, the printing press, was the principal tool of this process of pillarisation. It kept the group together and gave it, literally, a voice. There were Catholic, Protestant and Socialist dailies and weeklies and each group also had its own illustrated press. So when sound radio invaded the living rooms in the 1920s, the form of organisation was predetermined. Sound broadcasting was to be run in exactly the same manner as every other aspect of life.

The new medium, based on the tightly knit unity of each group, seemed a perfect way of strengthening the weakening will to move through emancipation towards the goal of conversion of the nation. The Catholics based their hopes on the rapid growth of their population, the Protestants on the historically Protestant character of the nation and the Socialists on the unity of the working class which, one day, would give them their numerical superiority. 'Our strength is our isolation', was one of the battle cries of the orthodox Protestants.

The 'bourgeois' wing, lacking significant religious or political ties, tried to acquire a monopoly position by founding, before any other group, a neutral broadcasting organisation which would provide opportunities for all, but their efforts were doomed from the beginning by the opposition of the majority of the religious parties in Parliament and by the resistance of the Socialists. Within a year each group founded its own broadcasting organisation. Five sprang up: a Catholic, a Protestant, a Socialist, a neutral and a smaller organisation of libertarian Protestants, each broadcasting according to its size. The government itself was not involved. It seemed a very democratic system, and indeed it was, in comparison with many other systems. The government left the media in the hands of those private groups which had a real following in the country; it only made the rules by which the broadcasting organisations had to operate. Each of them had to have *bona fide* members who would be able, at least in theory, to exercise influence through democratic participation. Broadcasting time was distributed proportionally. Could anything be more democratic?

But in fact it was less democratic than it seemed. The new medium did not have autonomy any more than the press did. It was not an opinion leader, it was the mouthpiece of the groups it belonged to. It was unable to weigh pros and cons, to judge and to reject, even to juxtapose different views. The Catholic broadcasting organisation not only excluded criticisms of Catholic dogma, it also suppressed every criticism of Catholic organisations. The Socialist broadcasting organisation supported the policies of the Labour Party and only allowed dissenting views provided they were also tolerated within the party or the trade unions. Inside each organisation the control was as rigorous as in a state broadcasting organisation.

Sound broadcasting too became part of the power struggle between the groups. Collections were made in the Catholic churches for the Catholic broadcasting organisation, prayers were said in Protestant churches for the Protestant broadcasting organisation and one was only a true Socialist or trade union member if one was a member of the Socialist broadcasting organisation. Although political parties and other social organisations had no direct influence in the broadcasting bodies, they were interconnected through personalities and membership lists.

Despite all these disadvantages the Dutch system had two great advantages: control in five organisations is preferable to control by a monopoly and the listener could tune in to five points of view. Each organisation was unitarian but the system was pluriform. A few even believed, without ever having heard of McLuhan, that the new medium would automatically provide for the 'message'. Radio was to penetrate the living rooms and the minds of the people. Radio would not demolish the 'pillars', but at least it would undermine them. The barricades between the various groups would be lowered. It appeared to be only a question of time. The process of emancipation was complete – or nearly so. Catholics were increasingly regarded as full citizens. The Protestant 'small folk' had risen in politics as well as in industry. Socialists were still seen by some as potential trouble-makers but many came to accept them as excellent administrators. Self-confidence was growing.

The war seemed to deal the broadcasting system a death blow. The organisations emerged discredited. In some areas the Nazis were unopposed. AVRO, the neutral organisation, had already dismissed Jewish staff before the Germans demanded it. The Catholic broadcasting organisation had been completely taken over by the Nazis before the Bishops, taking a firm stand, could intervene. The Socialist broadcasting organisation bowed before the Nazis with the exception of one official, Broeks (later Chairman of the European Broadcasting Union). The history of broadcasting during the occupation is a history of collaboration. To maintain the institutions was more important than to stand by the principles on which they were founded.

At the same time, a growing desire for greater co-operation, for breaking down the fences between the various groups, was expressed in the resistance movement. Catholics and Socialists, in particular, demanded unity, tolerance, respect for one another's viewpoints. The broadcasting system seemed on the verge of breaking up. But this was not to be.

The Restoration

When the first television transmission started in Holland in 1951 – with only 2500 television sets – it was a foregone conclusion that the transmissions should be produced by the same organisations which had started radio in 1925. VARA, KRO, NCRV, VPRO, the same old names, were competing for transmission time. How was this possible, how did it happen?

The first reason was that sound broadcasting had been far less effective than some had hoped and others had feared. Looking back, it was astonishing to see how in the pre-war years many had remained loyal to their own broadcasting organisation, some tuning in only to its broadcasts. And in as far as one did listen to other broadcasts, one was pre-disposed not to be influenced. But more importantly, the Dutch social system had created its own elite, interested above all in maintaining the system that had made it powerful. It was fully aware of the danger of removing one single stone and bringing down the entire building. It was the common interest of the various elites to prevent this. As early as the 1930s, the ultimate goal, the conversion of the nation, had disappeared from the scene. For however tightly organised each group, in its efforts to expand, it inevitably confronted another group. The one neutralised the other. It was therefore necessary to find a common ground to prevent the country from falling apart in warring factions. 'Pacification' became the catchword, a call to respect the boundaries of other groups through co-operation at the top. By keeping the pillars for their followers but bridging them for themselves, the leaders further strengthened their grip on the society.

So when, in 1933, the Dutch government punished the Socialist broadcasting organisation – the only time the government ever intervened in such a firm manner – by withdrawing one hour of broadcasting time because the Socialists had observed a one-minute silence after the execution of Van der Lubbe (the man accused of setting fire to the Reichstag), the government having judged this to be prejudicial to its policy of neutrality, the other broadcasting organisations boycotted the empty hour. Their common interest lay in taking a united stand.

Holland's much praised tolerance was based less on respect for others' convictions than on a gentleman's agreement to respect others' territories. The 'free social organisations' increasingly became vested interests, ruled by an inter-related elite. How vested they were, became clear in the early post-war years. When, a few days after the liberation, the board members of the various broadcasting organisations reclaimed the studios as their legal property, they were refused entrance on orders of the government; within a year, however, they were in complete control again.

Even before the liberation the orthodox Protestants had announced their intention not to allow a change in the system. And after the liberation the Catholic bishops, notwithstanding the feelings of many Catholics, strongly sided with them, saying in very clear terms that they 'wanted the reconstitution of the Catholic broadcasting organisation in accordance with the objectives of the organisation: to propagate the Catholic philosophy of life in every field as was done in the past'. The subordination of mass communication media could not have been defined more clearly. The bishops were strongly backed by the pre-war Catholic elite which had been in hiding during the Second World War and for which the maintenance of the old system was the only way of regaining power.

The Socialists who had been active in the Labour Party or the trade union movement in the pre-war years, supported the return of the broadcasting organisations for fear of being overwhelmed by the others. True, the Labour Party, at every congress, adopted resolutions asking for a more national broadcasting system but the argument was basically settled. The line that had been interrupted in 1940 was taken up again in 1945. Within a few years the pre-war elite had regained its previous power position in broadcasting as in other areas.

Although the present writer, for example, supported a more national broadcasting system in those years, I now admit it would have been a disaster. Because of the rigid organisation of each group, each opinion would have blocked the other and a pale form of broadcasting would have resulted. Every programme-maker would have avoided political and other contentious subjects in order not to offend a particular group. So there was no discussion about whether the existing five broadcasting organisations would move into television, although they had to make one concession. Those who were still nursing defeat in the immediate post-war years, particularly the more modern socialists, achieved the objective of having part of broadcasting time reserved for general or national programmes, including news, sport, and so on. The broadcasting organisations did not greatly object to this. It seemed to fit in with their policy of co-operation where co-operation was inevitable, to promote so-called 'roof' organisations for collaboration at the top. Television in the 1950s followed the classic pattern, an instrument for the propagation of ideas. Nobody was greatly interested as the number of television sets increased very slowly. Five years after the first television transmission there still were only 25,000 sets.

Those who still dreamed of a more autonomous broadcasting

system were cruelly woken in 1954, when the Catholic bishops published a pastoral letter forbidding membership of the Socialist trade union movement, attacking the Socialist Party and even forbidding 'frequent tuning in to Socialist broadcasts'. Such harsh words shocked even the dull and conformist Holland of the 1950s. It looked as if the bishops had overplayed their hand. The Labour Party, in a coalition government with the Catholics, made emotional protests against this 'vexatious' behaviour. The Socialist trade unions broke off co-operation with the Catholic and Protestant unions when these expressed support for the bishops. But the storm died down. Socialists and Catholics stayed in government, the Socialist trade union renewed co-operation at the top when the Catholic trade unions explained, without dissociating themselves, that they had not asked for the pastoral letter.

The extent to which the communication media were subordinated to the wishes of the establishment became clear in 1956. Stories appeared in the British and German press that Queen Juliana had called in a faith-healer to treat her daughter and this had disturbed the relationship with her husband, Prince Bernhard. The truth was more complicated and clearly carried political overtones. The Queen herself held pacifist views and a number of prominent figures in Holland (including the Queen's husband, as we now know) were preoccupied with quite different matters.

After the first publications in the foreign press, the Prime Minister – a Socialist – called a meeting of all chief editors. Television was not even invited to the meeting. The idea that it might pay attention to such things did not spring to anyone's mind. The Prime Minister requested the chief editors not to publish anything on the affair in view of the possible constitutional consequences. The editors obeyed, and the guilt still haunts Dutch journalists.

The real opinion leaders were the political and religious leaders. These were the village wisemen of whom Lerner writes.[1] The journalists were their servants as was shown by the pastoral letter of the bishops and the obedient behaviour of the newspaper editors. Everything seemed under control. Doubts were scarcely expressed. Peace had been signed. Even television seemed unable to disturb the calm. But matters quickly altered.

The Awakening

The 1960s came as an earthquake. It changed the entire landscape of Holland, old convictions giving way to new morals, old structures crumbling under the violence of spontaneous outbursts. The old power elite was losing its grip, it could no longer control events, its capacities, even its legitimacy being questioned. Old rules and arrangements were being broken. The closed society became the permissive society. Holland became the country where everything seemed possible, the leader in grass-roots democracy and in sexual freedom. Amsterdam became a magical centre of the world attracting thousands of young people. Similar changes occurred in every country in the industrialised world, but Holland was one of the first to be aroused and in no other country was the change so sudden, so abrupt, bringing so complete a break with tradition. How did it happen and what was television's impact? Did it have any? I think it did, in a decisive way.

James Strouse writes:[2] 'The effect of mass communication is still a mystery eluding social science.' One of the reasons is that a large part of the research is directed towards the short-term impact of television, particularly the impact on election results. All the intense study, in many countries, of the effects of the Kennedy-Nixon debates, have failed to detect a decisive influence on voting behaviour. The explanation is simple. Mass communication is not a separate power, able to stimulate or slow down developments in society at will. It takes place within a power structure. It may well influence government, parties, trade unions, etc., but it also influences itself. It stimulates and is stimulated, it criticises and is criticised. It is impossible to subtract the one factor, television, from the others.

That is why television cannot achieve detectable short-term changes in public opinion. The possibilities are less than the prophets of hope tend to think and the dangers are less than the prophets of doom try to make us believe. It does not change a mass into independent individuals and it does not change individuals into a helpless mass. Television tends to strengthen existing opinion. An ambitious series like 'Das Dritte Reich' hardly appeared to have changed any opinions at all. Sometimes even the opposite occurs. A few years ago Dutch television transmitted a well-made series of programmes about foreign workers, with the specific purpose of countering racial prejudice. When a study was made of the effects, the programme-makers were shocked to discover that they had increased the level of prejudice. Talking about foreign workers had been sufficient to strengthen the emotional predispositions. Television does have something more than a consolidating impact on existing opinion; it has the capacity to strengthen certain developments in the long term, working as a catalyst, speeding up and slowing down what is already under way. Those conditions were extremely favourable in the Holland of the 1960s.

The impact of television is at its greatest, as Sellers says,[3] when 'there are events with widespread and powerful impact and issues touching deep emotions'. Such events and issues were present in Holland: the rise of Pope John XXIII, touching deep emotions among Dutch Catholics, particularly the lower clergy; the ecumenical forces in the Protestant world; the emergence of a new generation questioning authority; rising doubt in the socialist world about the nature of traditional political activity; the end of the Dutch Empire with the loss of New Guinea, the growing mobility of the working class; creeping resentment against the establishment; the spectre of sexual freedom; the sudden conversion of Princess Irene, the marriage of Princess Beatrix to a German; all were events which, justifiably or otherwise, touched deep emotions.

Lazarsfeld, Gaudet and Berelson distinguish three types of cross-pressures:[4]

(1) Conflicting evaluation of political objects;
(2) Conflicts arising from tensions between the various social statuses a person might occupy; and
(3) Conflicts arising from the primary groups of which the individual voter is a member.

All these pressures and cross-pressures were present. One may distinguish three out of many:

(1) Growing secularisation. Between 1968 and 1975 the number of Catholics declined from 46 per cent to 30 per cent. The number of Protestants also declined from about 36 per cent to 30 per cent.
(2) Growing unity. The age-old differences between Catholics

and Protestants and between Christians and non-Christians became far less prominent. Even those who declared themselves Christian adopted a more tolerant attitude. Only some of them felt morally obliged to send their children to religious schools or to vote for a religious party or to be in favour of religious or political broadcasting organisations.

(3) Growing disunity. Differences and frictions appeared between Catholics who adhered to the old faith and Catholics who had a more open-minded attitude, between Protestants who stayed in their own group and Protestants who had thrown the doors wide open, between Socialists who kept to their old beliefs and Socialists who wanted more democratisation, between conservative Liberals and progressive Liberals. And growing disunity between those who stood for some ideals, old or new, and those who wanted not to be bothered at all.

Those were the conditions in Holland, giving television its new possibilities, making Holland an ideal laboratory in which to study the impact of television on society as a whole and on politics in particular.

Knock at Any Door

Television was bound to have a tremendous influence in a country where not only the doors of the living room were closed to strangers but also the doors of schoolrooms, union meetings, youth hostels, football grounds and dancing schools. Television in Holland did not only knock at the front door but at all doors. It confronted the masses with views, ideas and opinions from which they had been isolated. The shock value was greater than in any other country. For there was no way out, no hiding place, except by the difficult expedient of switching off. Television viewers could not even switch to a second channel because there wasn't one. Not before 1967 did a second channel get on the air and most viewers still could not receive it for years; it remained a second-best, in programming as well as audience ratings.

Television hastened the birth of a new unity. Catholics discovered that Socialists were not the dangerous atheists they had been warned about, Liberals had to conclude that orthodox Protestants were not the bigots they were supposed to be. Television at the same time sharpened the divisions in society between those who wanted to keep to their old beliefs and those who were looking for change.

There was another factor stimulating television's impact. Television arrived in Holland exactly at the right moment. It was born at the beginning of the 1950s and had its infancy during the rest of the decade. Its quality was doubtful, its transmission time limited, it was mainly regarded as an entertainment medium, with outside broadcasts as the ultimate miracle. Audience figures rose very slowly. And it occurred in the 1950s, a period of cultural and political stagnation when attention was focused on economic progress.

The dawn of television journalism was at the end of the 1950s with a monthly and popular forum, consisting not of representatives of the establishment but of various non-conformists. It sounded the bell for the transition to the 1960s.

The real breakthrough, in programming and audience figures, came at the beginning of the new decade, just at the moment when the first rumblings of the coming earthquake were audible. Bright, angry or simply open-minded journalists were entering television. They were not hampered by the strict rules surrounding the printing press, and had a virtually empty field. They were not allowed to cross various 'lines' but these lines had become less visible because the major broadcasting organisations could not find the right tools to draw new ones. The government, puritan at heart, right from the introduction of television, tried to hold back the sales of sets but the Philips concern broke through by invoking the argument of full employment. A third factor, strengthening the effects of television in Holland, was, paradoxically, the very closedness of the Dutch system itself. It exaggerated the shock of confrontation when it finally came. The programme-makers did not – and do not – have an obligation to give a balanced presentation pro and contra. The balancing of viewpoints is built into the system itself, through the variety of groups involved. Fairness and avoidance of bias were principles not laid down in the regulations but they were desirable ways of maintaining credibility. Programme-makers could be partisan, so long as they did not affront the viewers – and even that was not an absolute prohibition.

Walter Lippman once said: 'There is an essential and radical difference between television and newspapers. Networks, few in number, have a virtual monopoly'. That essential difference did not exist in Holland; there was no monopoly.

Those who were alarmed by the new developments were unable to withdraw inside the shell of their own group. Eager to show their independence, the journalists not only took the opportunity to interview opponents, they also pressed their own people hard. The old rule of Catholics with Catholics and Socialists with Socialists was broken and the authority of the groups' leaders was undermined. The journalists did not question the underlying beliefs, whether of Protestantism or Socialism, democracy or the rule of law but they seemed to question the institutions built upon them, and it was this, more than any particular programme, which tended to shock the Dutch. Old frames of references disintegrated, there was no longer an accepted set of standards. The social temperature was raised; opinions suddenly polarised.

Of course there was sometimes deep resentment. In every country, particularly in the first years of television, interviewers were criticised for showing a lack of respect for those interviewed. Criticism was even greater in Holland because of an almost biblical deference to authority. The deep contrasts in Holland between authority and freedom, between closeness and openness, may be one of the reasons why the pendulum swung so rapidly.

Attempts to Stem the Tide

The government tried but it could not do much against the prevailing trends. The Minister of Culture, Recreation and Welfare has no jurisdiction over the content of broadcasting programmes. This is the exclusive domain of the broadcasting organisations. He can only act when the broadcasting organisations do not fulfil the obligations of the 1967 Broadcasting Act; he may take action, for example against unauthorised advertising and against excessive self-advertising by the broadcasting organisations. In political matters the Minister can only act if a transmission is in breach of the law, that is to say if it threatens the safety of the state or public order or decency.

In 1963 the government tried to invoke this provision in a very clumsy way. It warned the Catholic broadcasting organisation, on the advice of the Foreign Secretary, Luns, later NATO's Secretary-General, that it would give orders to blank the screen if it broadcast a planned interview with Bidault, the head of the OAS. KRO bowed under pressure but the government was morally defeated. In a full-scale parliamentary debate – transmitted live by television – it was censured by a majority vote.

A year later the government announced on a Sunday evening that it was 'seriously considering taking action' when uproar broke out over an item in a satirical programme, of which more below. After that row died away, the government backed down.

In later years on two occasions the government formally 'deplored' certain programmes – without taking action: one in which VPRO showed a naked girl and one in which VARA showed wall paintings of the Pope standing with some pretty girls in a report of a Literary Ball. In 1969 it officially reprimanded VPRO – again without taking action – because it was alleged to have called for acts of sabotage in the army. Again in 1972 VPRO was reprimanded for an impersonation of the Queen. VPRO's appeal against the latter censure was upheld.

In a new draft Bill sent to Parliament in 1978, the Minister proposes to delete from the Broadcasting Act the words referring to withdrawal of the allocation of transmission time if programme material entails danger to the security of the state, public order or morals. This proposal arises from the acceptance of the principle that the government should not have more power over television and radio than over the press. Not the executive but the judiciary would in future decide whether the law has been infringed. At the time of writing, there seems to be unanimous agreement for this change.

Various business interests made attempts to block the tide of the era and bypass the whole existing system by pushing for commercial television. They came to the brink of success when the government – a coalition of the religious parties and Conservatives – sent a note to parliament proposing to give the second channel to a new group formed on similar lines to Britain's ITV. But when the Conservative ministers tried to press their point, the government fell apart and a new government, now including the Socialists, had to be formed.

The broadcasting organisations, sometimes under pressure from affiliated groups and parties themselves tried to stem the tide. AVRO, the neutral organisation which had little to do with the interplay between politics and mass communication in the 1960s, was subject to a good deal of internal censorship but that did not forestall all its difficulties. In 1964 it cancelled a literary programme which included a poem which used the word 'fuck'. In 1966 it cancelled a programme about an author of erotic books. A youth programme considered too 'risky' was cancelled in the same year. All of these programmes were removed when producers and editors refused to continue work on them. In 1968 a programme on the German occupation was cancelled because it featured a song by Mikis Theodorakis, the Greek composer, and the parallel between the Nazis and the Greek colonels was considered too dangerous.

The Catholic organisation which played an important role within the Catholic world with its debates on topical issues, had a period of conflict with producers who preceded an announcement of the marriage of Princess Beatrix with Prince Claus with the word 'Sondermeldung' (or 'Special Announcement', used by German headquarters during the war). In 1966 it banned a programme on birth control though the subject as such had been treated in other programmes. In 1968 it fired a well-known interviewer for not consulting the programme staff about showing naked females in a shot (as a reaction to the VPRO programme) and for making an untoward joke about the Royal Family.

The Socialist broadcasting organisation had more difficulties with the past than the present. It refused to transmit a play by Jakov Lind because of Jewish sensitivities; it banned an item dealing with certain shameful acts committed by Dutch citizens in the Dutch East Indies in 1941 during a transfer by boat of German prisoners of war. In 1967 it vetoed a satirical song about the American involvement in Vietnam.

Even the small VPRO, taken over by non-conformists in the second part of the 1940s, made certain cuts in its material and its producers tended to give it a hard time. After the row about the naked girls they wanted to show a girl undressing accompanied by the words used by the Prime Minister deploring the previous transmission. And when one month later they transmitted an appeal for a hundred 'fine specimens' willing to display their bodies, the programme disappeared from the screen altogether reappearing some time later with a scandal involving naked men. The VPRO did not completely deny its origins. A cabaret song entitled 'Tango with God' also bit the dust.

All these acts of interference were deeply resented in intellectual circles but the measures taken, or intended, were in reality only a rearguard action. What was possible was far more important than what was not. Even the powerful Dutch elite failed to stem the tide of the decade.

Superficially everything was as before. Each broadcasting organisation had a Board, plus a kind of Members' Council which in theory carried the ultimate power but which in practice had no influence except in the cases of VARA and VPRO. The Boards were the ultimate authority and consisted of representatives of respective sectors of the 'establishment', who stayed in power by a process of permanent co-option. But they too were unable to control the flow of events, and their front was no longer united. The power elite itself was afflicted with doubts, and found it had to move with the trend towards greater freedom and permissiveness. This elite, furthermore, had underestimated the importance of the mass media and had not put its most able and trusted people in the key positions. And so it had no real grip on the journalists who stood by their mandate and clung to their fundamental loyalty to the institutions they worked for. They managed the managers better than the real management did. Where the Dutch elite wanted to hold the dykes, it did not know how or where to do so. It was no longer clear who was friend and who was enemy. The once perfect machinery was failing.

Religion and Politics

The Catholic and Socialist broadcasting organisations were breaking the traditional rules, raising the temperature in the society, wooing those who were looking for new ideas, irritating those wanting to keep the old ones. Current affairs programmes played an important role, not only as programmes, but also because the broadcasting organisations came to regard them (because of the nature of the Dutch system) as their flag-ships.

They received prime time scheduling, just after the 8.00 p.m. news, the effect of which was all the greater because there was only one channel.

The Catholic broadcasting organisation was very active in both the religious and political sphere. The pastoral letter of 1954 had been counter-productive. Instead of closing the ranks more and more Catholics were asking questions about desirability. At first debate was restricted to intellectual circles, as it had always been, but the accession of Pope John XXIII gave it a practical dimension. In no country were people so fascinated with the ideas and personality of Pope John as in Holland. KRO found a man who resembled Pope John in many ways: Monsignore Bekkers, not a great theologian, not an original thinker, not an eloquent orator but a man of humble origin, a bishop but above all a pastoral man, open-minded, demonstrating his love and understanding for the common man. At first he followed tradition by delivering an epilogue at the end of transmission, but he soon moved over to the current affairs programme. He spoke, in carefully formulated phrases, about the acceptability of birth control, about the need to co-operate with Protestants and Humanists, about Christian guilt for injustice in the world, about the plight of priests wanting to marry, and, after the death of Pope John, about the differences of opinion with the Vatican, especially concerning celibacy. Then in 1964 he spoke out against the witch-hunt going on among Catholics against the producers of a satirical programme put on by the Socialist broadcasting organisation, VARA. He did not do it because KRO wanted him to do so. He acted on his own, after having sought advice and sometimes after having been advised by the people with whom he had surrounded himself: priests, laymen, medical people, social workers. Television again did not work as an engine but as a catalyst, reflecting and at the same time hastening developments.

As a Catholic organisation, KRO paid a great deal of attention to the Vatican Council meetings in Rome. While in other countries the Council was one item in a news programme and perhaps a subject for an occasional special report, KRO kept a team in Rome which made a constant flow of reports. It paid, almost systematically, more attention to new than to old ideas – an African bishop who treats celibacy as something typically European being more newsworthy than a German prelate who follows his traditional beliefs. The critics were in a way quite right: notwithstanding its Catholic background, KRO did not strengthen traditional Catholicism but undermined it. This approach immediately affected politics because of the traditional connections between religion and politics in the Catholic world. KRO could move more freely than the Socialist broadcasting organisation, always under the suspicion of trying to promote the Labour Party by criticising the party system. Paradoxically, the direct political impact of this religious broadcasting organisation was greater than that of the Socialist broadcasters.

It is hardly necessary to describe that impact without mentioning specific programmes. Catholic journalists hardly ever turned against the Catholic party and in so far as they did criticise, this was expressed more in an occasional ironical remark than in an elaborate item. The impact came mainly in interviews.

For years Catholics had been a very closed group. Nowhere else was the saying 'Don't wash your dirty linen in public' so meticulously observed. Internally, there was criticism but externally a united line had to be held. Conflicts between employers and trade unions were supposed to be solved in an atmosphere of 'natural harmony'. Radio was under the control of the leaders and the Catholic press pushed every internal conflict under the table.

Television broke that pattern. The politicians were constantly confronted with their own ideas and principles. Catholic leaders were interviewed in the same way as others – not by outsiders, but by their own people – the style of questioning being sceptical rather than critical. Conflicts and arguments were not covered up but used to stir up debate. KRO was the first to start a programme in Parliament, taking the same sceptical attitude. KRO was also the first to strike the same note in its treatment of American involvement in Vietnam.

Catholic politicians had to lick their wounds. They could hardly object to the Catholic broadcasters paying attention to problems that were alive in the Catholic world. Nor could they object to critical interviews as long as these were correctly conducted. And they had to take ironic remarks in order not to give the impression of being spoiled children.

Sometimes feeling ran high in KRO but the producers stood firm. On one occasion a member of the Board demanded a change in the editorial line to make it more consistent with Catholic tradition. KRO's director retorted: 'I can only do that by firing everyone. Is that what you want?'

The Taboos

The direct political impact of the Socialist broadcasting organisation VARA was less than that of the Catholic one. Its social significance was that it tried time and time again to break existing taboos and broaden the limits of public debate. It sometimes ran into great opposition because, unlike the KRO, it appealed in its programmes to all viewers, Socialist, or non-Socialist, whereas the primary concern of KRO was to reach the Catholic viewers.

In 1964 VARA had already made a programme on birth control, discussing and demonstrating the various methods of contraception. One year later it made a programme on homosexuality in which homosexuals participated. In a programme on suicide, people who had actually attempted suicide took part (a number of newspapers refused to accept an advert asking for participants in the programme – Dutch newspapers never mention suicide). Other programmes discussed divorce (then very rare in Holland), euthanasia and the reality of the sexual revolution. Today these problems find a place in normal public debate but in those years they were highly controversial.

The most important programme in this series was that on abortion. Until then abortion was the subject of an outright taboo in Holland. It was not for public discussion, either in Parliament or in the newspapers (which were anyway far behind television in the 1960s). The programme-makers did not take an explicit line as they might have done in Holland. All they did was to pay attention to the problem by letting women tell their stories, followed by a discussion with gynaecologists. The producers received hundreds of letters, very few abusive, which indicated the success of the chosen presentation. Six weeks later another programme on abortion was broadcast. Those programmes started up the public debate in Holland, one of the best examples of the agenda-setting function of television.

In 1963 VARA started a monthly satirical programme modelled upon the British programme, 'That Was The Week That Was'. Immediately after the first transmission the same thing happened as in England: heated opposition and delighted support. The crunch came in the third programme on the first Saturday in the New Year, in an edition which contained an item, three minutes in length, satirising television viewing as if it were a new religion. The script was a paraphrase of the Gospel of St. John: 'In the Beginning there was the Screen and the Screen was the New God.' The item ended with the Lord's Prayer: 'Blessed be the screen, your will is our will', etc.

All hell broke loose. Next day, priests and vicars fulminated from the pulpit against this 'blasphemous' programme. Parliamentary delegates of the religious and Conservative parties refused to wait until Monday to put their reactions directly on the national wire service. The Minister declared that same Sunday night that he was 'seriously considering taking action'. The wave of emotion grew higher and higher and the row developed certain hysterical features. On Monday, all but two newspapers turned against the programme. One leading newspaper, in a spirit of 'J'accuse', published the names of all the contributors to the programme. The Synod of the main Protestant church, in assembly next day, protested officially. All sorts of associations made declarations. The Socialist broadcasting organisation and the programme-makers were inundated with abusive telephone calls and threats. All those involved in the programme received police protection. A day later, there was another wave, now from people who were extremely indignant at the indignant. Institutes of mental health warned against the wave of intolerance. In a broadcast on KRO Mgr Bekkers expressed his regret for the lovelessness of many of the reactions. VARA bowed under the pressure but did not break. For a very brief moment, it considered stopping the programme but decided in the end not to go any further than to regret that the intention of the programme-makers had insufficiently come through. Four weeks later the programme was on the air again.

The programme lived on for almost three years, much longer than the British 'TWTWTW', without losing any of its sharpness. Excitement never grew so high as in 1964 but never ceased. One example: a well-known entertainment manager refused any further co-operation with VARA because the satirical show had exposed the war record of an artist he had under contract.

During the third year the programme-makers (all except the

responsible editor were freelance) decided not to continue with the programme the following season but the end came two months earlier amidst the smoke bombs, provo-activity and the counter-violence of the police, brought about by the marriage of Princess Beatrix to a German diplomat, an event which created a very tense atmosphere. VARA had some taste of this when transmitting 90 seconds of film, one week after the wedding, of riots which had occurred during the opening of an exhibition of photographs of the violence which had taken place on the Royal wedding day. The news programme had refused the film, a decision later regretted by its Editor in Chief. Although the presentation was matter of fact, the telephone lines were clogged by hours of abusive calls. The Socialist broadcasters announced a cooling-off period and a week later the satirical programme was transmitted. The programme-makers had written an item on Amsterdam's Mayor who had reacted very emotionally on the air. When this item was banned, the makers stopped the programme altogether.

In 1968, there was another important incident, the consequences of which shed some light on the complex relationship between television and politics. A young postgraduate had added a thesis to his dissertation (traditionally, a dissertation is supplemented by a number of theses which are not related to the subject) asserting that Holland had committed war crimes in Indonesia. In an interview he spoke about certain atrocities – torturing and shooting of prisoners – he had seen and partly committed himself. Desiring to get this dark period into open discussion, the producers kept the interview on their shelves to await suitable peak viewing. They waited until a Friday night after the News and just before a highly popular entertainment programme. Until that moment the entire subject had been taboo, as if a page had been torn out of the history books.

The shock was considerably less than in 1964 but more profound among those who had done military service in Indonesia and among their wives and children. Again there were threats and abuse, not so much from those directly involved but from an extremist fringe. The right-wing press heavily attacked the programme but many other papers started to publish stories about the period. The makers of the programme achieved their aim: a national debate, helped by some parliamentary delegates, asking what the government would do against the 'besmirching of the national honour'. They made two more programmes within a week, trying to put the responsibility where it belonged: on the shoulders of the politicians.

The programmes did not shift public opinion immediately. They strengthened the beliefs of those who already doubted the official version of that part of national history and antagonised those who did not want to hear about it at all. But the most important result was that it was now on the agenda and could not be removed. The following week there was a parliamentary debate. A proposal for a full-scale parliamentary enquiry did not get a majority but because of the outcry something had to be done to satisfy those who asked for an enquiry as well as those who wanted to save the honour of the nation. The government promised an independent enquiry into the files of the Dutch judiciary on the East Indies, and four months later the report was published. The Commission had only been able to explore the tip of an iceberg, those cases that had received the attention of the courts, but it became clear that more had happened in Indonesia than many had believed. The day before the parliamentary debate on the report, VARA again made a programme, now containing testimony from Indonesians and with more material and documents on the stubborness of the previous generation of politicians.

The programme-makers did not achieve what they had wanted, a parliamentary enquiry, but they did succeed in getting the subject talked about. The underlying thesis of the programme was accepted far more easily after those six months than before. It was not a complete success but a far greater one than programme-makers can normally hope for.

Finally, we consider VPRO. It started in 1925 as a small organisation of libertarian and progressive Protestants but in the mid-1960s it was completely taken over by non-conformists who defended the 'provo' and 'dwarf' cults, sometimes acting as armchair revolutionaries, sometimes as defenders of the old liberal traditions. Its support originated mainly in left-wing circles but it stood more for a mentality than for a Marxist ideology as its enemies claimed. It always experienced great difficulties in keeping sufficient members and its ratings were often low (this has changed during recent years), but it was highly popular among academics, students, social workers and other more volatile groups in society. It reached its peak in the 1970s because, as a small organisation, there needed to be a second channel before its share would amount to a whole evening a week.

The Protestant NCRV followed the Catholic KRO at a distance. It was far more careful and ran into difficulties with its own group not so much because of its outspoken views but because of its objecting to a naked shoulder or to a failure to show the characters of a play saying grace before meals.

The Results

KRO made a deep impact in its own Catholic circles. The impact in the non-Catholic world was far less, the non-Catholic viewers being outsiders, fascinated by what was going on, full of admiration for what proved to be possible but looking on more like non-supporters at a football match. It had, indeed, a certain impact in the Protestant world. The Socialist broadcasting organisation VARA had a lesser impact within its own group but one which spread further afield. Non-Catholics could ignore the KRO broadcast but they could not ignore the information given by VARA because it had direct bearing on problems affecting everyone.

VARA and VPRO had to cope with sometimes running into heavy opposition not only because of the message they brought but because it was they, VARA and VPRO, who brought it. No doubt, the same message given by a more national organisation, would have been more easily accepted. The question is theoretical since a national system did not exist, and if it had, it would not have brought the message. But it helps to show advantages and disadvantages inherent in Dutch television.

It touches another problem, valid for any television programme-maker in any country, assuming that neither absolute freedom nor absolute objectivity exist. He has to aim for objectivity, he has to show two sides of every coin, he has to put the incident in context and should not generalise from the exceptional; still, he is not an objective messenger because he has to aim at *something*, if it is only informing the public on this or that question; he has his own opinions that motivate him and he has to select what is and what is not in his report. Because he works in mass communication, he cannot avoid deciding what approach he thinks is the most effective.

The television producer or editor in Holland in the sixties had – and to a great extent still has – the freedom to select his means of communication and that means far more than studio design or camera angle. He can choose different approaches: partisan, less partisan, factual, pseudo-objective even under certain circumstances, provocative, provided he keeps the audience in mind. He has to face the question: what is more effective, a factual report which is more easily accepted but may be more easily forgotten? Or a more provocative approach which irritates more viewers but may have a deeper effect in the long run?

The 1967 programme on abortion would have been in danger of having the opposite effect if it had gone in for shock effect. But a similar approach regarding the Indonesian affair might have failed because an initial shock effect may have been needed to break through the walls long built around the issue. Only after having introduced the problem could its importance be weighed, evaluated and placed in the context of circumstances and responsibilities. The same can be said of television satire. It worked as long as conformity ruled and contrasts in the society were covered up. But it failed and it had had to fail when controversy was running so high that the lid flew off the kettle.

It was in particular the Catholic broadcasters at KRO who had a direct impact on politics. Their sceptical approach towards the Catholic establishment certainly hastened the downfall of the Catholic party which was reduced in ten years from fifty to twenty-seven seats. In a more indirect way, KRO created the conditions for the merger in the 1970s of the Catholic and Protestant parties in a Christian-Democratic party. VARA's impact was more indirect. By permanently hammering on the themes of freedom and democratisation it brought a new generation into power in the Labour Party, eliminating the old guard and bypassing the generation that grew up in the post-war years. It helped in this way to modernise the party.

Questioning the old ideas and criticising the establishment, the broadcasting system damaged the old parties and boosted new ones made possible by the proportional system. The House of Commons has 150 members, and any party that polls 0.8 per cent of the vote is assured of a seat in Parliament. All proposals to change the proportional system died before they could be voted on. Every election brought the success of a new party. In 1966 the Farmers Party gained support, a 'poujadist' party that also attracted disgruntled Socialists and even Communists in the big towns. In 1967, a resounding success went to the D'66 party of left-wing liberals fighting for more democratisation; in 1970 the success of DS'70, a party of disappointed social democrats and moderate conservatives and in 1972 the success of PPR, which started as a party of left-wing Catholics and became more and more a party of social workers and ecologists. It corresponds with the findings of Blumler and McQuail[5] on the British election of 1964 when the relatively tiny Liberal Party profited most from television, because there was a lack of clarity in the public image of the big parties.

Of course, there were the normal side effects of television. Politicians did things they probably would not have done without knowing the television cameras were focused on them, one politician getting a toupee, another sitting in the Amsterdam town square among the hippies. If it had any influence, it was a negative one. We are still a long way from a situation in which such tricks can determine the popularity of a politician.

It cannot be denied that television focused the attention on the party leader, that it personalised politics. But one should not exaggerate. No party leader in Holland, not even in the 1970s, was elected because of being 'telegenic' or of an ability to manipulate the power of television.

Parliamentary Transmissions and Political Broadcasts

Already at an early stage, in 1962, the President of the Second Chamber (House of Commons), after consultation with the government, gave permission to broadcast parliamentary debates. The decision concerned both live broadcasts and summaries. Permission was given to NOS which links all the broadcasting organisations. The initiative lies completely with television. The President has to give permission for each transmission but so far there is no refusal on record.

Direct broadcasts were of course no problem. The summaries had to meet the standards of fairness but these were not explicitly defined. What is 'fairness' when there are ten to fifteen parties represented in Parliament, varying from fifty seats to one? Practice dictated compromise. During the first years television tended to take speaking time as a criterion, in later years the importance of the party was taken into account also. The compromise was that the bigger parties got more coverage if speaking time was used as the basis for calculation while the smaller parties got more if the size of party was used. Over the years the rules were applied less strictly. Where it was permitted in the first years to record only with electronic cameras, nowadays it is also possible to use a film camera. Where in the beginning only NOS had permission to film, today the current affairs programmes of the various broadcasting organisations may also do so. In fact all restrictions have been lifted provided no material is used to stampede a single point of view.

There are now three types of parliamentary broadcasts:

Live transmission This is only done with 'hot' issues in which great public interest is expected. The Prime Minister's speech about the consequences of the enquiry into Prince Bernhard's wheeling and dealing was transmitted live. So were the parliamentary debates on this issue. So was the debate on the escape of Pieter Menten, accused of war crimes. In all such cases, the broadcasting organisation with transmission time that day puts it at the disposal of NOS.

Summaries Summaries are made of important but less newsworthy debates. Summaries are always made of the debates after the Speech from the Throne (the Queen's speech, announcing the government's plans for the following year). These are broadcast before and after the evening programme (about 6.15 p.m. and 11.00 p.m.). Sometimes if the debate on the last day continues, the debates are picked up live because usually the end is the most exciting part: the last replies, voting on motions, etc.

Flashes There are sometimes news flashes of a debate, sometimes interviews during and after debates. For NOS's parliamentary magazine on Tuesdays, Wednesdays and Thursdays, Parliament is conveniently in session. The current affairs programmes of the broadcasting organisations can also make use of this facility.

During the first years parliamentary transmissions undoubtedly worked against the established parties. To many viewers Parliament looked like a badly managed boarding school with a great many pupils who did not show up or, if present, displayed so little interest in what was going on that they read newspapers or even fell asleep, some being so impertinent as to continually interrupt the teacher. On top of that many spoke a language an ordinary person could hardly understand. The transmission strengthened the feelings of disquiet about the existing parties. However, this was not a permanent feature. Public understanding of parliamentary proceedings has increased with the years, though some disquiet remains. Empty benches still irritate but less than in the past because live transmission being of great importance, practically all members are present. But when during the Menten debate the Minister of Justice was sharply attacked, many viewers asked why he alone had to face the attack and why the Prime Minister or one of his colleagues was not present. Those with knowledge of state affairs know that the Prime Minister's presence would indicate the possibility of a crisis and the necessity to ask for a vote of confidence. But some viewers give pity or sympathy for the lonely man behind the government's table, irrespective of what he says or has done.

In general parliamentary transmissions have stimulated interest in and understanding of Parliament. The live transmissions have a relatively high audience rating. Those viewers who reacted furiously when their beloved film series was cancelled because of the Menten debate, were rather contradicted by the ratings, which were higher than for the film series. Summaries attract fewer viewers but about 10 per cent stay viewing deep into the night after the switchover to live transmission. The parliamentary magazine usually attracts 6 to 10 per cent of the audience and is highly appreciated by those interested in politics.

Without being chauvinistic, it must be said that parliamentary broadcasting in Holland seems to have found the ideal formula: rather scarce live broadcasts, only when a great following is expected, with summaries of important debates and news flashes for daily business.

Less need be said about party political broadcasts and ministerial broadcasts, about which Mrs Wyndham Goldie[6] writes so authoritatively, because they were and are of less importance for Holland than Britain. Party political broadcasts started in the middle of the 1960s, one ten-minute broadcast every week except in the summer. Every party, irrespective of its size, gets the same number of transmissions, the Labour Party with fifty-three seats getting no more than a one-man party. (There are now eleven parties represented in Parliament: 53 Socialists, 49 Christian Democrats, 28 Conservatives, 8 Liberals, 3 Radicals, 3 Fundamentalists, 2 Communists, 1 Pacifist-Socialist, 1 Social Democrat, 1 Farmer and 1 Fundamentalist of another type.) The ratings are extremely low and the influence nil.

During election time every party that puts up candidates in all districts (during the last elections, eighteen) receives the same amount of transmission time. The problem was solved by transmitting most of them at the end of the day's programmes so that nobody would be disturbed, who did not want to watch. It must be added that the broadcasting organisations and the NOS, during election time, organise numerous debates and interview politicians whenever they deem necessary. One Dutch student received his degree for a dissertation on party political broadcasts the conclusion of which was that it was in the interest of political parties to abolish them. There are people who, without research, come to the same conclusion. Party broadcasts are important only for the smaller parties.

The Prime Minister can ask for a *ministerial broadcast.* He rarely does. In 1970 the Prime Minister asked time to explain why the government increased the NATO contribution by 150 million guilders. He was widely criticised because the occasion did not merit it. During the oil crisis the Prime Minister went on the air to explain why the old times would never recur. That is all. But why should he do more? By agreement with the broadcasting organisations he is interviewed every Friday night after the Cabinet meeting by one of the interviewers of the broadcasting organisation with transmission time that night.

Party conferences are not transmitted live in Holland. They are dealt with in the news and current affairs programmes of the broadcasting organisations.

Some Loopholes

Television in Holland was and is the 'Athenian "agora" where the political contenders are to be heard and where the citizens' decisions are formed' as the American National Committee for an Effective Congress stated in 1967. But did it and does it meet that other democratic criterion, perhaps a more pragmatic test for the level of freedom in society: how much freedom there is to criticise its most sacred institutions?[7]

Television used that freedom in the 1960s, asking old and new questions, shedding light on old and new problems, giving a free flow to old and new ideas, thus setting the agenda for public debate. It could exercise that tremendous influence because society was already moving. The old order disappeared and gave way to a more daring and dynamic society. But because the broadcasting system itself was a part of the old order, it undermined its own position making itself obsolete for the future. This was made possible by the deficiences, the contradictions and the loopholes of the Broadcasting Act, drafted after commercial television had been rejected in 1965 and passed in 1967. At that time the Act was seen as if it were a complete victory for the broadcasting organisations – and strangely enough was seen by them as such – but it was a Pyrrhic victory. In fact, it was an unworkable compromise between the defenders of the broadcasting organisations and business interests (it introduced advertising, and made steps towards a more national system by creating and defining the NOS).

Besides the provisions already mentioned and the re-defining of the qualifications for getting transmission time the Act licensed a new body – STER, the Advertising Foundation, to transmit commercials daily except on Sundays, Christmas, etc., in blocks before and after the news at 7.00 p.m., 8.00 p.m. and 9.30 p.m. to a total of 180 minutes a week. The Act also made provision for improving television income. There are two sources: first a licence fee for radio and television with increases subject to Parliamentary approval (as in all countries, Parliament is very reluctant to increase it); secondly, STER generates revenue, amounting to something more than a quarter of the total income of television. Until 1970, 40 per cent was paid to the press as compensation for the loss of advertising revenue. This compensation was later reduced and came to an end on 1 January 1977.

The Act states that the Minister of Culture, Recreation and Social Work is in charge of general policy. He is advised by a Broadcasting Council. Day-to-day supervision is carried out by a Government Commissioner who, however, is not allowed to attend meetings of programme bodies of the NOS so as to avoid government interference with the contents of the programme. The Minister, bound of course by certain rules, has to approve the distribution of transmission time. He may allocate transmission time, in addition to broadcasting organisations, to the churches for church services, to political parties and to institutions which aim at 'satisfying cultural, religious or spiritual needs which are not otherwise adequately provided for'. The importance of this clause should not be exaggerated. It relates to organisations such as the Seventh Day Adventists, Moral Rearmament, etc., which get five or ten minutes every four or eight weeks. Most lose their transmission time after a period. Problems arise, however, from other sections of the law.

The Act introduced 'candidate' organisations, that is, broadcasting organisations which fulfil the requirements (non-profit-making, etc.) and are in the process of building up their membership. Under the Royal Decree it was ruled that membership must be at least 15,000 (later raised to 40,000) to get one hour of transmission a week or a whole night a month. Within two years the candidate organisation must have 100,000 members, otherwise it loses its transmission time.

The transmission time, after deducting time for NOS, churches, political parties, etc., is divided between three categories of broadcasting organisations: (A) organisations with 400,000 or more members; (B) organisations with more than 250,000 and less than 400,000 members; and (C) organisations with 100,000 but less than 250,000 members. It is divided in proportion of 5 to 3 to 1, the minimum allocation being 2½ hours a week for an organisation falling in the (C) category. Members are those who subscribe to the radio and television guide of any broadcasting organisation (only these are allowed to publish the weekly schedules; newspapers are permitted to publish only a brief statement of the daily schedules) and so-called 'paying members' who pay a certain sum without having a subscription to the television guide.

The new Act constituted a single body for radio and television, NOS, with among other things the following tasks: co-ordination of television programmes, providing and operating radio and television studios and all other technical facilities, establishing contact with foreign countries but also producing its own television programmes, designated as 'transmissions which are particularly suited for joint preparation' (news, sport, Eurovision, national events, etc.) and also 'programmes which serve as meeting places'. Because NOS does not have members, the Minister has to allocate transmission time to it: a minimum of 25 per cent and a maximum of 40 per cent. It is now 26 per cent; in 1967 it was 36 per cent.

The most important body is the Executive, consisting of thirty members: a Chairman, seven members nominated by the Crown, seven members of cultural organisations such as the Netherlands Sports Federation, the Federation of Artists, the Consumers' League, etc., and fifteen members of the broadcasting organisations.

The complex organisation of broadcasting has led to a growth of committees, sub-committees and various bodies and working groups for every programme type such as entertainment, drama, current affairs, etc. To give two examples of the difficulties involved. First the allocation of transmission time: this is not only a question of total time but also of what broadcasting organisation receives which day of the week. Problems are solved, mostly after very lengthy discussions, by a rotation system: the organisation which has Monday evening one year on one channel, will get Friday evening next year, and so on. Another problem arises from the so-called claim system. Every broadcasting organisation has to register a 'claim' at the NOS claim bureau if it has an interest in a certain project, subject or foreign programme. The current affairs programme which wants to make a given film report must deposit a 'claim'. The first to register its claim, may make the report. Of course there are limits. A claim cannot override topicality and it cannot prevent current affairs programmes featuring the same subject in different ways.

The combination of the open door policy, the absolute necessity to hang on to members, the prominent position of television guides and the dual character of the NOS have led to many problems and ultimately to the decline of Dutch televiaion.

The Decline

In 1967 the neutral broadcasting organisation AVRO, losing members and afraid of slipping under the crucial membership limit of 400,000, suddenly merged with an illustrated weekly that had always succeeded in getting hold of the details of radio and television programmes but feared to lose this privilege through legal action taken by the broadcasting organisations. The solution was quite simple: the fee was automatically enclosed in the subscription for the magazine, which remained unchanged if the subscriber stated he did not object. At a stroke AVRO gained 400,000 members, making it by far the largest organisation. In legal terms, the action was dicey but a weak minister did not dare to interfere. The *coup* proved how unsound the system actually is. But as the law did not differentiate between 400,000 and 800,000 members and as AVRO hardly changed its programme, there were no immediate consequences.

This was not the only contradiction in the law. There was built-in conflict between the NOS and the broadcasting organisations, the NOS being the co-operative body but at the same time a competitor because it produces programmes. Years were spent in discussing what exactly was meant by the 'meeting programmes' which the NOS had to produce. There was continuous conflict on the question of whether someone could be interviewed in the NOS news programme and for how long so as not to obstruct the current affairs programme of the broadcasting organisations. There were constant quarrels in the NOS Executive, the representatives of the broadcasting organisations trying to restrict the independence of NOS programme-makers, objecting especially to its more popular programmes like film series, and trying to push back the total transmission time of NOS.

The system was undermined even further with the advent of new broadcasting organisations. The first was the EO, an organisation of religious fundamentalists who found the existing Protestant organisation too modern. It knows but one task: to propagate the message of the Gospel. Its audience ratings are very low but it has the support of a firm group of 100,000 paying members, amongst whom is a small number of Catholics opposed to changes within the Catholic church. EO fights against drugs, abortion, homosexuality, the World Council of Churches, strikes and left-wing critics of South Africa. It returned completely to the old pattern: opponents are never given the opportunity to express their opinions.

But the most important event was the foundation of TROS. It originated from a pirate transmitter that had produced television from an artificial island off the Dutch coast. It avoided all political or controversial programmes and avoided also, with the aid of a government afraid to take unpopular measures, its legal obligation to broadcast a 'comprehensive' programme by counting wild life films and leisure time programmes as 'information'. It received strong support from the newspaper *Telegraaf* (comparable to the German *Bild*) which took care of the initial losses of the TROS programme guide and of the recruitment of members.

TROS had but one aim: to enlist members. No one expressed the philosophy of this new offspring better than its Chairman: 'The essence is to give the people the programmes they want to see. So, no politics. I say to the viewers: we are here for you, not for ourselves. The viewer is the boss.' To give another example of TROS philosophy: the credits of one of its programmes once read: 'editor – the Dutch people'. From the start TROS had excellent contacts with the record industry. Because it applied very few qualitative standards, this industry could 'plug' any artist. Unauthorised advertising was rife and acted against only when it was too late. Critics fulminated vehemently against the quality of the programmes but this only strengthened TROS's popularity, becoming the favourite of all those who did not want to hear about politics, who were frustrated by the new developments, who detested nakedness but laughed heartily at indecent jokes and who were fed up with all those 'intellectuals' who 'dominated' the screen. TROS excluded the world from the living room, it did not ask for the viewer's interest nor did it appeal to his intellect. It was no longer necessary to switch over to avoid the world and possible feelings of guilt, for the viewer can avoid all that by watching TROS. It became the ideal broadcasting organisation for Wright Mills' man 'who loses the desire to be independent', Riesman's 'other-directed man' and Fromm's 'empty-vessel to be successful'. TROS not only attracted viewers and members among the working class for which daily work is so boring that in the evenings they want only to sit back with beer and peanuts but it attracted also members among the young executive class who did not want to be distracted from the pursuit of their careers by the problems of the world.

This was the basis of the phenomenal growth of TROS. In 1971 it had passed the 250,000 limit, in 1974 it had reached the 400,000 limit, and is now (excluding the AVRO *coup*) by far the largest broadcasting organisation. Commercial insight helped to achieve this by marketing a small and relatively inexpensive television guide using the American format. TROS's political position is to brainwash the viewer with the thought that politics are dirty, to speculate on his prejudices and to confirm the viewer in his attitudes. Potentially, TROS was right-wing from the start. But this did not show up before its position had become unassailable. And it had to show its true face when later a more vigilant minister insisted that TROS transmitted a current affairs programme.

It would be hard to imagine a greater contrast than between EO and TROS. The former preaches the Gospel, the latter the gospel of bread and circuses. But the success of both stems from the same cause: the uneasiness with the new world. What had been proper for years suddenly seemed bad. What had been forbidden for years, suddenly seemed proper. The group one had been born into was not the same any more and had lost its hold on the individual. Respected leaders of the past proved to be fallible people who had either been shunted aside or, worse, no longer had any answers. The climate was ideal for what has come to be called 'cognitive dissonance'.[8] This dissonance was especially blamed on television. Television had introduced all this misery into the living room, it had shaken all certainties. Therefore, television's fate had to be that of the messenger in classic times who was decapitated for having brought bad news.

EO made television more palatable by offering its viewers a return to the old certainties. TROS did it by denying the problems. It offered the viewers the opportunity to turn away from information that would increase their feelings of insecurity or guilt. It speculated on a mood which can best be described as follows: 'You can't understand it all anyhow and you can't change it anyway, so better leave it to others.' TROS's certainty is the taste of the masses. The similarities between EO and TROS were characterised strikingly by a cabaretier who called EO 'God's own TROS'.

All this made the broadcasting system lose its dynamics. It could not hold its own against a new broadcasting organisation that was the very negation of the broadcasting system based as it was upon the conception of giving broadcasting time to groups that had something to say. It did not know how to react to an organisation that had nothing to say but nevertheless became a great success.

In mass communication the principle that nothing breeds like success is very strong. Almost automatically other broadcasting organisations try to copy a successful rival using his weapons. The fear of the consequences of TROS's success had a paralysing effect on television in the 1970s.

'Trossification'

Intellectuals even invented a new word, 'Trossification', to describe the phenomenon of making everything fit the lowest presumed public common denominator. But the discussion of this subject, mainly among people without great knowledge of mass communication, obscured the issue more than illuminated it. The broadcasting organisations were blamed for paying too much attention to ratings, and to entertainment programmes, for directing their programmes to the whole of the public instead of to their own group. But that was not the crux of the problem. In all countries, attention is paid to ratings and entertainment and already in the 1960s the Dutch broadcasting organisations were looking beyond their own groups. The problem was the system itself. It compelled the broadcasting organisations to react to TROS's success. Feverishly, they tried to win the masses and at the same time to keep hold of their own members. The result was disastrous. Entertainment became boring and information weak.

The arrival of new organisations led to chaos in programming. It became increasingly difficult to accommodate all those entitled to broadcast, let alone to harmonise the broadcasting policies of all the organisations concerned. Even now, the end is not in sight. In 1976 a new organisation, Veronica, stemming from a pirate radio transmitter, applied for transmission time. The Minister refused, invoking the article of the Act which says that a broadcasting organisation has to satisfy cultural, religious or cultural needs. He was overruled by the Council of State who decided that the size of membership is a sufficient indication. Later on, Veronica applied for (C) status (100,000 members) but this was refused because it was established (every year the membership figures are inspected) that half of the membership had not paid the registration fee. The final arbitration is still to come. (The Council of State, consisting of elder statesmen, has to judge whether the government's decisions are according to the laws.)

The openness of the Dutch system led to anarchy, as 'regulated competition' became a 'free for all'. The administrators of the broadcasting organisations lacked a plan for the changed situation. Panicking, they all turned on NOS, the co-operative organisation which, in their view, had too much broadcasting time. Strange coalitions developed, such as between TROS and VARA – TROS because it opposed all collectiveness, the Socialists because they assumed apparently that all problems would be solved if everyone received an extra one or two hours of broadcasting time. The negative symptoms of the Dutch system became even more evident. Competition for members was fought out with cheap and attractive television guides, with special offers, holiday trips, roving disc-jockeys and seductive hostesses. When VARA was in danger of falling below the 400,000 limit, its programme-makers went out into the streets to offer red roses to passers-by.

All this was bound to have a paralysing effect on the programmes. Does it make any sense to exhaust oneself to produce good programmes when a good colour print of the television guide seemed to be more important? Does it make any sense to make controversial programmes when the only result is to drive the public into the hands of TROS?

One broadcasting organisation totally disregarded that problem: VPRO. It continued to make high quality programmes and did not shun controversy. It introduced a new style of entertainment, mocking the old and smooth forms. It produced a satirical programme not at all in the style of the old 'TWTWTW', far less political and moralistic, but socially motivated and of a consistently high quality. Sometimes it devoted a whole night to one subject. It could disregard the problem because it was and wanted to remain a small organisation. As soon as it was in danger of falling under the 100,000 limit, there were always enough people at hand to keep it on the air.

But the big broadcasting organisations felt TROS breathing down their necks, felt themselves slipping down the slope. They did not lower their programme standards purposely in order to take the wind out of TROS's sails. The quality dropped because the programme-makers were dragged along in the general climate of depression and insecurity. Of course, the mood of the 1970s was quite different from that of the 1960s – in most countries television has become less exciting. But the decline in Holland was steeper than in most countries and also went deeper in television than in other spheres. Politics in Holland was less exciting in the 1970s than in the 1960s but at least it was still exciting, alive and full of spirit.

The broadcasting organisations did not know what to do. Did they have to compete with entertainment and quizzes to keep sufficient members or did they have to accentuate their own specific differences to prevent their members joining TROS? This question led to an identity crisis in several organisations. VARA was torn apart by bitter personal conflicts between those who believed that it should be more socialist and those who believed that it should be socialist but at the same time appeal to a larger audience. The Catholic broadcasting organisation, on its fiftieth anniversary in 1975, published a booklet with vague articles on the position of the KRO in a changing world. The Protestant organisation completely kissed away the 1960s in a volume of reminiscences. All of this discussion on old and new identities was doomed to remain non-productive. The problem had nothing to do with the broadcasting organisation as such but with the broadcasting system.

The Dutch system seems to be the complete opposite of the American. But the definition of the American system in the British Annan report on the future of broadcasting applies to the Dutch system too:

> Competition in excellence is admirable. But competition solely to gain audiences has less desirable effects. Broadcasting in the United States [*read* Holland] strongly suggests two conclusions. The first is that competition between three [*read* at least seven] broadcasting organisations narrows the range of programmes. The second is that competition for the same range of finance [*read* members] lowers programming standards so as to satisfy the lowest common denominator.[9]

That is what has happened in Holland during the 1970s. Virtually unrestricted competition has forced the broadcasting organisations to use the same means and the same methods to maintain themselves. One quiz led to another, one Top Ten to the next Top Twenty. In this battle, programme standards inevitably suffered. Informative programmes were pushed into the background. Their numbers were not actually reduced – although the situation is less favourable than is usually claimed – but they were practically all scheduled at unfavourable times. There are few countries where so few informative programmes are scheduled in prime time. The information too has changed in character. Informative programmes in the 1960s took the initiative, focusing on internal and external dialogue. Information in the 1970s has been defensive, focused on maintaining the group. Programmes are designed to give their own supporters just enough to prevent them from running away and but not enough to irritate outsiders. Television has completely lost its agenda-setting function. It has fallen behind the printing press, which has opened up all the new issues of recent years: the Lockheed affair, the Menten affair and its ramifications in the post-war period. It was the printing press which exposed the power structures and confronted the politicians with their faulty decisions. Television lost its autonomous function. It became more and more subordinated to the politicians, did not dare any longer to take an adversary stance if this stance disagreed with that adopted by its own group or might irritate too large a section of the audience. In this process it lost its watch-dog function too. There was a growing affinity between the new power elite – more open, more democratic, more tolerant than the old power elite but still an elite – and the television journalists. Their socio-cultural proximity became stronger. Interaction reduced the distance between them. It may be typical that the monthly parliamentary programme of the Socialist broadcasting organisation is called 'The Hague Circles'.

Interviewing in the current affairs programmes of the broadcasting organisations has changed in character. They now prefer to interview their own people and give them a less difficult time than before. Sharp questions are directed only at adversaries. Interviews seem to have become more friendly, more civilised, but in fact bias has increased. Unlike the 1960s, producers' opinions have disappeared more into the background although the Dutch system seemed to meet the requirements of the Annan report perfectly: 'Public affairs programmes should be clearly distinguished from news programmes, and programmes which reflect strongly committed views should be labelled and, over the course of time, balanced by other expressions of opinion.' They were distinguished, they are labelled by the name of the broadcasting organisation which transmits them and they are balanced by programmes of other organisations.

But television mainly limited itself to registration, and where the programmes were committed, the commitment was that of the group. In theory Dutch television met the criterion of democratic opportunity: there was and is much freedom to criticise its most sacred institutions. In practice, it has failed that test in the 1970s because it has not used the opportunity. It was bound to fail since the broadcasting system forced television into a straitjacket. The advantage was lost. The openness led not to democratisation but to the dictatorship of membership figures. The freedom encouraged conflicts between the organisations and NOS rather than co-operation. The advent of TROS led not to diversity and enrichment but to restriction and impoverishment. This does not mean to say that everything about the Dutch system is wrong. The straitjacket of membership figures is still preferable to that of the state. Freedom is still great compared to other countries. Attempts at direct influence by politicians occur less frequently in Holland than in Western Germany, let alone France or Italy. Parliamentary broadcasts have strengthened political consciousness. The parliamentary magazine contributes to political analysis. The current affairs programmes continue to offer the politicians the most important way of communicating with a modern voting public. If political interest in Holland is still considerable, this also is thanks to the 'forum' function of television.

Conclusion

The Dutch broadcasting system has performed well and sometimes excellently as a public service for the nation. It has kept television free of government interference and overt commercial exploitation. It guarantees a freedom of expression unheard of in most other countries. It assures free access in television to differently orientated groups, either religious or non-religious, political or non-political, conformist or non-conformist, left or right. Television played a major role in the 1960s in setting the agenda for public debate, stimulating freedom of expression, opening new horizons, boosting inventiveness by regulated competition. In doing so, it destroyed its own foundations, rooted as they were in the society television helped to change. The broadcasting system made itself obsolete. Giving differently orientated groups a right to mass communication changed into giving pressure groups free room for manipulation. A good marketing department became more important than a good public affairs department; the television guide became more important than the well-made programme. Programming standards were subordinated to the struggle for existence fought out by essentially commercial methods. It led to creeping commercialism, to cultural stagnation and political inertia. Television lost its leading role in public debate, registering what others did or said, leaving to the printing press the task of challenging or defending, also perhaps the right to publish and be damned. The solution for Holland does not lie with making television responsible to Parliament. The broadcasting system should rest on the principle of free organisation, with Parliament setting the rules within which the organisations have to work. However, television in Holland can only reach a new momentum by eradicating certain absurdities in the system, restricting differences and competition to those spheres in which they really count. It can only be done by encroaching somewhat on the autonomy of the broadcasting organisations.

A new television authority should have – by law – the authority to arrange the programming plan for the whole of Dutch television, stipulating what kind of programmes should be transmitted how often and when, and to produce all programmes which bear no direct relationship to the various constituencies of the country – films, series, quizzes, most entertainment programmes. By giving – again, by law – the broadcasting organisations the right to nominate the Board of Directors (apart from the Director General) even in these areas differences in outlook can be respected. This authority should be answerable to a television parliament, consisting half of representatives of the broadcasting organisations, including those of the workers and employees, and half of representatives of cultural, political and other organisations nominated by the Crown.

The broadcasting organisations should produce on the basis of the programme scheme those programmes in which their own opinion and outlook play a dominant role: current affairs, documentaries, drama and some entertainment programmes. The programmes of the television authority could be transmitted under the name of the broadcasting organisation of the day except in those cases where that organisation does not want to accept the responsibility. This would not only make effective programming possible, it would also restore the original idea of the Dutch system: giving a free voice to different opinions and competition on the basis of this different orientation. It would eradicate its excesses: commercialisation, chaos in programming, competition between programmes that have nothing to do with differences in ideology, leading to the lowering of programme standards. It would preserve and strengthen the great achievements of the Dutch system: freedom of opinion and free access for all the various groups in society. It would free the public affairs people from constant pressure and stimulate discussion and enquiry.

I am not for bias, for manipulating, for constantly disseminating group philosophies. I am for fair treatment, for taking into account more than one view, for respecting the foundations of a society. But I also strongly believe in commitment, in the right to give one's own opinion, in a pluriform society as well as in a pluriform television, where the balance is more in the whole schedule than in a single programme, in the autonomy of the various sectors which make up our society. These need to be safeguarded at all costs.

7 Some Conclusions

Anthony Smith

What stands out from the preceding essays is the remarkable way in which television has developed along similar lines since the 1950s in so many different countries. In each decade the broadcasting systems and professions have been obliged to respond to fundamentally the same set of pressures and demands from the outside world. The norms and practices of television became set in the early 1970s when it seemed to have completed its exploration of the 'genres' and formats to which its technology seemed peculiarly suited. At the same moment television had become organisationally mature, its career patterns fairly clear to all those passing through them. It was no longer the young man's medium which it had been in the heady days of 1968. Its faces were more lined; its hands hardened; it had acquired its own history and mythology. Within the broadcasting professions much of the 'mystery' is shared among practitioners everywhere although the tensions they experience in their own societies give a national complexion to their transmitted work.

In the 1960s television had seemed for a moment to escape from all its bonds and become a free and international medium, operated by an almost autonomous profession *despite* its legal and constitutional background. The most important change which appears to have taken place since then is the realisation everywhere that the practices of television will inevitably and necessarily be subjected to political scrutiny and politically

imposed change. The genie has been put back in the bottle. In all
of the countries written about in this book there has been an
obvious taking stock of the supposed freedoms which reached
their peak in about 1970; the growth of terrorism has been an
important source of a new sobriety about the social impact of
television, certainly in Germany, Italy, Sweden and Britain. The
fear of unemployment and economic stagnation has made many
more think again about the mere level of seriousness with which
television should deal with affairs of state. All of the essays in this
book bring out the sense of bafflement rather than disillusionment
which is affecting television, the sense that, even where it has
equal *rights* with the printed press, freedom of expression in
television is far more difficult to locate than was supposed before.
In other words, television is trying to change the primary analogies
which have surrounded the evolution of its journalistic content.
The privileges of the fourth estate are as desirable in 1980 as in
1960, but where they appear to have been achieved (Sweden,
Holland) they are undermined by other pressures which bear
down upon the broadcasters, pressures from media researchers,
from groups of viewers, from Parliaments, from the press itself.
The television world has become the object of much telling
criticism and finds that it has acquired a role and status in society
which makes the very privileges of journalistic freedom less valid,
less *à propos* to the actual task of the era.

Reith, the founding Director General of the BBC, used to
describe its status as that of 'an organisation within the
constitution', and by this he implied that, despite its independence
(its condition of not being a department of state), it took a
protective view of society and its institutions. Britain has always
improvised its constitution and to be 'inside' it can only mean that
broadcasting discerns from time to time those practices and
institutions which comprise the settled external order which it
deems it its duty not to disturb. Reith, in other words, saw to it
that the BBC grew up inside the world of power, its greatest
moments of independence being those at which it could operate a
brokerage within that world. It helped to shape the political
culture of the society, and presented its great audience with an
image of that culture, held up as an icon to be revered.
Broadcasting in Britain has continued to perform this function but
in a vastly changed set of political circumstances. Trade unions are

also today 'inside the constitution' in most respects, and so are a much larger number and variety of groups and institutions: it is among all of these that the broadcasters now minister the sacrament of public communication. It is easier today to define the 'constitution' by reference to those not inside it: the National Front is not, nor the Communist Party, nor the Scientologists, nor the IRA, nor the paedophiles, nor those who seek to legalise LSD and cannabis. Any of these groups could theoretically force their way into the arena of plausibility, within which the broadcasters' law of impartiality operates, but until they do so, they remain untouchables, beyond the law, and may be addressed only in terms of disdain. They must be 'distanced' as they speak. Broadcasting retains taboos even in the most open of societies, and, indeed, it is possible to feel that broadcasting, in all the societies this book has dealt with, has now become the main fashioner and communicator of the prevailing taboos.

We have seen how rapidly society can inject a new area of taboo into broadcast content. Perhaps the response of German television to the great reaction against terrorism which took place in 1977 is an example, or the treatment of politicians by British broadcasting after the great row of 'Yesterday's Men' or after the wave of television satire had spent itself in the mid-1960s. One has the feeling that in each society boundary walls are constantly being erected as a result of the interactions between the practical professional world of broadcasting and the world of politics. The politicians patrol the perimeters; occasionally an escapee is captured or shot, to concentrate the minds of those behind the walls upon their proper task. In France many of the producers who showed their hand in 1968 have never been readmitted to television. We have seen, in the case of Holland, how difficult it is for any group in society to retain its desired taboos if it cannot express this desire in television; broadcasting has become the essential means for asserting, reinforcing, the perimeter values of a society, be they political, moral, economic.

Societies have gone about the task of institutionalising this function in very different ways, and sometimes the differences help to point up the taboos and values themselves. In Britain, for instance, it is felt that cultural activity has to take place within a private depoliticised sphere – utterly different from the position in France or Italy, where art is almost acknowledged to be politics carried on by other means. In Britain it is felt that politics must be kept out of the control of broadcasting by all means; the very thought that groups of politicians could occupy executive roles over broadcasting is a source of general horror; there exists in Britain an acceptably neutral territory on which cultural institutions may be built. Not so in much of Europe, where political and cultural traditions are very different, and where a visible and collective political sanction (in the case of Italy and Germany) is the prerequisite for the construction of any stable institution at all in the cultural sphere; in other cases, such as France, the government has retained the power of appointing and dismissing all of the seven Director Generals within an internally competitive system, so deep-seated is the belief that without an umbilical cord to government, broadcasting will inevitably construct links of a political kind with opposition.

The 1970s have not, therefore, finally settled the question of the political locus of television, and most countries now have accepted that there will be continuing debate on this question, at least as long as television messages occupy a scarce natural resource in the course of transmission.

The fact that this discussion continues vexedly into the future is taken no longer, as it once was, as a sign of political immaturity. There is, in all political contexts, a real problem arising from the pursuit of independence, from the attempt by broadcasters and politicians to legitimise the function of public information through the electro-magnetic spectrum. The countries we have examined have all chosen one or a combination of various possible points of sovereignty from which the operations of television and radio journalism can be validated: the state can itself supply the location of sovereignty, or can create a market-place in which free and competitive transactions can take place, or can establish self-governing institutions operating through a kind of state-founded autogestion. In the 1970s the countries of Europe have refined their techniques in broadcasting management, despite frequent collapses, and have come more clearly to recognise the narrowness of choice available and the implications of each. All of the countries concerned have learned that none of their current attitudes is anything more than an interim or improvised response to the problem. Public service broadcasting systems may well be partly or completely commercial by the end of the century; the financial support of all existing systems may change in any or all of the countries concerned. At least in the difficult experiences which have followed the rise of television to a position of dominance in political information, national administrations have realised that no system is sacred in itself. In a way the total monopoly of a country like France can be supported by people with similar social and cultural attitudes to Italians supporting the complete abolition of monopoly and the freeing of the air to all comers. The very flexibility which has crept into national discussions in the 1970s is a kind of progress, a kind of professionalisation of the discussion of policy.

There is another major strand which must be teased out of the discussion: in each society a set of broadcasting professions has now emerged which operate according to standards and ideals that are to a great extent international. Television producers and reporters, linguistic problems excluded, can work equally well in any society with adequate technical resources. The emergence of general professional values helps to concentrate the minds of makers of policy on the same issues in different societies. The flexibility just referred to in the discussion of policy is partly the result of this growing internationalisation of the professions. To some extent this is reinforced by the growth of co-production and co-financing of a certain segment of television output between countries.

One may re-state the problem of broadcasting governance in the late twentieth century, in fact, as that of a profession in search of legitimacy, where previously it had been that of a medium in search of institutional independence. Today independence as such emerges partly from the professional business of broadcasting; there is a new partner in the debate, who was absent for the most part in the 1950s and the early 1960s. National enquiries into broadcasting today have to start with the *a priori* existence of programmes and programme-makers. It is this fact which helps to diminish the tensions which arise from social fears about the effects of broadcasting. It is an activity which no one is going to *stop*; the debate about its attitudes, methods, incentives, occupies a similar position to the debate about the role of educators in society and their institutions and legitimacy. The argument about broadcasting effects, which is referred to in several of these chapters is defused today, not merely because its conclusions are thought to be non-definitive, but also because the medium itself and its professions are no longer under threat, in any primary sense.

This is not a very pessimistic book. None of the writers feels that the events which it describes are tantamount to disaster in terms of journalistic freedom. Television is not slipping back into a generalised subservience. Politicians are, if anything, still improving in their realisation that the medium of television must be allowed to proceed with its various journalistic tasks. However, there is a danger that the re-thinking which has characterised the years since 1970, and which has led to reorganisation of parts of broadcasting internally and externally, will slip imperceptibly into another period of self-censorship and damaging restraint. The genre of investigative radio and television journalism is not being permitted to develop in very many societies. Interviewing, anxious to establish professional norms, has tended to be less rigorous in a period in which television journalists feel themselves on the defensive. Above all, the subtle powers which reside in broadcasting authorities to push and hold back the careers of individual journalists are widely available for the purposes of adding a covert set of controls to the statutory ones.

What one hopes the reader will carry away is the realisation that behind the complex questions of broadcasting governance lies the shaping of the main sources of political information in all the societies of Europe. If there is any overriding criterion which should be applied it must be to enquire whether the viewer is being helped towards a complete citizenship through the medium of television. He requires a coherent and permanent flow of images of (and information about) those contending for power and holding it; he needs to have access to the main lines of the major arguments of his time in the field of social administration and foreign policy. He needs to know that a group of professionally trained but not tightly knit or inward-looking journalists are uninhibitedly saying whatever they know and that simultaneously there is scope for organised groups to offer wholly new conceptions of the society and the directions it is taking. In no single country considered in this book can it be said that all of these aids to citizenship are yet provided by television, though it has greatly improved in comparison with the past. There is a danger that the evolution of the forms and skills of television may stand still during the prolonged period of doubt through which we are currently passing. Doubts must not be permitted to become excuses.

Notes and References

Chapter 1: Britain

1. *Report of the Committee on the Future of Broadcasting,* Cmnd. 6753 (London: HMSO, 1977).

2. Ibid., para 4.31, p. 39.

3. The quotation with which Lewis Namier begins his classic work, *The Structure of Politics at the Accession of George III* (London: Macmillan, 1929, 1970) p. 1.

4. For this see *BBC Handbook 1978* (London: BBC Publications) and *Television & Radio, 1978* (London: IBA).

5. 'Licence and Agreement', Treasury Minute dated 7 July 1969, para 13(2).

6. Ibid., para 13(4).

7. There are plans to publish more of the proceedings at future refranchisings.

8. Three examples are Lord Simon of Wythenshawe, *The BBC from Within* (London: Gollancz, 1953); Charles Stuart (ed.), *The Reith Diaries* (London: Collins, 1975) and Lord Hill of Luton, *Behind the Screen* (London: Sidgwick & Jackson, 1974).

9. In a Royal Society of Arts Lecture, reprinted in the *Listener,* 17 Jan 1974.

10. For a detailed analysis of the literature of the 1926 crisis, see Michael Tracey, *The Production of Political Television* (London: Routledge and Kegan Paul, 1977) pp. 142–56.

11. *Facing the Nation – Television and Politics 1933–76* (London: Bodley Head, 1977).

12. Ibid., p. 328.

13. Circulating internally since 1969.

14. Published in April 1972.

15. The texts of both are published as Appendixes to Goldie, *Facing the Nation.*

16. See, in particular, Jay Blumler and Michael Gurevitch, *The Challenge of Election Broadcasting* (University of Leeds Press, 1978) for a detailed analysis (and comprehensive set of proposed reforms) to the whole of election coverage in British television, including the advocacy element.

17. For a description of the evolution of relations between pressure groups and media at a local level in Britain, see David Murphy, *The Silent Watchdog – the press in local politics* (London: Constable, 1976).

18. 'Principles and Practice in News and Current Affairs', para 9 (c) – quoted in Anthony Smith, *British Broadcasting: a book of documents* (Newton Abbot: David & Charles, 1973).

19. *Report of the Committee on the Future of Broadcasting,* para 28.7, p. 435.

20. Ibid., para 17.57, p. 287.

21. For a detailed account of this development in the 1969–72 period see Anthony Smith, 'Television Coverage of Northern Ireland', *Index on Censorship,* vol. 1, no. 2 (1972).

22. Professor Tom Burns, *The BBC* (London: Macmillan, 1977) p. 296.

23. Ibid.

Chapter 2: France

1. Jean Montaldo, *Tous Coupables* (Paris: Albin Michel, 1974) p. 39.

2. *Le Monde,* 28–29 June 1959.

3. *Le Monde,* 4 Jan 1977.

4. *L'Année Politique,* 1972, p. 406.

5. J. Thibau, *La Télévision, le Pouvoir et l'Argent* (Paris: Calmann Lévy, 1973) pp. 31–3.

6. *Journal Officiel,* AN 16 June 1972.

7. *Le Monde,* 3 Jan 1975.

8. *Le Monde,* 4 Jan 1977.

9. *Correspondance de la Presse,* 28 Sept 1976.

10. The PTT had made some experimental broadcasts before 1939, but there were then only a few hundred receivers.

11. F. O. Giesbert, *François Mitterrand* (Paris: Le Seuil, 1977) p. 103.

12. *Le Monde,* 6 Feb 1958. See also for the whole of this period, Montaldo, *Tous Coupables.*

13. Thus, in 1963, the Communist group in the Senate submitted proposals for a law to govern the RTF, which proposed the creation of a supervisory committee on information, four of whose five members were to be appointed by the Authorities. See Montaldo, ibid., p. 140.

14. *Journal Officiel,* AN session of 26 May 1964.

15. One can find a very complete account of this period in Ruth Thomas, *Broadcasting and Democracy in France* (Bradford University Press, 1976). See also Jacques Thibau, *Une Télévision pour tous les Français* (Paris: Le Seuil, 1970).

16. *Journal Officiel,* AN Debates 30 April 1965.

17. *La Nation,* 5 Jan 1966.

18. *Notre République,* 22 Dec 1967.

19. Jean Diwo, *Si Vous Avez Manqué le Début* (Paris: Albin Michel, 1976) p. 14.

20. Quoted in Jean Diwo, ibid., pp. 161–2.

21. Denise Bombardier, *La Voix de la France* (Paris: Laffont, 1975) p. 89.

22. *Rapport de la Commission d'étude du statut de L'ORTF* (Paris: Documentation Française, 1970).

23. *Journal Officiel,* AN 16 June 1972.

24. Arthur Conte has made a picturesque and detailed description of the period when he was Chairman of the ORTF in *Hommes Libres* (Paris: Plon, 1973).

25. Jean Diwo, *Si Vous Avez Manqué le Début,* p.258.

26. Articles 12, 16, and 17 of the directives for TF 1 and A 2.

27. Jean Diwo, *Si Vous Avez Manqué le Début,* pp. 264–5. Jean Diwo's account has never been contradicted.

28. *Journal Officiel,* AN session of 18 Nov 1975.

29. F. O. Giesbert, *François Mitterand.*

30. *Lui,* April 1977.

31. M Elkabbach gave his version of this strange affair in an interview published in *Lui,* April 1977.

32. *Rapport d'information de la délégation parlementaire,* Sénat n 28 1976, pp. 12, 13.

33. Ibid.

34. Ibid.

35. *Le Monde,* 20 Feb 1977.

36. This influence of television on the organisation of debates provoked a recent incident. The independent Republicans withdrew their speakers in protest against the timetables which had been established in accordance with the demands of television (*Le Monde,* 27 April 1977).

37. All the same, it is worth noting that, in a recent poll conducted by SOFRES in June 1976, 39 per cent of the people declared their trust in

political news on television as against 23 per cent for radio and 18 per cent for the daily newspapers.

38. *Télé 7 Jours,* 29 Nov 1975.

39. A parliamentary report published in October 1977 tried to assess the effect of the 1974 reform on programme content (*Rapport Le Tac,* Assemblee Nationale, n 3131, annexe 49). According to this document, the percentage of current affairs programmes compared to the total output has increased from 29.2 per cent to 35.8 per cent. Documentary and artistic programmes dropped from 15.6 per cent to 12.1 per cent; fiction dropped from 29.3 per cent to 23.8 per cent, while games and variety programmes increased from 9.8 per cent to 14.9 per cent. During the first six months of 1977, series of American origin accounted for 3.6 per cent of programmes on TF 1, 5.4 per cent on Antenne 2 and 0.6 per cent on FR 3. As the Le Tac report emphasises, the television companies have developed low cost programmes such as games and variety programmes, to the detriment of fiction and documentaries which demand much greater human and financial commitment.

Chapter 3: Italy

1. See *L'Editore,* vol. 1, no. 2 (February 1978) p. 95.

2. Franco Cazzola, *Governo e opposizione nel Parlamento italiano* (Milan: Giuffré, 1974) p. 99.

3. Law 395 of 30 June 1910, quoted in Roberto Zaccaria, *Radiotelevisione e Costituzione* (Milan: Giuffré, 1977) pp. 19–20.

4. Law 1067 of 8 February 1923. See Zaccaria, ibid.

5. Law 103 was followed by an agreement between the Ministry of Posts and Telecommunications and RAI which was approved by Decree 425 of 11 August 1975. The first para describes the aims of the concession; para 28 sets out the sum which RAI has to pay to the Treasury and the Ministry of Posts in exchange for the concession; para 32 fixes the length of the concession at six years, renewable for a period not exceeding the same. Para 8 states that the licence fees to be paid by the owners of a radio and/or a television set plus advertising – not to exceed the 5 per cent of the transmission hours – constitute the RAI-TV's revenue. Every two years the Ministry of Posts, in co-operation with the Treasury, verifies the adequacy of the licence fee. RAI-TV may, however, ask for a revision of the fee before the two-year term expires. These texts may be found in *Il Diritto delle Radiodiffusioni e delle Telecomunicazion,* vol. 1 (1975) pp. 109–36 and vol. 2 (1975) pp. 329–63.

6. Royal Decree 2207. The previous company was URI (Unione Radio-fonica Italiana) which was the result of a merger between RADIOFONO and SIRAC, the first of which derived from the Marconi Group, the second from Western Electric. The creation of EIAR marks the exclusion of foreign interests in broadcasting.

7. Zaccaria, *Radiotelevisione,* pp. 23–5.

8. One of the first directors of EIAR was a rich industrialist who was subsequently appointed by the fascist regime to be the head of the 'Ente Radio Rurale', 'whose aim was to spread radio broadcasting into the countryside'. See Zaccaria, ibid., p. 28 and Philip V. Cannistraro, *La Fabbrica del Consenso* (Bari: Laterza, 1975) p. 237.

9. See on this question, Leo Valiani, *L'Avvento di De Gasperi* (Turin: De Silva, 1949) p. 23.

10. Constitutional Court, Decision 59, 6 July 1960, in *Gazzetta Ufficiale,* 174, 16 July 1960. See, in this matter, Art. 21 of the Constitution: 'Everyone has the right to express his own ideas, freely, in speech, in writing, and by any other means of dissemination'.

11. Constitutional Court, Decision 59, 6 July 1960. It is perhaps worth quoting Article 43 of the Constitution in full: 'In the public interest, the law can reserve or transfer to the state, to public bodies or to consumer groups, by expropriation or through the payment of a fee, certain undertakings or categories of the same which constitute essential public services, sources of energy or monopolies, which are of especial common interest.'

12. Apart from the period immediately after the Second World War, when all the parties of the 'Committee for National Liberation', from the Liberals to the Communists, joined to form a coalition government.

13. Raffaele Simone, 'RAI, il vuoto dietro le parole', in *La Repubblica,* 13 Sept 1977.

14. Francesco Alberoni, 'Risultati di un'indagine sperimentale sui contenuti dei principali mezzi di comunicazione di massa negli anni 1969–1970', Quaderni del Servizio Opinioni, 23, RAI-Radio-televisione Italiana, 1973. A careful study of this excellent enquiry allows us to perceive the full extent of the characteristics we have mentioned in the content of the programmes examined.

15. See Decree 180 of 26 January 1952 in *Gazzetta Ufficiale,* 82 (5 April 1952).

16. These bills foundered with the end of the legislature in 1972. For a description and critical analysis of these first proposals, see Roberto Giannone, 'Verso una riforma della RAI-TV', in *Politica del Diritto,* 3 (June 1971), pp. 357–81.

17. Decree 782 of 15 December 1972 in *Gazzetta Ufficiale,* 326 (18 Dec 1972).

18. Parliamentary records, Discussions in the Chamber of Deputies for

the session of 13 December 1972, 'Questions on the possible renewal of the agreement between the State and the RAI-TV'.

19. Published in *Il Diritto delle Radiodiffusioni e delle Tele-comunicazioni*, 1–2 (1973) pp. 135–314.

20. In order of appearance: Decree 796 of 20 December 1973 – *Gazzetta Ufficiale*, 327 (20 Dec 1973) and Decree 113 of 30 April 1974 – *Gazzetta Ufficiale*, 112 (30 April 1974).

21. Pulished in *Il Diritto. . .*, 1–2 (1974) pp. 251–64.

22. A useful and exhaustive synopsis of this proposal and those of the PCI, PSI and of the Regional administrations is to be found in *La Rocca*, 15 Nov 1974 (Assisi).

23. Decisions 225 and 226 were published in *Gazzetta Ufficiale*, 187 (17 July 1974).

24. Decree 603 of 30 November 1974 – *Gazzetta Ufficiale*, 313 (1 December 1974). It can also be found in *Il Diritto. . .*, 3 (1974) pp. 451–79.

25. 'Decrees become redundant right from the start if they are not converted into law within sixty days after their publication', Article 77 of the Italian Constitution.

26. Decree 3 of 22 January 1975 – *Gazzetta Ufficiale*, 20 (22 January 1975).

27. Parliamentary records, Chamber of deputies, 6th legislature, Bill 3448, February 1975 proposed by Messrs Piccoli (DC), Mariotti (PSI), Cariglia (PSDI) and Biasini (PRI), 'New Regulations governing Radio and Television broadcasting'.

28. See note 5 above.

29. This document, which has never been published, is part of the material collected for this chapter.

30. See the PCI proposals dated 20 March 1973 in *La Rocca*, 15 Nov 1974.

31. Zaccaria, *Radiotelevisione*, p. 73.

32. Ibid., p. 104.

33. Decision 225, *Gazzetta Ufficiale*, 187 (17 July 1974).

34. Zaccaria, *Radiotelevisione*, p. 127.

35. The quotation comes from Paolo Barile, 'Un monopolio riformato a metà', in *Problemi dell'Informazione*, vol. 1, 3 (1976) p. 362.

36. For the meetings of the Parliamentary Commission, see *Il Diritto. . .*, for 1976 and 1977. The figures for the meetings of the Board are drawn from a confidential interview.

37. Piero Pratesi, 'I Nuovi Signori della RAI', in *Problemi dell'Informazione*, vol. I, 1 (1976) p. 8.

38. Ibid., p. 8.

39. Marina Tartara, 'Ricostruire un'azienda', in *Problemi dell'Informazione*, vol. I, 3 (1976) p. 395.

40. See Law 103, Article 4, and *Documento di Ristrutturazione*, approved by the board of the RAI-TV on 22 November 1975 and published in *Il Diritto*. . . , I (1976) pp. 170 ff.

41. These documents are dated respectively 19 February 1976, 2 July 1976, 3 July 1976, and 11 November 1976. They are to be found in *Il Diritto*. . . , I (1976).

42. An expression which refers to a form of sharing which favours the parties in power. It was first used by C. Pedrazza–Gorlero. See the collective work, *La Nuova RAI-TV* (Bologna: Il Mulino, 1975) p. 32.

43. The list of names is published in *Corriere della Sera*, 9 August 1977.

44. *Corriere della Sera*, 19 July 1977.

45. *L'Unità*, 30 July 1977.

46. See *La Stampa*, 30 July 1977 and *La Repubblica*, 31 July 1977.

47. *L'Unità*, 2 Aug 1977.

48. *Corriere della Sera*, 4 Aug 1977.

49. *The Times*, 5 Aug 1977.

50. Constitutional Court, Decision 202 of 28 July 1976 – *Gazzetta Ufficiale*, 205 (4 Aug 1976).

51. See *Prima Comunicazione*, VI, 51 (February 1978) p. 73.

Chapter 4: Federal Republic of Germany

1. See, inter alia, the three speeches pronounced in 1975–76: 'Das demokratische Geschichtsbild', 'Dreissig Jahre nach dem Krieg' and 'Zum Mythos der deutschen Geschichte', in Walter Scheel, *Vom Recht des Anderen* (Thoughts about Freedom) (Düsseldorf: Econ, 1977) pp. 11–54. See also A. Grosser, 'Mitverantwortung für eine gemeinsame Zukunft' (Address in the Bundestag on the occasion of the Day of National Mourning, 1974) in *Wider den Strom* (Work for Enlightenment as a Policy for Freedom) (Munich: Dtv., 1976) pp. 11–22.

2. List 1958–67 in Georg Feil, *Zeitgeschichte im deutschen Fernsehen* (Osnabrück: Fromm, 1974) pp. 47–9.

3. Structural scheme and pictures in a Rororo-volume, Hamburg, 1977. Particularly stern criticism in W. Wenders, 'That's entertainment: Hitler', *Die Zeit*, 5 Aug 1977. Defence by J. Fest, 'Revision des Hitler-Bildes?', a leading article in *Frankfurter Allgemeine Zeitung*, 29 July 1977 (he is one of the directors of the paper). On the effect: 'Berliner Schüler loben die Objektivität des Fest-Films und bemängeln die Oberflächlichkeit', *Die Zeit*, 19 Aug 1977.

4. See the justified attack by Dieter E. Zimmer, 'Die Weisslacher: Wie die Fernsehunterhalter unsere Vergangenheit bewältigen', *Die Zeit*, 6 Jan 1978.

5. All texts published by Wolfgang Lehr and Klaus Berg (eds.), *Rundfunk und Presse in Deutschland* (Legal Foundations of the Mass Media) (Mainz: v. Hase und Koehler, 1976) 2nd rev edn 607 pp.

6. The problems are accurately described in Rudolf Rass and Jochen Witting, 'Die Rolle der Parlamente als Delegationsorgane der Rundfunkgremien' in *Rundfunkpolitische Kontroversen* (Frankfurt: Europäische Verlagsanstalt, 1976) pp. 76–8.

7. Figures in *FUNK-Korrespondenz*, 12 Nov 1977.

8. *Die Zeit*, 9 Dec 1977.

9. Descriptive analysis in the monthly *Das Capital*, Oct 1977. Regarding budget equalisation and the problem of the North German corporation, see the account published in *FUNK-Korrespondenz* of 6 Oct 1976 and 13 July 1977, as well as the discussion published in *Die Zeit*, particularly on 23 Dec 1977.

10. The expert opinion on the West German corporation is dealt with in detail in *FUNK-Korrespondenz* of 3 Nov 1977.

11. Amusing satirical counter-programmes in a reader's letter to *Der Spiegel*, 8 Aug 1977 (Caricature of the 'Red' Hesse corporation) as well as in *Frankfurter Rundschau* and *Süddeutsche Zeitung* (the 'black' broadcasting institutions in Schleswig–Holstein and Bavaria), both reprinted in *Der Spiegel* of 1 Aug 1977 and 2 Jan 1978.

12. See the well-documented case history by Hannelore Keidel, 'Politische Aspekte der Aufsicht über den Rundfunk', in *Rundfunk und Fernsehen*, 1–2 (1976) pp. 15–38.

13. Complete text in *epd-Kirche und Rundfunk*, 11 Dec 1977.

14. Klaus Simon, 'Thesen zur Unabhängigkeit des Journalisten', in A. L. Heygester and E. Maseber (eds.), *Fernsehkritik* (Mainz: v. Hase, 1975) pp. 147–51.

15. Title of a very one-sided contribution by J. Brüning and W. Nax in *Rundfunkpolitische Kontroversen*, pp. 99–114.

16. H. H. Boelte, 'Thesen zu Kontrolle und Einfluss', *Fernsehkritik* (1975) pp. 143–6.

17. Quotation from the transcript of the speech.

18. See 'Informationsprobleme in den deutsch-französischen Beziehungen', *Bulletin de Liaison* of the Deutsch–Französisches Jugendwerk (German–French Youth Action), June 1976, 106 pp. See also Georg Jurgens, *Politische Auslandsberichterstattung im deutschen Fernsehen*, which gives correspondents' reports about the USA as an example (F. U. Berlin: Fachbereich Politische Wissenschaften, 1974) particularly Chapter 4, pp. 44–68.

19. Text of a prize-winning programme in *Journalistenpreis Entwicklungspolitik*.

20. See *inter alia* P. Ch. Hall, 'Auf dem langen Marsch in die Ernüch-

terung. Zur Entwicklung und Situation der fernsehkritischen Fernseh-sendungen', *Medien* + *Erziehung*, 1 (1977) pp. 18–26; M. Wiebel, 'Medienkritik im Fernsehen', *Rundfunkpolitische Kontroversen*, pp. 231–41; 'Was darf "Glashaus" noch?', *FUNK-Korrespondenz*, 25 Jan 1978.

21. *FUNK-Korrespondenz*, 13 Jan 1978.

22. Good critical review in *Funk-Korrespondenz*, 7 Dec 1977. Position of the ZDF set out in *FUNK-Korrespondenz*, 5 Jan 1978. Sharp reaction in the aggressive monthly of the DGB (Trade Union) Youth Section, *Ran*, February 1978.

23. See *epd-Kirche und Rundfunk*, 19 Feb 1977 and 4 June 1977.

24. E.g. in *Stern*, 8 Dec 1977 and even more so in the aggressive analysis of an insider 'Piep! Piep! Piep!' in *Lui* [*sic*], February 1978.

25. Special edition 'Das "Wort am Sonntag" vom 25. Juni im Widerstreit der Meinungen', *epd-Dokumentation*, 29 Aug 1977.

26. See the analysis by W. Ruhland about the parties in the political current affairs programmes, in the 'Tele-Forum' of *Das Parlament*, 15 Jan 1977, and the analysis 'Der Wahlkampf als Wahlkampf im Fernsehen. Läuft alles scheif?', *FUNK-Korrespondenz*, 9 Sept 1976.

27. Good report by Kurt Reumann, *Frankfurter Allgemeine Zeitung*, 23 April 1977, review by F. W. Hymmen, *Allgemeine Deutsche Sonntags-zeitung*, 6 Feb 1977.

28. Title of the contribution by Hanno Beith, *Rundfunkpolitische Kontroversen*, pp. 194–205.

29. See *inter alia* H. Ch. Buchholtz, 'Offentlichkeitsarbeit in der Auseinandersetzung um das Atomkraftwerk Wyhl', *Medium*, May and June 1977, as well as the analyses in *FUNK-Korrespondenz*, 1 Dec 1976 and 5 Oct 1977.

30. Excellent short description by Cornelia Bolesch, 'Der Fall Schleyer: erlitten, erlebt, ferngesehen', *D.A.S.*, 18 Sept 1977. The fundamental views of intelligent television executives such as Franz Wördemann ('Terrorismus und Medien') and Dieter Stolte set out in 'Das Fernsehen als Medium und Faktor in Krisenzeiten', *FUNK-Korrespondenz*, 21 Nov 1977 and 11 Jan 1978.

31. See A. Grosser, 'Die Bundesrepublik: der innere und der äussere Frieden', speech upon being awarded the 1975 Peace Prize, in *Wider den Strom*, pp. 181–93.

Chapter 5: Sweden

1. Riksdag debates, Second Chamber, 1966 No. 117, Wednesday 14 December 1966, p. 27.

2. Ibid., p. 22.

3. The overseas and educational services are financed through taxation.

4. Government Bill 1977/78: 91 on continuance of radio broadcasting services, etc.

5. His Majesty's Bill No. 136 of 1966 on continuance of radio broadcasting services, etc.

6. Government Bill 1977/78: 91, p. 195.

7. Ibid., p. 196.

8. In the bill of 1977/78 the new Government suggests an important though enigmatic change of this formula. They want it to read: SR should 'assert the basic ideas of the democratic system'.

9. 'On Being Neutral', stencil, transcript of radio programme.

10. Centre, Liberals, Conservatives, Social Democrats, Communists.

11. The source of the table is Ivar Ivre, *I väntan på en mediepolitik* (Stockholm: Tidskiften Tiden, 1977).

12. *Radio Sweden Year Book* (1968) p. 14.

13. Memorandum of Proceedings of the Board of Governors.

Chapter 6: Holland

1. Daniel Lerner, *The Passing of Traditional Society* (New York: Free Press, 1958).

2. James C. Strouse, *The Mass Media, Public Opinion and Public Policy Analysis: Linkage explorations* (Columbus, Ohio: Merrill, 1975).

3. *Public Opinion Quarterly* (1965).

4. Paul F. Lazarsfeld, Bernard Berelson and Hazel Gaudet, *The People's Choice – How the Voter Makes up his Mind in a Presidential Campaign* (New York: Columbia University Press, 1944).

5. Jay G. Blumler and Denis McQuail, *Television in Politics – its Uses and Influence* (London: Faber, 1968).

6. Grace Wyndham Goldie, *Facing the Nation – Television and Politics 1936–76* (London: Bodley Head, 1977).

7. See, for example, Jerome A. Barron, *Freedom of the Press for Whom?* (Indiana University Press, 1973).

8. Leon Festinger, A Theory of Cognitive Dissonance (New York: Harper, 1957).

9. *Report of the Committee on the Future of Broadcasting,* Cmnd. 6753 (London: HMSO, March 1977) p. 290, para 17.64.

Bibliography

Britain

JAY G. BLUMLER and DENIS MCQUAIL, *Television in Politics – its Uses and Influence* (London: Faber, 1968).

TOM BURNS, *The BBC – Public Institution and Private World* (London: Macmillan, 1977).

STEVEN H. CHAFFEE (ed.), *Political Communication – Issues and Strategies for Research* (London: Sage, 1975).

EDWARD JAY EPSTEIN, *News from Nowhere, Television and the News* (New York: Random House, 1973).

GLASGOW UNIVERSITY MEDIA GROUP, *Bad News* (London: Routledge & Kegan Paul, 1976).

GRACE WYNDHAM GOLDIE, *Facing the Nation: Television and Politics 1936–1976* (London: Bodley Head, 1977).

STUART HALL, 'Media Power – the Double Bind', *Journal of Communication*, Autumn, 1974.

LORD HILL, *Behind the Screen, the Broadcasting Memoirs of Lord Hill* (London: Sidgwick & Jackson, 1974).

STUART HOOD, 'The Politics of Television' in Denis McQuail (ed.), *Sociology of Mass Communications* (Harmondsworth: Penguin, 1972).

KURT LANG and GLADYS ENGEL LANG¿ *Politics and Television* (Chicago: Quadrangle Books, 1968).

ROBERT MACNEIL, *The People Machine: the Influence of Television in American Politics* (New York: Harper & Row, 1968).

HAROLD MEDELSOHN and IRVING CRESPI, *Polls, Television and the New Politics* (Scranton, Pa.: Chandler Publishing Co., 1970).

COLIN SEYMOURE-URE, *The Political Impact of Mass Media* (London: Constable, 1974).

MICHAEL TRACEY, *The Production of Political Television* (London: Routledge & Kegan Paul, 1977).

E. G. WEDELL, *Broadcasting and Public Policy* (London: Michael Jospeh, 1968).

LORD WINDLESHAM, *Communication and Political Power* (London: Jonathan Cape, 1976).

France

General Studies

ROGER ERRERA, *Les Libertés à l'Abandon* (Paris: Le Seuil, 1975).

E. SULEIMAN, *Politics, Power and Bureaucracy in France* (Princeton University Press, 1974).

Historical and Descriptive Studies

DENISE BOMBARDIER, *La Voix de la France* (Paris: Laffont, 1975).

ARTHUR CONTE, *Hommes Libres* (Paris: Plon, 1973).

JEAN DIWO, *Si Vous avez Manqué le Début* (Paris: Albin Michel, 1976).

PIERRE MIQUEL, *Histoire de la Radio et de la Télévision* (Paris: Editions Richelieu, 1973).

JEAN MONTALDO, *Tous Coupables* (Paris: Albin Michel, 1974).

RUTH THOMAS, *Broadcasting and Democracy in France* (Bradford University Press, 1976).

JACQUES THIBAU, *Une Télévision pour tous les Français* (Paris: Le Seuil, 1970).

JACQUES THIBAU, *La Télévision, le Pouvoir et l'Argent* (Paris: Calmann Lévy, 1973).

Reports on French Broadcasting

Rapport de la Commission d'Etude du Statut de L'ORTF (*Commission Paye*) (Paris: Documentation Française, 1970).

Rapport de la Commission de Contrôle de L'ORTF (*Rapport Le Tac*) (Paris: Assemblée Nationale No. 2291, 1972).

Rapport de la Commission de Contrôle de la Gestion de L'ORTF (*Rapport Chinaud*) (Paris: Assemblée Nationale No. 1072, 1974).

Rapport sur la Radiodiffusion et la Télévision (Paris: Assemblée Nationale No. 3131, Annexe 49, 1977).

Italy

AA. VV., *Televisione e Vita Italiana* (Torino: ERI, 1968).

AA. VV., *Libertà d'Espressione e Organizzazione Radiotelevisiva,* 2 vol (Milano: Giuffré, 1970).

AA. VV., *Radiotelevisione, Informazione e Democrazia* (Roma: Editori Riuniti, 1974).

G. BASSI (ed.) *Sindacato e Riforma della RAI-TV* (Roma: Editrice Sindacale, 1972).

GIUSEPPE CARBONARO, *Indagine Statistica sui non Possessori di Televisore* (Torino: ERI, 1970).

GIOVANNI CESAREO, *Anatomia del Potere Televisivo* (Milano: Angeli, 1970).

GIOVANNI CESAREO, *Televisione Sprecata. Verso una Quarta Fase del Sistema Communicazioni di Massa?* (Milano: Feltrinelli, 1974).

FURIO COLOMBO, *Televisione: la Realta come Spettacolo*, (Milano: Bompiani, 1974).

FERNALDO DI GIAMMATTEO, *Televisione, Potere, Riforma* (Firenze: La Nuova Italia, 1973).

FEDERICO DOGLIO, *Televisione e Spettacolo* (Rome: Studium, 1961).

R. FAENZA and F. SILIATO (eds) *Attenti al cavo! Rivoluzione nella Televisione dopo le Sentenze della Corte Costituzionale* (Firenze: Guaraldi, 1974).

GUIDO FANTI, *Radiotelevisione: Informazione e Democrazia* (Milano: Feltrinelli, 1973).

AUGUSTO FRAGOLA, *Radiotelevisione nella Giurisprudenza* (Padova: CEDAM, 1971).

ANTONIO PAPA, *Storia Politica della Radio in Italia, 1924–1943* (Napoli: Guida, 1978).

F. ROSITI (ed.), *Lavoratori e Televisione* (Milano: Angeli, 1970).

ROBERTO ZACCARIA, *Radiotelevisione e Costituzione* (Milano: Giuffré, 1977).

Germany

ULRICH EGGERT, *Tele-Lexikon, from ARD to ZDF* (Berlin: Haude & Spener, 1971) 112 pp.

HEIKO FLOTTAU, *Hörfunk und Fernsehen heute* (Munich: Olzog, 1972) 294 pp.

ALFRED GROSSER, *Geschichte Deutschlands seit 1945,* 5th edn (Munich: Dtv, 1977) 535 pp. (Television, pp. 350–4). Revised edition, written in 1974–5, of *Germany in Our Time* (New York and London: Praeger, 1971) 378 pp.

Arthur Williams, *Broadcasting and Democracy in West Germany* (Bradford University Press; and London: Crosby Lockwood Staples, 1976) 198 pp.

Statutes and Legal Topics

Konrad Berendes, *Des Staatsaufsicht über den Rundfunk* (Berlin: Duncker & Humblot, 1973) 272 pp.

Ilse Dygutsch-Lorenz, *Die Rundfunkanstalt als Organisationsproblem* (Düsseldorf: Bertelsmann University, 1971) 230 pp. (about the Bavarian Broadcasting Corporation).

Ernst W. Fuhr, *ZDF-Staatsvertrag* (Mainz: v. Hase & Koehler, 1972) 336 pp.

Rüdiger Hoffmann, *Rundfunkorganisation und Rundfunkfreiheit* (Berlin: v. Spiess, 1975) 2 vols.

Wolfgang Lehr and Klaus Berg, *Rundfunk und Presse in Deutschland* (Legal Foundations of the Mass Media, Texts) 2nd rev. edn (Mainz: v. Hase & Koehler, 1976) 607 pp.

Discussion and Criticism

Henry Broder (ed.), *Die Schere im Kopf* (About censorship and self-censorship) (Cologne: V. Bund., 1976) 205 pp.

Walter Jens, *Fernsehen* (Themes and taboos) articles written as 'Momos', 1963–73, Munich, 1973, 288 pp.

Christian Longolius (ed.), *Fernsehen in Deutschland. Gesellschaftspolitische Aufgaben und Wirkungen eines Mediums* (Mainz: v. Hase und Koehler, 1967) 352 pp.

Christian Longolius (ed.), *Fernsehen in Deutschland: Macht und Ohnmacht der Autoren* (Mainz: v. Hase und Koehler, 1973) 444 pp.

Mainzer Tage der Fernsehkritik (Published regularly since 1969 by v. Hase und Koehler).

Rundfunkpolitische Kontroversen (On the occasion of the eightieth birthday of Fritz Eberhard) (Frankfurt: Europäische Verlagsanstalt, 1976) 495 pp.

Miscellaneous

P. Borowsky, B. Vogel and H. Wunder, *Gesichte in Presse, Funk und Fernsehen* (Opladen: Leske, 1976) 132 pp.

MANFRED DELLING, *Bonanza & Co. Fernsehen als Unterhaltung und Politik* (Hamburg: Rororo, 1976) 110 pp.

GEORG FEIL, *Zeitgeschehen im Deutschen Fernsehen* (Analyses of television programmes on historical themes, 1957–1967) (Osnabrück: Fromm, 1974) 183 pp.

EGON NETENJAKOB, *Anatomie der Fernsehserie* (Television workers examine their working conditions) (Mainz: v. Hase und Koehler, 1976) 376 pp.

HANS JÜRGEN WEISS, *Wahlkampf im Fernsehen* (Examination of the role of the great television debate in the 1972 federal election campaign) (Berlin: v. Spiess, 1976) 292 pp.

BERNWARD WEMBER, *Wie informiert das Fernsehen?* (Munich: List, 1976) 176 pp.

Current Documentation

ARD-Jahrbuch (ARD yearbook) (Cologne, since 1969).

FUNK-Korrespondenz (Cologne: Katholisches Institute für Medien-forschung) fortnightly. *epd-Kirche und Rundfunk* (Frankfurt: Gemeinschaftswerk der Evangelischen Publizistik) – both cyclostyled publications.

WDR COLOGNE, *Hörfunk und Fernsehen.* (Register of essays published in periodicals and anthologies) Annual 1975/76, 1977, 300 pp. (Appears annually; cyclostyled, monthly part editions before the appearance of the volumes.)

ZDF-Jahrbuch (ZDF yearbook) (Mainz, since 1962).

Sweden

Literature in English

OLOF HUTLEN and IVAR IVRE, 'Sweden: Small but Foreboding Changes, European Broadcasting in Transition', *Journal of Communications,* Summer 1978.

IVAR IVRE, 'Conflict and Resolution in Sweden', in *Mass Media Policies in Changing Cultures,* ed. George Gerbner (New York: Wiley & Sons, 1976).

Laws and Basic Regulations (Stockholm: Sveriges Radio, 1972).

EDWARD W. PLOMAN, *Broadcasting in Sweden* (London: Routledge & Kegan Paul, 1976).

254   *Television and Political Life*

Radio and TV 1978–1985. Proposals of the Swedish Broadcasting Commission 1977 (Stockholm: The Ministry of Education and Cultural Affairs, 1977).

Literature in Swedish

LARS BERGMAN, *Radionämnden anser* . . . (Opinions of the Radio Council) (Stockholm, 1977).

LARS GRAHN, BENGT NERMAN, and SVERKER TIRÉN, *Programmedarbetarnds Dilemma – en Undersökning av Opartiskhets – och Saklighetsfrågor* (The Dilemma of the Programme Producer – an Investigation into Impartiality and Factuality) (Stockholm, 1976).

GÖRAN HERMERÉN, 'Kvantitativ Objektivitetsmätning' (Quantitative Measurement of Objectivity), *Statsvetenskaplig Tidskrift* (1973).

IVAR IVRE, *I Väntån pa en mediepolitik* (In Expectation of a Mass Media Policy) (Stockholm: Tidskiften Tiden, 1977).

'Jag vill vara neutral, säger radion', Utskrifter av tre radioprogram 1976 ('I want to be neutral', Transcripts of three radio programmes 1976).

Kungl. Maj:ts proposition nr 136 år 1966 angående rundradions fortsatta verksamhet m m. (Government Bill on the development of radio and television 1966:136).

Regeringens proposition 1977/78:91 om rundradions fortsatta verksamhet m m (Government Bill on the development of radio and television 1977/78:91).

Riksdagsdebatterna, Andra kammaren, 1966 Nr 117. (Record of Parliamentary Debates, Second Chamber 1966:117).

Sveriges Radios Årsböcker (Yearbooks of Sveriges Radio).

Tvåkanalssystemet i tv (The Two-channel TV System. An Evaluation of TV 1969-1974) (Stockholm: Sveriges Radio, 1975).

JÖRGEN WESTERSTÅHL, *Objektiv Nyhetsförmedling* (Objectivity in the News) (Stockholm: Scandinavian University Books, 1972).

Holland

J. BANK, 'Een halve eeuw omroephistorie in hoofdlijnen' [A half century's history of broadcasting in outline], *AVRO 50: historie en perspektieven* (Hilversum: AVRO, 1973) pp. 9–48.

J. BARDOEL, J. BIERHOFF, B. BANSCHOT and P. VASTERMAN, *Marges in de Media: het verbroken contact tussen omroep en publiek* [Margins in the Media: the broken contact between broadcasting and the public] (Baarn: Het wereldvenster, 1975).

CHR DE BRAUW, 'Broadcasting in the Netherlands: Institutionalised Access with Limitations', *Journal of Broadcasting*, 18 (1974) pp. 453–63.

D. R. BROWNE, 'Citizen Involvement in Broadcasting – Some European Experiences', *Public Telecommunications Review*, 2 (1973) pp. 16–28.

W. B. EMERY, 'The Netherlands: Pluralism with Freedom', Chapter 8 of *National and International Systems of Broadcasting: Their History, Operation and Control* (East Lansing: Michigan State University Press, 1969) pp. 140–57.

K. VAN DEN HAAK and J. SPICER, *Broadcasting in the Netherlands* (London: Routledge & Kegan Paul in association with the International Institute of Communications, 1977).

J. HEMELS, 'Zur Lage des Niederlandischen Rundfunks' [The Situation of Dutch Broadcasting], *Publizistik*, 3 (1976) pp. 343–60.

J. H. J. VAN DEN HEUVEL, *Nationaal of Verzuild: de strijd om het Neder-landse omroepbestel in de periode 1923–1947* [Nation or Pillarization –the Struggle for Netherlands Broadcasting, 1923–1947] (Baarn: Ambo, 1976). FRANCA KLAVER, *Media in the Netherlands* (Strasbourg: Council of Europe, 1976).

PETER M. LEWIS, *Community Control of Local Radio* (Strasbourg: Council of Europe, 1976).

A. LIJPHART, *The Politics of Accommodation: Pluralism and Democracy in the Netherlands* (Berkeley: University of California Press, 1968).

MINISTER VAN CULTUUR, Recreatie en Maatschappelijk Werk, Omroep, Chapter 4 of *Nota over het massamedia-belied* [Memorandum on Mass Media Policy] ('s-Gravenhage: Staatsuitgeverij, 1975).

NOS PUBLICATIONS, *Broadcasting Act and Broadcasting Decree* (Hilversum: NOS, 1976).

NOS PUBLICATIONS, *Radio and Television in the Netherlands* (Hilversum: NOS, 1976).

H. VAN PELT, *De omroep in Revisie; ontwikkeling van het radio en tele-visiebestel in Nederland en Belgie* [Broadcasting in Context: the development of radio and television institutions in the Netherlands and Belgium] (Louvain: Acco, 1974).

J. VAN SANTBRINK, Legislation and the Broadcasting Institutions in the Netherlands', *EBU Review*, 98B (July 1966) pp. 55–8.

J. VAN SANTBRINK, 'Legislation and the Broadcasting Institutions in the Netherlands. Part II: The Transitional System (1965) for Sound Broadcasting and Television in the Netherlands', *EBU Review*, 102B (March 1967) pp. 53–9.

J. VAN SANTBRINK, 'Legislation and the Broadcasting Institutions in the Netherlands. Part III: The Netherlands Broadcasting Act, in Force from 29 May 1969, and the Replacement of the NRU and the NTS by the NOS', *EBU Review*, 116B (July 1969) pp. 46–50.

H. SCHAAFSMA, *Geschiedenis van de omroep – karakteristiek van de omroep* [History of broadcasting – characteristics of broadcasting] (Amsterdam: Wetenschappelijke uitgeverij, 1970).

H. SCHAAFSMA, 'Knelpunten in de omroepwet' [Bottlenecks in the law of broadcasting], *Massacommunicatie*, 2 (November 1973) pp. 20–9.

H. SCHAAFSMA, 'Mirror of a Pillarized Society: Broadcasting in the Netherlands', *Delta*, IV, 4 (winter 1966/7).

D. VERKIJK, *'Radio Hilversum 1940–1945'* (Amsterdam: de Arbeiderspeps, 1974).

Index

Annan Committee 1, 24–5, 39
AVRO, Holland 191, 222, 224
  self-censorship 205

BBC 1
  at odds with Labour Party
    11–12, 234
  attitude to reporting from
    Northern Ireland 26, 30,
    31–2
  Charter 5
  Complaints' Commission 12
  defies government on 'A
    Question of Ulster' 28–9
  documents on broadcasting prac-
    tice 15, 16
  finances 6–7
  governing body 5, 10
  managerialism in 1970s in 38
  news and current affairs 31–2,
    34–5
  on staff and impartiality 25
  position during General Strike
    13
  producers' impartiality 16
  reflector of issues 26, 27
  stance on Suez incident 13
  statutory obligations 5–6

Tudor-style 'royal privilege'
  of 37
Bekkers, Monsignore 207, 210
Bernabei, Ettore 92, 93, 96
  controls RAI for Christian
    Democrats 97–8, 90, 91, 95
Britain
  condemnation of political control
    of broadcasting 235
  overlapping groups in society
    4
  politicians' right to the air 6, 16
  relations between broadcasters
    and politicians 1–2
  unified area of public debate
    2–3
  see also BBC; broadcasting,
    British; IBA
broadcasting
  and collectivity of politicians 2
  groups among 3
  internationalisation of 236
  need to follow broadcasting
    authorities' line 24–5
  political skills needed 15
broadcasting, British
  'access' 19
  committees of enquiry into
    13–14
  constraints on 37

broadcasting, British – *continued*
coverage of elections   20
election broadcasts   17–18, 19, 28
impartial within prevailing system   21–2
ministerial broadcasts   16, 17
part of public life   4
party conferences   28
party political broadcasts   16, 17–20
relation between authorities' Chairmen and Directors General   9, 10
tensions between institutions and creative workers   39

Chaban Delmas, Jacques   61, 62
TV reforms in France   53–4
Conservative Party
attitude to broadcasting   40

de Gaulle, General   44, 51, 53, 65

EO, Holland   192, 222–3, 224

France
'manichean consensus' in   41, 73
political broadcasting   65–9
political liberalisation after 1968   44–6
pool of broadcasting journalists   71–2
post-1945 belief in state control of broadcasting   42–4, 73
post-1974 broadcasting companies   58
post-1974 distrust of broadcasting by politicians   62–5, 70
post-1974 supervision of broadcasting   61–2
regional news   67–8
riots of 1968   52
taboo subjects for television   70
television right of reply   67
television starts, 1948, under government control   47
see also ORTF; RTF

Germany, Federal Republic of
anti-Communism of   116–17
attitude to GDR   117–18
composition of Bundestag   120
financial problems of television   126–7
importance of democratic concept to   118–19
Laenders' responsibility for broadcasting   120–1
licence fees   126
origin of state   114
party struggles for control of television   130–5
problem of freelance television contributors   127–8
problem of Nazi past   115–16
restrictive tendencies in television   136–8
role of political parties   119–20
television conformism in 1970s   140
television influence on elections   138–9
television institutions   122, 123, 127
television programme achievements   135–6
see also ZDF
Giscard d'Estaing, President Valéry   45, 57
television appearances   67, 70–1

Holland
beginnings of radio   193
broadcasting discredited in Second World War   195
broadcasting finance   219–20
broadcasting organisations   191–2, 195–7
broadcasting system   191, 229–30
historical reasons for Dutch broadcasting system   192–5
ministerial broadcasts   218
new unity in 1960s   201–2
parliamentary transmissions   215–18

Holland – *continued*
party political broadcasts 218
'pillarisation' in 192, 193, 196
post-1945 establishment control
of broadcasting 198
pre-1945 radio as mouthpiece of
groups 194
provisions of Broadcasting Act,
1967 219–21
reactions to revolutionary 1960s
203–6
revolutionary 1960s in 199–200
television advertising 219
television decline in 1970s
222–5, 227–9, 230
see also AVRO; EO; KRO;
NCRV; NOS; TROS;
VARA; VOO; VPRO

IBA 1
complaints panel 12
franchises 7
governing body 7, 10
Independent Television News
32, 34, 35
programme companies 8
programmes on Northern Ireland
30, 31
supervisory role 8–9
Italy
development of television 76–7
enthusiasm for cable television 102–3
foreign television transmissions
103–4
idea of broadcasting as government 'concession' 83–5
moves on private radio and television stations 112–13
philosophy of proportional representation in 81–2
political fruits of reform of television 108–9, 110–11
political party system 78–9, 82,
108
political phases since 1948 80–1
post-1972 party proposals for
television reform 96–102

provisions of Law 103, 1975, on
broadcasting 105–7, 108
see also RAI

Kennedy, President John F. 182
KRO, Holland 191, 195, 204, 206,
227
Catholic unorthodoxy on 207–9
impact of 213, 214
self-censorship 205

Labour Party
at odds with BBC 11–12, 234
view of broadcasting 40

NCRV, Holland 192, 195, 213,
227
self-censorship 205
news and current affairs
arguments for bridging gap between 35–6
division between 32, 35
historical separation of fact from
comment 33–4
NOS, Holland 192, 215, 219, 220,
221, 222, 227

ORTF, France 45, 46, 74
birth of 49–52
break-up in 1974 57–8, 73–4
crises and scandals, 1968–74 53,
55, 56–7
finance 58–9
government control 50, 51–2
Parliamentary influence on
59–61
Presidential Election broadcasts
51
shaken by French riots of 1968
52–3

Palme, Olof 162, 163, 166, 184
television ideals 144, 145, 166
Parliament, British
broadcasting of 20
Fourteen Day Rule 27–8
relations with broadcasting
14–15

politicians
  desire to dominate television 143–4
  eager to broadcast 15
  ideas on political broadcasting 20–1
  television regulars 69, 71
  undue influence ascribed to television by 185
Pompidou, President Georges 44, 56, 57, 71
  on ORTF 53
pressure groups 22–3
  influence on programme-makers 23–4
proportional representation 81–2

Radio Sweden
  at odds with politicians, 1976 159–60, 170, 177, 181–2
  Board of Governors 148, 172–7 *passim*
  budget reduction and restoration 171
  climate in late 1970s 186–7
  coverage of miners' strike, 1969 169
  development of 145, 187–90
  financing of 146
  first allowed to transmit news 147–8
  government's *de facto* reserve powers over 163
  impartiality and factuality demanded of 151–3
  increased freedom, 1950s and 1960s 160–1
  independent television channels 145
  lack of hearing for minorities 164–6
  pressure from 'popular movements' 155–9
  radio 'access', 1978 149
  reporting public scandals 178–80, 181
  Riksdag's bill to reorganise, 1978 149–50
  scrutinises labour movement, 1960s 169–70
  shareholders 146
  similarity with BBC 163
  taboos 178, 180
  tradition of budget addresses 161–3
RAI, Italy
  Christian Democrat 'occupation' of 82–3, 85, 87–8, 90, 91, 94–5
  internal censorship 92–3
  main source for Italian viewers 78
  monopoly limited, 1974 98, 103–5, 107–8
  monopoly upheld, 1960 88–90
  organisation, 1948–60 85–6
  Parliamentary Commission's supervision of 87–8, 100, 105, 106
  political struggle for control of 77–8
  reformed in light of Law 103, 1975 98, 109–10
  seeds of revolt against Christian Democrat control 95–6
  status 77
  subscribers 76, 77
  television expansion, 1960s 90
Reith, John 13, 38, 39, 233
RTF, France 43
  information services 47
  problems of censorship and administration 48
  rise in importance of television 49

social visibility 3, 4
Sträng, Gunnar 178, 179
  budget addresses on Radio Sweden 161–2, 163
Sweden
  anti-Communism during cold war 165
  election of 1976 143, 184–5
  effects of revolutionary 1960s in 166–71

Sweden – *continued*
   fall in costs of radios and tele-
      visions, 1970s 172
   left-wing movements, 1960s
      167–8
   miners' strike, 1969 167, 168
   political parties' right of veto by
      abstention abolished 154,
      173
   'popular movements' 146–7,
      155–9
   prosperity and stability to 1970
      142
   Radio Act provisions 151–2
   Radio Council 148, 154, 176,
      177
   signs of policy to direct broad-
      casting, 1978 150–1
   Social-Democratic 'affairs', 1970s
      178–81
   see also Radio Sweden

television
   develops own news style 34
   dramatic distortion of news by
      69–70
   early division between news and
      current affairs in Britain 34
   effect on political tactics 181–4
   freedom in 1960s 233
   moulding public opinion
      139–40
   outlook for 237
   political regulars on 69, 71
   similar worldwide development
      232
   stagnation in 1970s 233

   strengthens existing opinion
      199–200
   taboos 234
TROS, Holland 191
   style of programmes 223–5
   'trossification' 225–9

United States of America
   concept of separation of fact from
      comment 33
   early news broadcasts 34
   Kennedy–Nixon television con-
      frontations 182

VARA, Holland 192, 195, 206,
   226, 227, 228
   attempts to break taboos
      209–12, 214
   controversial programmes 204,
      209–10
   impact of 213, 214
VOO, Holland 192
VPRO, Holland 192, 195, 205,
   206, 213, 226
   controversial programmes 204
   self-censorship 205–6
   style of 212–13

ZDF, West Germany
   basic tasks 123–4
   central establishment owned by
      Laender 123
   directives about programme-
      making 126
   finance 126
   governing structure 124–6

Television and Political Life

Studies in six European countries

Edited by
Anthony Smith
for Writers' and Scholars' Educational Trust

M

First published in 1979 by
THE MACMILLAN PRESS LTD
London and Basingstoke
Associated companies in Delhi Dublin
Hong Kong Johannesburg Lagos Melbourne
New York Singapore and Tokyo

Photoset and printed in Great Britain by
LOWE AND BRYDONE PRINTERS LTD
Thetford, Norfolk

British Library Cataloguing in Publication Data

Television and political life.
  1. Television in politics – Europe
  I. Smith, Anthony, b.1938
  384.55′4′094   HE8700.7.P6

  ISBN 0–333–24327–7
  ISBN 0–333–24328–5 Pbk